KING ALFRED'S COLLEGE
WINCHESTER
Library: 01962 827306

To be returned on or before the day
marked below, subject to recall

WITHDRAWN FROM
THE LIBRARY

UNIVERSITY OF
WINCHESTER

KA 0201133 6

BIBLE AND LITERATURE
SERIES

Editor
David M. Gunn

FORM AND MEANING

Studies in Literary Techniques in
THE BOOK OF JONAH

JONATHAN MAGONET

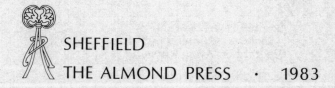

SHEFFIELD
THE ALMOND PRESS · 1983

LA SAINTE UNION
COLLEGE OF HIGHER
EDUCATION, SOUTHAMPTON

ACC. 137877

CLASS 224.92066 Mag

DATE REC.   CAT.
26. 0 . 1993

KING ALFRED'S COLLEGE
WINCHESTER

224/92
MAG   KA0201336

BIBLE AND LITERATURE SERIES, 8

Copyright [this edition] © 1983 The Almond Press

This book first appeared in 1976 in the series Beiträge zur biblischen Exegese und Theologie, edited by Jürgen Becker and Henning Graf Reventlow and published by Herbert Lang (Bern) & Peter Lang (Frankfurt/M), by whose kind permission it is now reprinted.

Second edition 1983 incorporating corrections and supplementary bibliography, an additional chapter by the author, and a Foreword by James S. Ackerman.

Line Drawings by Leah Hellner

Line Drawings Copyright © 1983 Leah Hellner

ISBN 0 907459 25 0
ISSN 0260 4493; 8

Published by
The Almond Press
P.O. Box 208
Sheffield S10 5DW
England

Printed in Great Britain by
Dotesios (Printers) Ltd
Bradford-on-Avon, Wiltshire
1983

FOR DORO

TABLE OF CONTENTS

FOREWORD

In 1976 two major works on the Book of Jonah appeared, with methods and results that are almost diametrically opposed to one another. One volume is a sophisticated continuation of the traditional approaches and concerns of historical-critical scholarship.* The other volume, based partially on studies by Lohfink (1961), Trible (1963), Good (1965), Landes (1967), O. Kaiser (1973) and especially on the major works of H. J. Kraus (1965) and Cohn (1969), represents a major contribution to biblical studies in general and to the interpretation of the Jonah story in particular.** It illustrates a general trend in biblical studies today: many scholars are turning to "outside" disciplines to enrich their understanding of the text. And for those of us who are attempting to apply literary criticism to the Bible, this second volume stands as an exemplary work. In 1980 S. Bar-Efrat listed it as one of the important recent contributions to this rapidly developing approach, along with the works of such scholars as Alter, Fishbane, and Fokkelman [VT 30 (1980) 154]. I certainly concur with this assessement.

A comparison of these 1976 works illustrates the radically divergent interpretations that result when two scholars approach the same text with differing methodological presuppositions. Schmidt's analysis of the Jonah story is based on the shift of divine names. Chs. 1-2 focus on YHWH, who is distinguished from other gods, whereas Elohim is the god of all peoples in Chs. 3-4. A traditional argument against multiple authorship has been that the two names indicate different aspects of God's personality. Pointing out that the Elohim of Chs. 3-4 has the same characteristics as the YHWH of Chs. 1-2 (lord of nature, merciful), Schmidt concludes that only multiple authorship can account for the changing of names. The two halves of the story, he believes, are loosely joined together: only 1:2 points ahead to the second half, and 4:2 points back to the first.

*Ludwig Schmidt, "De Deo". Studien zur Literarkritik und Theologie des Buches Jona, des Gesprächs zwischen Abraham und Jahwe in Gen. xviii 22ff. und von Hi. i. (BZAW, 143; Berlin: de Gruyter, 1976). 198pp.
**Jonathan Magonet, Form and Meaning: Studies in Literary Techniques in the Book of Jonah (Beiträge zur biblischen Exegese und Theologie, 2; Bern and Frankfurt/M: H. & P. Lang, 1976). 169pp.

This line of reasoning leads Schmidt to reconstruct a basic source: 1:2, 3:3-10, 4:1, 5a, 6-11 - omitting "YHWH" in 4:6a, the YHWH phrase in 3:3a, and changing "YHWH" to "Elohim" in 4:10. Because of its ties to 1 Kings 19, Jer. 18, and Ex 32, the Jonah story can be dated to the exile. It is a didactic narrative aimed at probing the nature of God. Rather than turning to Israel's sacred-history traditions for his resources, the writer explores divine forgiveness in terms of a creation theology derived from Israel's wisdom traditions. God's pity, Schmidt concludes, is motivated by the helplessness of the entire created order. The writer moves away from a God acting through a particular people, towards the concept of a redemptive grace that extends to all creation.

In the "basic source" the issue is not Jew versus Gentile, so the writer is not combatting the particularist tendencies developing in Diaspora Judaism. Both Jonah and the Ninevites are related to "Elohim." Moreover, Nineveh is de-historicized. It is not depicted as the capital of Israel's enemies, the Assyrians; it is rather an ancient "great city" during the time when all people worshipped the same god (cf. Job 1). The writer shows no interest in Jonah's personality. Jonah's sole function in the story is to enable God to broaden and redefine the nature of divine mercy. He doesn't even get to answer God's question at the end of the story. Thus the focus is not on Jonah as particularist Jew who resents God's sparing Gentile oppressors; nor is it on Jonah as frustrated prophet whose oracles are undermined by divine caprice. The sole interest of the basic source is on the universal mercy of the deity who creates qiqayon plants and great cities.

At a later time, says Schmidt, the basic source was expanded to include the storm scene and the great fish (1:1, 3-16, 2:1, 11). He theorizes that this segment never existed as an independent story, but was put together from folklore motifs by the person who reworked the basic source. Jonah's "confession" in 1:9 sounds the central theme of the addition: YHWH's power, versus the impotence of all other deities. There is literary unevenness in Ch. 1 (e.g. 1:10), but this is due to folk motifs that have been patched together rather than to a variety of sources. The reviser has thrown in whatever enhances YHWH's power. It is even irrelevant who speaks - Jonah, the captain, the sailors; it only matters that all the characters experience the divine power.

Some scholars see Jonah's struggle against his prophetic commission as a central theme. But Jonah's "confession" in 1:9 deals only with the universal Creator who is universally powerful. When Jonah realizes and admits his guilt in 1:12, he does not say "Take me back to shore, and I will go to Nineveh." Crushed by the divine power and helplessly awaiting death, Jonah must learn what he had earlier confessed and what the sailors also finally apprehend: YHWH rules both land and sea. If the issue had been Jonah's prophetic commission, YHWH would have allowed the sailors to return Jonah to the land. The segment concludes with the sailors' recognition of the power and freedom of YHWH, who then can proceed to rescue Jonah. The reviser gives Jonah no opportunity to speak or to act.

Although the basic source stresses divine mercy and the additional segment stresses divine power, both sources presuppose a creation theology. By appending 1:1, 3-16; 2:1, 11 to the basic source, the reviser is affirming that divine mercy is coterminous with divine power. This theme is further developed in 4:2-4, where a second "confession" is inserted and elaborated. In 4:2 Jonah is not claiming a special status for Jews because of Israel's covenant relationship; he is affirming the futility of proclaiming judgement when God's basic characteristic is mercy. Thus the thematic structure of the story is based on two confessions (1:9 and 4:2), and Jonah functions as the work's straw man whose words and actions serve to underline the theological message. The reviser makes no attempt to entice the reader to identify with Jonah, because there are no groups in his community whose views the story is intended to combat. The Book of Jonah is neither satire nor polemic. Who could possibly consider escaping from God's presence or denying God's mercy?

Schmidt sees the final stage of the story's development taking place when a later redactor added Jonah's prayer in 2:2-10. This insertion, focusing on human disobedience overcome by YHWH, moves the story close to the prophetic legend genre. The end result is to shift the reader's interest away from God and towards Jonah. Tracing parallel developments in the redactions of Jonah, Job 1, and Genesis 18, Schmidt sees a common tendency to transform stories that orginally focused on God's nature and activity into stories that emphasize the human response.

Schmidt's source analysis is easy game for criticism. Without textual warrant he must remove three YHWH's from his "basic source" in order to create the clear separation he seeks to find. And when he concludes that multiple authorship explains why God (whether called YHWH or Elohim) has the same characteristics throughout the story, this is source criticism gone awry!

A far more serious deficiency, however, is Schmidt's failure to interpret the meaning of the Jonah story with any depth and fullness. This is strange, because De Deo focuses on the theologies of the strata in the story. And surely the Book of Jonah has a theological meaning. For Schmidt, theological viewpoint is one further means of distinguishing between his sources. And, once established, he shifts over to an elucidation of how that theological viewpoint functioned within the assumed historical and cultural context in which it arose. I see this as a major shortcoming of the historical-critical approach to the biblical text. We are more interested in the theology of the text as an important datum in source analysis and as an element in the history of Israel's religion than we are in opening up a text's full theological richness through close reading. And this is Schmidt's problem: he has abstracted theological dogmas from a text that was written to be read as a story. The result is a thin, superficial reduction of the revised story's meaning: the powerful Creator who rules over land and sea is also the Creator whose mercy extends to all beings. That's the equivalent of describing the Sistine chapel ceiling as a picture of two people almost touching hands.

Most of us biblical scholars will read De Deo with satisfaction, because it gives us what we are used to: a clear, brilliantly conceived, neatly packaged theory of the text's redaction process. We will weigh and debate the merits of his case. We may even disagree with his conclusion that the story is not combatting Jewish particularism of the post-exilic period. But we will not fault him for his failure to probe and explicate the full richness of the story. His theological reduction has satisfied our needs for historical reconstruction. Anything further - anything "purely literary" that looks for richer, more complex meanings - risks moving away from the objective world of the text into the subjective mind of the reader.

The second 1976 volume is a parade example of the contribution that literary interpretation can make to supplement (and in some cases to challenge/correct) the results of historical-critical scholarship. Unlike De Deo, Form and Meaning finds out what the text is saying by focusing on how the story is told. Magonet begins with objective realia of language usage (e.g. Leitwörter) to show how word repetition and variation establish structural linkages, thematic patterns, and characterization. He is sensitive to a wide range of stylistic devices that give subtlety and complexity to the work.

Only in the final two chapters does Magonet broaden his analysis beyond the language, style, and structure of the Book of Jonah. Ch. 4 notes how the story relates to other parts of the biblical tradition and the effect these allusions have in shaping the story's meaning. When coming to an elucidation of the story's major themes in his concluding chapter, Magonet carefully incorporates the results of the four preceding chapters. The structure of his book is a gradual move from the specific to the general, so that his concluding interpretation has rich theological dimensions that are solidly based on close analysis of how the story is constructed.

The past two decades have witnessed great progress in interpreting the Jonah story, primarily because scholars are increasingly moving towards literary analysis. Although I do not agree with all of the results in Magonet's work, I have no doubt that it has made a major contribution to Jonah research. Yet by and large the world of biblical scholars seems not to have taken note. Whereas De Deo was reviewed in many of our major journals,* I could find only one review of Form and Meaning.**

My special thanks, therefore, goes to David M. Gunn editor of the Almond Press "Bible and Literature" series, for helping to give this important work the widespread distribution it deserves.

James S. Ackerman
Indiana University
Bloomington, Indiana

---

* E.g. In JBL, JSS, RHPR, and VT.

**By Robert Murray in the 1978 Heythrop Journal.

PREFACE TO THE SECOND EDITION

In the nine years since the completion of this Doctoral Dissertation there have been enormous advances in the "literary" approach to Biblical studies - both in evaluating individual texts and in exploring the theoretical aspects. It is difficult to remember how isolated and out of step one felt at the time. It is very much to the credit of Professor Rolf Rendtorff that he agreed to supervise it - and what I felt at the time as a healthy scepticism on his part forced me to justify each step of the analysis by producing new methodologies and rigorously applying them. The attempt to combine what was essentially an intuitive feeling about the text with a scientific self-discipline gave the study its inner dynamic and tension.

In re-reading it, it is interesting to see how much has remained a regular part of my teaching of the book, and the new post-script indicates how far the figure of Jonah has become part of my religious consciousness. If I have questions about some of the detailed conclusions, it seems that they come from an over-zealous need at the time to nail down each nuance and give it a definitive implication. Nevertheless the approach to questions like how one evaluates "quotations" within a text or how to find a framework for assessing the different potential meanings of a passage is still valid and needs to be taken further. In retrospect I find the analysis of the "Psalm" the most satisfying in that it opened up new ways of unravelling the structure. To the best of my knowledge I came to it with no preconceived theory, and what emerged emerged. The same applies to the question of its "authenticity", which I think the study proves, as far as such things can be proved, though - with a few notable exceptions - this has yet to enter either scholarly or popular consciousness.

In retrospect what was most shocking in my research was to see how far scholarly views from an earlier age were mechanically (even word-for-word) reproduced in study after study without serious re-evaluation. If "Form and Meaning" broke new ground and still encourages a fresh approach to the text of the Hebrew Bible, then this second edition will be justified.

I would like to thank Jim Ackerman for his kind Foreword and David Gunn for making this second edition possible and preparing the additional bibliography. Our gratitude is due to him and his colleagues in Sheffield for their remarkable publishing ventures that have furthered in particular this sort of approach to Biblical studies.

The line drawings in this edition are by Leah Hellner and I take this opportunity to express to her my thanks and appreciation.

Jonathan Magonet
Leo Baeck College, London   June, 1983

PREFACE

This work was accepted as a doctoral dissertation by the Philosophisch-
Historische Fakultät of the University of Heidelberg in May 1974. I am
happy to have this opportunity to acknowledge my gratitude to Professor
Dr. Rolf Rendtorff who supervised it, and to Professor Dr. G. Ch. Macholz
who was Korreferent.

Many have helped over the years in formal and informal ways in the pre-
paration of this work. I would like to express my thanks to at least a few
of them:

The late Dr. Ellen Littmann, Lecturer in Bible at the Leo Baeck College,
London, since its inception, who gave me my first impetus towards Bible
study and watched over my earliest work on "Jonah".

Professor D. Dr. Hans Walter Wolff who gave much helpful critical advice.
Professor Dr. H. Graf Reventlow who accepted the Dissertation for publication and advised on the presentation.

The Leo Baeck College, and in particular Rabbi Dr. Albert Friedlander,
the Director of Studies, for encouraging me in this project by providing a
research grant and for allowing time from my teaching commitments in
the latter stages.

Mrs. Carol Roundtree for typing the original manuscript.

Herr Jurischka und Frau Lehmen of the Verlag Peter Lang for their patience
in dealing with the difficulties that arose in preparing the manuscript for
publication.

For grants which enabled me to pursue my research in Jerusalem and Heidelberg, I am indebted to the Memorial Foundation for Jewish Culture,
New York, and the Jewish Educational Development Trust, London - my
particular gratitude going to the Chief Rabbi, Dr. I. Jakobovits and Mr.
Moshe Davis.

The publication of the thesis in its present form would not have been possi-
ble without the generous help of Mr. Marcel Mann, and the Publications
Committee of the Leo Baeck College, under the Chairmanship of Mr. Louis
Littman.

Jonathan Magonet
Leo Baeck College, London

INTRODUCTION

This study of the Book of Jonah is the result of several years' preoccupation with the book, and with certain questions that have repeatedly emerged, above all the contrast between the apparent simplicity of the narrative and the vast range of interpretation it has yielded. Behind the simplicity it soon becomes clear that a highly complex structure exists, beginning with a system of repetitions (of words, phrases and complete sentences), culminating in structural patterns over whole chapters. This study is concerned with the interrelationship of these various levels of construction and the ideas they convey; the form and the meaning.

At the outset we are faced with two problems of methodology. On the one hand we are trying to examine the complexity of the book as a whole, and the multiple levels of interconnection between the various parts which contribute to this. Yet in order to do so, we must concern ourselves with the unravelling of innumerable details of word usage and meaning, of construction and interplay, so that with so much material it is difficult to find the right point at which to "break into" the book without presenting from the beginning a partial, and hence unbalanced, picture. Secondly, the method of analysis we have used has been largely empirical, depending upon the accumulation of detailed notes over a period of years, based upon repeated attempts at a close reading of the text, augmented at various times by a study of the relevant literature. Yet in order to convey what we have found, a more formal presentation is necessary which distorts both the "history" of the research and, more importantly, the way in which the book itself repeatedly reveals new facets and remains fresh and surprising despite a long and detailed preoccupation with it.

In view of these problems, we have opted for the system shown in the Table of Contents. Thus we have started in Chapter One with the smallest units, words and phrases, examining particularly their repetitions and interrelationships, upon which the larger structural units of the book are built (1). Since the question of the authenticity of the "psalm" in Jonah 2:3-10 remains a problem for exegesis, a chapter is devoted to it at an early point in the analysis.

In the third chapter we have taken larger units and attempted to analyse the structure and interrelationships of the chapters themselves.

From our earliest studies, before even reading the work of Feuillet (2), we had noticed the appearance in Jonah of material from elsewhere in the Bible, and thus felt that this, too, must be introduced before any attempt was made to integrate our findings into an evaluation of the book as a whole. The relevant material can be found in Chapter Four.

In the course of study we became more and more aware of certain ambiguities in the book which enabled quite widely divergent interpretations to emerge, all of which appear to have some justification in the text itself.

This in turn led to a re-examination of the word-usage, where the source of certain ambiguities lay, and the nature of the problem is discussed in some detail in the fifth chapter.

In this same chapter we have tried to synthesise the material gathered throughout the book. The result was not, as originally intended, to show a single, unified "book", but rather a series of "divergent" yet closely-interrelated "books", all of which are in some sense "Jonah" (3); none of which are the "only" reading possible. Again it should be stressed that this conclusion was reached initially by paying attention not only to the book's structure, but also to the "reader effect", both upon this writer and upon other exegetes who have contributed such widely differing readings to the literature. Only then did we begin to search more formally for explanations of these phenomena in the work of contemporary literary criticism as it applies to general literature and to the Bible itself. If we have laboured this point, it is only to emphasise once again that our starting point, and the source to which we have continually returned, is the book itself, going beyond it for "answers", as and when new problems emerged. Our intention has primarily been to let the book speak for itself.

Chapter I

ANALYSIS OF LANGUAGE

A number of studies of the Book of Jonah in recent years reflect the
growing emphasis on literary analysis of Biblical texts (1). What these
studies have in common is a concern with the relationship between the
form of the Book and its content. Thus the use of language, verbal forms,
sentence construction, rhythmic aspect, dramatic construction, etc.,
are brought into relationship with the overt meaning of the text, and the
way they complement, and reinforce, the meaning or meanings, is displayed.

As our starting point, we shall attempt to tackle the use of words, and
particularly the repetition of words, used by the author of "Jonah". Inevitably this means repeating the work of others, and whenever possible
this will be indicated. However, it is interesting to note that many of the
same observations were made independently (though often with different
conclusions), which reflects a common approach to studies in Biblical
narrative that seems to be currently "in the air".

We shall begin by examining as a preliminary measure the distribution
of verbs throughout the Book. This has the advantage of presenting certain materials in a readily available form for future reference, and giving
an overall view of certain patterns of word repetition. Though we are thus
separating rather artificially the distribution from the meaning to be
attached to the various word usages, the latter will be examined in subsequent sections.

The Distribution of Verbs

One of the first concerns of literary analysis is the defining of the literary
unit to be studied. Thus if we take an overview of "Jonah", we see the
symmetry of its division into two more or less equal parts (Chapters 1-2,
3-4), and could validly examine each half separately. Moreover each
chapter itself can be seen as an independent unit and examined by itself.
Within the chapters individual "scenes" can be recognised (e.g., Jonah's
call; Jonah aboard the ship, in Chapter 1) and these scenes can also constitute a unit for analysis. Our first concern, however, is the relationship between certain repeated words and the specific chapter or chapters
in which they are to be found. The structural implications are that the
presence of these words helps to define and encapsulate a particular unit,
and conversely to provide linkages between various chapters, thus defining
wider units. For this study we have taken into account all forms of a verbal
root (including nouns and adjectives derived from it) which appear more
than once. The results of listing these roots can be seen in Tables 1-4
(overleaf).

Table 1 — Verbs which appear in a single chapter only

Chapter 1	Chapter 2	Chapter 3	Chapter 4
ירא (6)	סבב (2)	כסה (2)	טוב (5)
טול (4)		טעם (2?)	מות (4)
סער (4)			קדם (3)
נפל (3)			שמח (2)
נתן (2)			נכה (2)
רדם (2)			חוס (2)
נגד (2)			חיה (2)
שזק (2)			
נשא (2)			

Table 2 — Verbs which appear in two chapters

Chapter 1	Chapter 2	Chapter 3	Chapter 4
ירד (3)	ירד (1)		
זבח (1)	זבח (1)		
נדר (2)	נדר (1)		
קום (3)		קום (3)	
הלך (4)		הלך (4)	
זעק (1)		זעק (1)	
שוב (1)		שוב (4)	
ברח (2)			ברח (1)
	מנה (1)		מנה (3)
	פלל (2)		פלל (1)
		ישב (1)	ישב (2)
		נחם (2)	נחם (1)
		ראה (1)	ראה (1)
		חרה (1)	חרה (4)

Table 3 — Verbs which appear in three chapters

Chapter 1	Chapter 2	Chapter 3	Chapter 4
קרא (3)	קרא (1)	קרא (5)	
באה (3)	באה (1)	באה (1)	
עבר (1?)	עבר (1)	עבר (1)	
עלה (1)	עלה (1)		עלה (1)
יבש (2)	יבש (1)		יבש (1)
אבד (2)		אבד (1)	אבד (1)
ידע (3)		ידע (1)	ידע (2)
רעה (3)		רעה (3)	רעה (3)
עשה (4)		עשה (3)	עשה (1)
דבר (1)		דבר (4)	דבר (1)

Table 4 — Verbs which appear in four chapters

Chapter 1	Chapter 2	Chapter 3	Chapter 4
גדל (6)	גדל (1)	גדל (4)	גדל (4)
אמר (9)	אמר (3)	אמר (3)	אמר (6)

A glance at Table 1 shows immediately the interesting feature that although in Chapter 1 four verbs appear more than twice (סער סול ירא and נפל) and three verbs do so in Chapter 4 (קדם מות טוב), none do so in Chapters 2 and 3. It is only when we include verbs which appear twice that a single verb can be included from Chapter 2 (סבב) and one from Chapter 3 (כסה) (2). That is to say that in the construction of the Book the technique of repeating a verbal root several times, yet restricting it to a single chapter, occurs in Chapters 1 and 4, yet not in 2 and 3. Thus from a purely technical point of view, there is a feature which distinguishes this former pair of chapters from the latter, an observation that will become significant at a later stage of this work (3). We shall examine the particular verbs which are contained in these chapters, and the meanings they convey, in the discussion on "meaning" (4).

Table 2 shows the verbs which appear in two separate chapters. We can recognise immediately two of the "call words" of Jonah (קום הלך) which occur in Chapters 1 and 3, the latter chapter being the occasion when the call is repeated. However, it is noteworthy already that in addition to their use in the call itself and its repetition (1:2, 3:2) and fulfillment (3:3, 4), these roots reappear a number of other times in the same chapters. A glance at Table 3 shows that the third call word, קרא , similarly appears several times in these chapters, and additionally in Chapter 2. Thus together there are six appearances of קום , eight of הלך and nine of קרא , yet they are all contained within Chapters 1-3, and do not reappear in the last chapter. It is clear that Chapters 1-3 contain the account of the call and its ultimate fulfillment, which explains at least one set of uses of these three verbs. But in no case is this exclusively so, and it is interesting that though the verbs are used for other purposes in the Book, they are nevertheless restricted to these three chapters. We may thus make a provisional note that a unit is hereby defined covering Chapters 1-3, and excluding Chapter 4.

The appearance of ברח in Chapters 1 and 4 reminds us that Jonah's explanation of this flight is delayed until this latter chapter. Thus the appearance of ברח in both places is no surprise, but nevertheless forms a further connecting element which distinguishes these two chapters from the others.

We have seen already the linkage between Chapters 1 and 3 provided by the repetition of the "call words" to Jonah. Yet it is interesting to note that certain other words, by their repetition in two chapters, might also serve to link them together. Particularly significant are words which link the "Psalm" to other parts of the Book. It shares ירד , זבח and נדר with Chapter 1; עבר with Chapter 3; פלל with Chapter 4 (Chapter 2 as a whole shares פלל and מנה with Chapter 4). It contains also קרא and באה in common with Chapters 1 and 3 (5); עלה in common with Chapters 1 and 4.

Chapters 1 and 3 are further linked by the verb זעק (one appearance each); and we shall see below the important relationships between the sailors and Ninevites established by the use of זעק and קרא (6). It comes, however, as a surprise to note a further connection between these two chapters. The fourfold appearance of שוב in Chapter 3 accords well with the problem of repetance with which it deals. But its single appearance in Chapter 1 alerts us to a possible extension of the idea to the earlier context (7). The appearance of מנה in Chapter 2 and 4 serves also to link the events in both chapters (8).

Finally, we can note the four verbs shared by Chapters 3 and 4 (ישב, נחם, חרה, ראה) and we shall see the interrelationship of these below (9). Altogether, if we include the verbs which occur over three chapters as well as two, eight are shared by Chapters 1 and 2 (נדר, זבח, ירד, עבר, יבש, עלה, באה, קרא) and eight are shared by Chapters 3 and 4 (חרה, ראה, נחם, ישב, עשה, רעה, ידע, אבד). (Three are shared by Chapters 2 and 3; seven by Chapters 1 and 4.)

The last Table (No. 4), shows the presence in all four chapters of גדל , whose 14 appearances in the book have been frequently commented upon (10). In addition, אמר appears 21 times.

The Repetition of Verbs

We shall now examine in more detail the verbs which repeat themselves, but which are restricted to a single chapter, so as to see the possible implications of these repetitions. Of the verbs used in Chapter 1, we can say at once that both סער and נפל are used here, in a sense, as technical terms. Since a storm at sea is being described in its mounting fury, the repetition of the word for "storm" is only to be expected (11). Likewise נפל is used three times to describe the stages involved in the "casting" of lots by the sailors. However, with the use of ירא six times, one can say at least that there is a strong undercurrent of "fear" that runs throughout the chapter (one not emphasised elsewhere in the book, though it would be relevant, for example, in Chapter 3), which serves to underline, almost subliminally, the fearsome situation in which the sailors find themselves. We shall return to this "fear" later in the section on the "growing phrase" (12) where we will see how it "develops" throughout the chapter.

With the fourfold usage of the root טול a significant new factor enters into the pattern. Although it might be argued that it is also a "technical term" for "hurling", it is curious that it is used here with two separate subjects; and that whereas it could be argued that the acts of hurling the vessels overboard by the sailors (verse 5) is comparable to that of hurling Jonah overboard (verse 15) and, indeed, his request that they do so (verse 12), it is surprising to find the same usage with regards the act of God in hurling a wind onto the sea. However, if we examine the sequence of events we can see a causal relationship between all four uses: God hurls the wind; the sailors are forced to hurl the vessels overboard; Jonah (whether to save the sailors, or to kill himself) is forced to ask to be hurled overboard, and the sailors have no other choice but to hurl him into the sea (13). That is to say that the act of God in sending the storm has consequences which are revealed not merely on the level of the narrative itself, but also on the "subliminal" level of the word that repeats and repeats itself through the episode (14). We can state this same idea in a slightly different way - namely that the "word" of God once expressed (whether as command or action), remains somehow present, "in the air," until it comes to be fulfilled (15). To confirm this we must turn briefly to a second set of repetitions within the chapter. In the call to Jonah, three verbs are used in the imperative form: וקרא .... לך, קום (16) "Rise up! Go!...and call!" These same words, as we have noted above, are repeated at the beginning of Chapter 3, when God's word comes a second time to Jonah. That is to say they are still "in the air" waiting till the prophet carries them out. But when Jonah descends into the innermost part of the boat and falls into a deep sleep, he is roused by the captain of the crew awakening him with two of the call words: "Rise up! Call!" Thus the call words are repeated, but in an ironic fashion, meaning, as they do, different things to Jonah (and the reader), who hear in them God's original command repeated, and to the captain, who intends only that Jonah pray to his God (17). Thus we can see that the repetition of these words both echoes the original commands of God in a clearly recognisable way, and at the same time shows how they are unconsciously present, "disguised" within the course of other external events (18). The effect of this technique upon the reader is to force him from the beginning onwards to read the story on at least two levels.

Since we have opened up the problem of the repetition of words serving to underline and "comment upon" the overt action, it is worth pursuing it through the examination of another verb. The root ירד occurs three times in Chapter 1 (19). When Jonah attempts to flee to Tarshish, he "went down" to Jaffa, found a boat and "went down" into it. When the storm breaks, Jonah "went down" (20) into the innermost parts of the ship. Once again it is possible to dismiss the threefold repetition as a mere technical usage of the verb; however, in view of what we have seen so far, it is likely that we have here a description of a continuing act of "descent" by Jonah which can therefore be interpreted in both "physical" and "spiritual" terms (21). In support of the latter, we can bring the fourth usage of ירד , namely in the "Psalm" (2:7), where the context gives to the description of a physical descent (in the sea) a spiritual dimension. We shall return later to the problem as to whether the "Psalm" is an integral part of the book (22), but suggest for the moment that at least a link is provided by this word (both from a "technical" and "meaning" point of view) between the events in Chapter 1 and the "Psalm," and that a "spiritual" interpretation of Jonah's flight is reinforced by the occurrence of ירד in both chapters (23).

To sum up what we have found so far, the repetition of a verb within a single chapter may have one of the following effects:

i. The neutral effect of the repetition of a technical term, e.g., נפל

ii. The emphasising of an underlying <u>atmosphere</u> within a chapter, i.g., ירא , סער

iii. The reinforcing of the <u>ideas</u> expressed in the overt narrative, e.g., נטל , קום , קרא , ירד

If we now turn to Chapter 4 where we have noted that three verbs are repeated more than once, two of them immediately force themselves upon our attention, namely מות "death" and טוב "good" precisely because of their contrasting meanings. In fact, as we take into account the other verbs which are present here, further violent contrasts are everywhere apparent: מות and חיים ; רעה and טוב ; חרה and שמח חוס ; נכה, יבש , אבד (24) and נחם, חסד,רחם , חנן (25).

Expressed in this form, the violence of these contrasts is almost shocking, yet a brief reconsideration makes it clear that this is only because the way the final scene has been composed by the author has taken the edge off our consciousness of its violence. On several levels a great conflict is taking place. The will of Jonah is yet again being matched against the will of God - a conflict formerly expressed by the violence of a storm at sea (26). Expressed in another way, we are dealing with the rage and frustration of Jonah (sometimes characterised as "childish" rage) (27) which has to be admitted by him, despite the prophet's unwillingness (he only answers God's question in verse 4, in verse 9), and thus exorcised - a highly traumatic psychological exercise. The means God employs are violent - both in themselves and in their contrasts: the God who is described as "compassionate, long-suffering and abundant in mercy" inflicts controlled, disciplinary measures upon His prophet; Jonah is thus forced through wildly changing emotional states, from extreme anger to extreme joy to death-seeking despair; finally as if in order to teach Jonah the implications of the destruction he wished to see inflicted upon Nineveh, God lets him suffer the pain of the wind and burning sun on his head, so that physical violence is present as well. So much are we concerned with the prophet that we hardly even notice the depiction of the background of violence in nature itself, here "speeded up" by the sudden blossoming and equally sudden destruction of the gourd, "struck" (נכה verse 7) by the worm, just as Jonah is "struck" (נכה verse 8) by the sun.

Thus here no single word sets the emotional atmosphere (as did ירא in Chapter 1), but rather the various levels of conflict situation are underlined by the multiplication of verbs with contrasting meanings. These, however, are never actually set in direct opposition to each other in the final composition, but are placed within, or in successive, contrasting contexts. For example, Jonah's first angry outburst, his "prayer" ending in a plea for death (4:2-3), contains within it the description of God's attributes of compassion; the sequence of "constructions" (Jonah builds his <u>succah</u>, sits comfortably in the shade of the gourd, Jonah rejoices) is succeeded by the series of "destructions" (the appointing of the worm, the striking of the gourd and its withering, the appointing of the wind, the sun striking Jonah till he faints, and his second request for death).

Thus we have seen how the use of language, the choice of words and their repetitions, can both reveal "subliminally" the atmosphere being created, and at the same time conceal it, through the form of composition itself. Furthermore, they help "seal off" a unit by their presence and alternatively provide linkages across two separate units. Various other examples of this latter effect will become apparent as this analysis continues, but we will turn how to a separate, though related, effect of these repetitions, namely the comparison it allows between different characters in the book.

Comparison and Contrast

The order to Jonah to "rise up" is a familiar introduction to a prophetic call (28), and the reader expects with the repetition of the verb in the following verse, "and he rose up," the usual continuation in which the prophet does what he is told (29) only to be shocked by the appearance of "to flee to Tarshish" (30). Thus the author has created a latent tension built into this repetition, which will act upon the reader when he encounters the same repetition in Chapter 3. Will the Jonah who "rises up" now finally fulfil his mission? There is thus a second level of linkage created by the repetition. Yet the sixth occurrence of the same root, and the same form ויקם is probably not accidental, for it is the verb used to describe the immediate response of the king of Nineveh on hearing of the message of Jonah and his people's response, he rises up...and himself does penitence. We thus have here at the very least a connection between the king and Jonah, contrasting their first immediate response to a message from God (31). It is thus an element in the theme expressed throughout the narrative of the contrast between the behaviour of Jonah and all the pagans (sailors and Ninevites) that he encounters.

However, this is not an isolated instance where the same verbal form is used with regard Jonah and the king of Nineveh. The response of the king after he rises up is to take off his robe, to cover himself with sackcloth and to sit in ashes (3:6):

ויגע הדבר אל מלך נינוה ויקם מכסאו ויעבר אדרחו מעליו ויכס שק
וישב על האפר

"And the tidings reached the king of Nineveh, and he arose from his throne, and laid his robe from him, and covered him with sackcloth, and sat in ashes."

When Jonah is challenged by God about his anger at the non-destruction of Nineveh (4:4), he does not answer with words, but leaves the city and sits down to the East of it (4:5):

ויצא יונה מן העיר וישב מקדם לעיר ויעש לו שם סכה וישב תחתיה בצל
עד אשר יראה מה יהיה בעיר

"Then Jonah went out of the city, and <u>sat</u> on the east side of the city, and there made him a booth, and <u>sat</u> under it in the shade, till he might see what would become of the city." The repetition of וישב here draws attention to this verb. One notes that "he sits," and then sets about making himself comfortable, building the booth, and then "sits" again. As we shall note again later (32), while the king of Nineveh sits in ashes inside the city hoping it will be spared, Jonah sits in the shade outside the city, hoping it will be destroyed.

We can thus recognise a technique of the author that has emerged from this analysis. By using the same verbal form, with two different subjects, he brings them into contrast: Jonah in response to God's command - the king in response to God's threat; the king's concern that the city be spared, at considerable discomfort to himself - Jonah's concern that it be destroyed, while he himself is comfortable (33).

A variant of the same technique is used to compare, and thus identify with one another, the two groups of pagans mentioned in the story - the sailors and the Ninevites. Both "call out in prayer" to God using the verb קרא (34) (1:14; 3:8); both use the same verb זעק - though, as we shall see below (35), with contrasting meanings. Most significantly, in the face of imminent disaster (the sailors from the storm, the Ninevites from God's decree) their respective leaders (the captain, the king) in similarly constructed sentences express the identical hope (1:16; 3:9) "that we perish not" ולא נאבד . Thus we are led to see both groups that Jonah encounters in their dissimilarity (the evil Ninevites, the "neutral" sailors) and conversely in the elements that they have in common - a readiness to respond to the will of God with prayer, the ultimate helplessness of all mankind in the face of death.

The technique is also used to compare the actions of God and man. The most obvious example is in fact stated explicitly in the text in God's final question to Jonah (4:10-11): אתה חסת על הקיקיון ..... ואני לא אחוס על נינוה: "You had <u>pity</u> on the gourd...should not I have <u>pity</u> on Nineveh....?" The use of the same verb, emphasised by the use of the personal pronouns, lead us to compare and contrast a quality in man and in God (36). Nor is this, again, an isolated case, because one other verb is used in relation to a quality in God and Jonah, namely חרה , "anger," used here for the "righteous anger" of God חרון אפו (3:9), and ironically for the "self-righteous anger" of Jonah (37). Not only do God and Jonah share these two verbs of emotion, but they also share the sense of "sight" (38). In 3:10, after the repentance of Nineveh: וירא האלהים את מעשיהם "And God saw their works....." God sees "objectively" what happens in the city, and is persuaded by it to "change His mind." Jonah also "sees" the city of Nineveh, but from a totally subjective point of view (4:5):

..... וישב תחתיה בצל עד אשר יראה מה יהיה בעיר
"...and he sat under it (the booth) in the shade, till he might <u>see</u> what would be in the city." Thus God and Jonah are matched against each other on a subliminal level, in addition to the overt conflict recorded in the

CHAPTER I - ANALYSIS OF LANGUAGE

narrative itself. A similar "subliminal" device is easily overlooked through the familiarity of the word used: דבר . Though אמר "to say" appears through-out the Book, and is in fact the commonest verb employed, דבר is used far more selectively. The דבר of YHWH comes to Jonah in 1:1 and a second time in 3:1. The second time it is reinforced by the reminder that he may only say the words which God "speaks" (דבר) to him (3:2) (39). This "mat-ter" דבר reaches the king of Nineveh (3:6), and God ultimately repents of the evil which he "said" (דבר) to do to them (3:10). Thus in all these usages, the "word" is that of God, echoing throughout the chapters - a word that on-ly God Himself can cancel. Furthermore, the significance of the דבר is strengthened by the usage of the formula: ויהי דבר ה' אל יונה.......
"Now the word of YHWH came unto Jonah...." with all its rich associations with the call to the prophets (40). With the fulfillment of his task, Jonah finds himself free to voice his complaint, which he opens with the words (4:2):....הלא זה דברי "Was not this may saying....?" Literally, "Now the word of Jonah came unto YHWH," this "appropriation" of the divine "word" emphasising even more strongly the significance of the quarrel between Jonah and God (41).

In passing it is worth noting two other techniques which contribute to this effect. When God hurls the storm onto the sea, the word order puts parti-cular emphasis on YHWH (1: 4): וה' הטיל "And YHWH hurled ..." Two verses later, when we learn that Jonah goes down into the innermost part of the ship, the identical structure recurs (1:5): ויונה ירד "And Jonah went down..." As we noted in the discussion on ירד (42), the act of Jonah can thus be seen as a direct "answer" (43) to the act of God. Furthermore, in the symmetrical construction of Chapter 4 (44), the same number of words are given to Jonah (4:2-3) and God (4:10-11) in their major sentences, and in the intermediate dialogue. The wider meaning of this conflict between God and Jonah will be discussed in the chapter on the Analysis of Themes (45).

A third set of comparisons, obtained by the use of a shared verb, links the pagans and God (46). One of the central themes of the book is "repentance," characterised by the verb שוב to "turn". It is used here in the sense of "turning away" from evil (the Ninevites turn away from the evil in their hands); and in God's responsive "turning" from his anger (47). The four occurrences of שוב in Chapter 3 are found in three tightly interrelated sentences (3:8b-10) (48), containing part of the king's proclamation and God's response.

וישבו איש מדרכו הרעה ומן החמס אשר בכפיהם......
מי יודע ישוב ונחם האלהים ושב מחרון אפו ולא נאבד.
וירא האלהים את מעשיהם כי שבו מדרכם הרעה וינחם האלהים על הרעה
אשר דבר לעשות להם ולא עשה.

"... let them turn every man from his evil way, and from the violence that is in their hands. Who knoweth whether God will not turn and repent, and turn away from His fierce anger, that we perish not? And God saw their

COMPARISON AND CONTRAST   21 works, that they turned from their evil way; and God repented of the evil, which He said He would do unto them; and He did it not."

The initiative for "turning" comes from the people of Nineveh - away from their evil way and the violence in their hands. Their hope is that God will Himself "turn," also in two ways - to "reconsider" (both שוב (49) and נחם having no object when used the first time in 3:9); and then specifically "turn away" from His fierce anger. In the event God sees them "turn" from their evil way, and indeed repents of the evil He said He would do to them. The verb שוב is thus used equally with the Ninevites and with God, the intention to "turn" and the "turning" itself of the Ninevites bracketing (50) the "turning" of God. An interesting feature of the structure thus coincides with the lesson being conveyed in the narrative itself, namely the hope that lies in repentance as a way of influencing God, yet at the same time the provisional nature of this hope - "Who knows...?" God indeed "turns," but the key word of God's "repenting" (נחם) of the evil, the punishment He has prepared, remains outside the bracketing, thus emphasising its provisional nature, beyond the automatic control of man. Nevertheless the balance between the acts of God and of man, suggested by the equal distribution of the verb שוב , is confirmed by the balanced chiastic structure of the final sentence in this text, which hinges on the use of the words עשה and רעה(51). God saw their "doings," that they turned from their "evil" way; in exact response God repents of the "evil" He said He would "do" to them. Again an exact balance is achieved between the acts of man and of God, God responding "measure for measure" to the initiative of man.

Multiple Meanings

With the introduction of the word רעה (52) into our discussion (a word which is used in relationship to all three "characters" in the book: God, Jonah, the pagans), in addition to the element of comparison and contrast it evokes, a further dimension appears. This is the problem of translation, since the word itself has a number of different meanings throughout the book - yet remains recognisably the same word. That is to say that although the author could have chosen a different word each time to express different shades of meaning, by retaining this one, he allows each usage to interact with the other, multiplying the levels of correspondence and contrast between the respective subjects or contexts related to the word.

In its first appearance there is already a certain ambiguity:
קום לך אל נינוה העיר הגדולה וקרא עליה כי עלתה רעתם לפני
"Arise, go to Nineveh, that great city, and proclaim against it that their evil is come up before Me." (1:2). Does רעתם refer to the evil performed by the Ninevites (as most translations suggest), or does it refer to the "evil" which God is about to bring down upon their heads? (53) The ambivalence is suggestive, and already points to the problem of the "localisation" of evil that we shall see recurring in the book.

Diagram 1

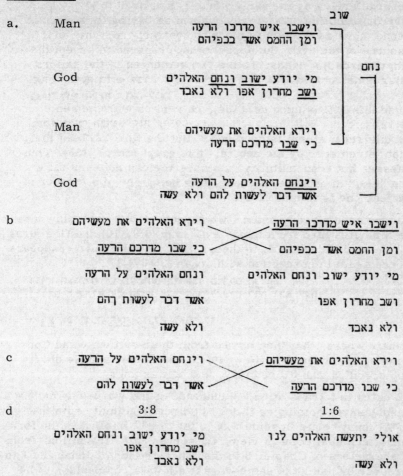

a) Shows how שוב recurs four times in 3:8b-10, the two "turnings" by man bracketing the two "turnings" of God. נחם is both inside and outside these brackets. See page 22.

b) Shows the parallel construction in the same verses between the words of the king and what God subsequently saw and did. Note the chiastic relationship of the first pair of sentences, and the parallel relationship of the second pair – based on נחם and the final verb.

c) A further chiastic relationship in which the words עשה and רעה relating respectively to man and then God, form the pivot. See page 22.

d) An additional sign of the complexity of construction – the parallel between 1:6 and 3:8.

MULTIPLE MEANINGS

23

The consequence of Jonah's flight is the storm, and the "evil plight" of the sailors is characterised by the same word (1:7, 8) הרעה הזאת . But in their question to Jonah this רעה is recognised as having its source in the act of someone, thus an attempt is made to abstract from the "evil situation" the source of the evil. But Jonah is not prepared to accept the label "evil" with regards his deeds. To the two sentences of the sailors with their similar construction (1:7, 8):

בשלמי הרעה הזאת לנו

באשר למי הרעה הזאת לנו

("for whose cause this evil is upon us") (54), he replies with the same construction (1:12): בשלי הסער הגדול הזה עליכם

"because of me this great storm is upon you." But the word רעה of the sailors' question is replaced by the neutral "this great storm" (55). Thus Jonah both confesses his responsibility, yet nevertheless does not fully acknowledge the "evil" of what he has done, this being one of a number of "partial confessions" he is to make (56).

In Chapter 3, as we have already noted, two aspects of רעה interplay with each other: the Ninevites turn from their "evil" way (3:8, 10) and God turns from the "evil" He said He would do to them (3:10). But the word reappears immediately, once again in connection with Jonah (3:10-4:1):

וירא האלהים את מעשיהם כי שבו מדרכם הרעה

וינחם האלהים על הרעה אשר דבר לעשות להם ולא עשה.

ויֵרַע אל יונה רעה גדולה ויחר לו

"And God saw their works, that they turned from their evil way: and God repented of the evil, which He said He would do unto them; and He did it not. But it 'displeased' Jonah exceedingly, and he was angry."

It is difficult to catch in a translation the innuendo of the word-play here - for Jonah's "displeasure" coming as it does in direct continuity with the other uses of רעה must relate in some way to the "evil" implied in the former (57). From a technical point of view, 4:1 serves as a "transition" from the events and characters of Chapter 3 to the concentration of Jonah in Chapter 4 (58). Moreover by using the same word it allows a comparison to be made between the relationship of all three "characters" and this concept. Thus it puts into contrast the "acknowledged" evil of the Ninevites and the "unacknowledged" evil of Jonah (which we have seen in Chapter 1), and prepares us for the discussion of this in Chapter 4 (59).

The subtlety of this interplay of ideas becomes apparent with the next usage of the word, in Jonah's statement about the attributes (60) of God in 4:2. He quotes a version of the attributes (found elsewhere only in Joel 2:13) (61) in which the closing phrase is ונחם על הרעה"and repentest Thee of the evil." In its overt meaning, Jonah's words refer back directly to God's "repenting of the evil" He said He would do to Nineveh (3:10), thus making a further bridge between the two chapters. In the context, however, it provides an ironic commentary on God's relationship to the prophet himself. For God repented of the evil He would do to Nineveh in response to their turning from their "evil" - this very "grace" of God, however, being even more extended in His dealings with the "unacknowledged" evil of His prophet. This becomes even more clear in the final usage of רעה , which once again has a double meaning (and is related in its context to yet another word-play). Jonah refuses to answer God's question (4:4) and sits outside Nineveh in the shade of his booth.

וימן ה' אלהים קיקיון ויעל מעל ליונה להיות צל על ראשו
להציל לו מרעתו

"And YHWH God prepared a gourd, and made it to come up over Jonah, that it might be a shade over his head, to deliver him from his evil." (4:6.) The word play on צל / להציל (to be a shade/to deliver) alerts us to the double purpose of the gourd (62). By providing a shade it is to comfort Jonah and help cool his "displeasure" (רעה). In this it succeeds, for Jonah rejoices greatly in the gourd (4:6b). But at the same time it is to deliver him from his "evil" (63) (his anger at the non-destruction of Nineveh) by providing a tangible, physical example for Jonah of God's pity, which man should also attempt to imitate.

We have thus here a highly complex interweaving of ideas about the nature and source of evil. If "evil" is the wickedness of Nineveh, what can we say of the "evil" of Jonah? Is his unwillingness to see them saved really as bad as the deeds of Nineveh itself? Why is the just punishment that God is about to mete out discribed by the same term; in what sense is it evil? What is important from our analysis is the recognition of the ambiguities implicit in such multiplicity of meaning (64). "Evil" is no longer a static thing to be ascribed to the "wicked Ninevites" "out there," but a dynamic thing, admitted and unadmitted, constantly changing as does the relationship between the characters of the book. The reader is caught up in these changing currents, and must frequently adjust his perspective. We shall examine the nature of these ambiguities in the Analysis of Themes (65), but would draw attention now to what is the essential paradox of the author's technique: namely that he uses what is overtly a very precise and economical technique of word usage, but at the same time succeeds in conveying reverberations and ambiguities that dissolve any oversimplified reading of the story.

A second example of this effect can be seen in the use of קרא , the third of Jonah's "call words." The command of God to Jonah to "call out" קריאה (1:2, 3:2) gives the word the meaning "proclaim." (so also the form "proclamation" in 3:2). In this sense it links together the two commands to Jonah, in Chapters 1 and 3, to proclaim God's word against Nineveh. Here the speaker calls out from a position of knowledge and self-confidence on behalf of God. Yet by the paradoxical methods of our author, the same root is used to serve a totally opposite meaning: the cry of prayer in distress when self-confidence is totally lacking, a cry addressed to God. The transition point naturally hinges on the figure of Jonah himself, in the ironic situation we have already noted (66) - the captain of the ship telling Jonah to "cry out" to his God, thus repeating unknowingly God's call word to Jonah. The interplay between these two meanings seems to be deliberately developed. In the sense of "pray" it introduces the prayer of the sailors to YHWH in 1:14, and reappears significantly in Jonah's "psalm" (2:3) serving among other things to link the "Psalm" to the rest of the book.

However in Chapter 3, its first meaning is "restored" in the repetition of God's call to Jonah (3:2) and Jonah's actual fulfillment (3:4) of his task. As if in further accordance with God's will (like the repetition of הטיל) the word continues to carry this sense of proclamation, as the people of Nineveh proclaim a fast (3:5). But again the sense of prayer reappears in the words of the king (3:8): "and let them <u>cry</u> mightily to God." As we have noted above (67), this serves the additional purpose of comparing and linking the response of the people of Nineveh to that of the sailors. With this prayer of the Ninevites, the verb recurs no more, and we can say that with their prayer the "call" of God (and the call words themselves) reach their fulfillment and need no longer remain "in the air."

It is worth noting, however, that a similar but reversed interplay of meanings takes place with the other verb of "calling" which is used by our author, זעק , whose primary meaning is "to call out in need." The response of the sailors to the storm is to "cry out" to their gods (1:5)

וייראו המלחים ויזעקו איש אל אלהיו

"And the mariners were afraid and cried every man unto his god." Under the influence of זעק , the mood is set for the new meaning with which the captain uses קרא in speaking to Jonah. Conversely in Chapter 3, after Jonah has "proclaimed" (3:4), and the people have "proclaimed" (3:5 - using קרא both times), the king has it "proclaimed" (זעק) so that the meaning of זעק is now "under the influence" of קרא . Certainly the use of זעק with regards both the sailors and the Ninevites is another technique for linking these two sets of representatives of the pagan world. It is possible, however, to see in addition a certain significance in the switching of the words קרא and זעק , as well as their changing meaning. Had Jonah obeyed the first time, there would have been no need for the other meaning of קרא to be used - he would have proclaimed, and events would have transpired in Nineveh, as indeed they did, in Chapter 3. However, his flight led to the storm, and the fear of the sailors, and all the opposite meanings latent in קרא (under the influence of the "cry" of the sailors), became released - thus God's word is still "fulfilled," though in a quite contrary sense.

Before leaving this section we can consider one more verb which is used both for comparisons between two sets of characters, and to convey extra ideas through the multiplicity of its meanings - namely ידע "to know." When the storm rages, and all their prayers and skill have failed them, the sailors set out to discover the source of this evil (1:7)

ונדעה בשלמי הרעה הזאת לנו

"...that we may know for whose cause this evil is upon us." They wish to <u>know</u> a fact, a piece of technical information obtained through "technolocigal" means (68), the casting of lots, which can be used for determining their next step. Their technology works, and Jonah is revealed as the guilty party. But in their quest for more information, a new dimension enters into what they <u>know,</u> opening up quite different perspectives (1:10):

וייראו האנשים יראה גדולה ויאמרו אליו מה זאת עשית כי ידעו
האנשים כי מלפני ה' הוא ברח כי הגיד להם

"Then the men were exceedingly afraid, and said unto him: 'What is this that thou hast done?'" For the men <u>knew</u> that he fled from the presence of YHWH, because he had told them." The change in the nature of their knowledge is heralded by the change in the nature of their questions. Those in Verse 8 are all "technical" ones, aimed at obtaining necessary information - where is he from, of what people, etc. Now their question is also an exclamation, uttered in great fear, and it concerns the behaviour of Jonah himself and his attempted flight from YHWH - for the men <u>knew</u> that he fled from the presence of YHWH. They are no longer <u>outside</u> of Jonah's situation, trying to ascertain objective knowledge of <u>what</u> has happened; they are themselves <u>inside</u> Jonah's situation, trying to explain out of their own subjective knowledge <u>how</u> it could have happened.

With the third use in this chapter comes a third development (1:12b):

כי יודע אני כי בשלי הסער הגדול הזה עליכם

"...for I <u>know</u> that because of me this great storm is upon you." Now the speaker is Jonah, and we have the first hint at what he "knows," the first overt clue to his motivations (69). Furthermore, with the extra ironic dimension we have already noted (70), he only makes a partial confession of his guilt, so that the question arises about how much he really "<u>knows</u>," and how much he is prepared to "<u>acknowledge</u>" - the latter being the new dimension of meaning added to ידע in his statement.

The development in the "knowledge" of the sailors has been matched by their growing "fear," fear that will change into "fear of YHWH" (1:16) (71). Nevertheless their "knowledge" is restricted to the human plane: facts and human motivations. In this respect the speculation of the king of Nineveh (3:9) brings us to the borderline between human knowledge and knowledge of the divine will.

מי יודע ישוב ונחם האלהים ושב מחרון אפו ולא נאבד

"...Who <u>knoweth</u> whether God will not turn and repent, and turn away from His fierce anger, that we perish not?"

With this statement he goes one step further than the captain of the ship, whose parallel "perhaps" (1:6) is limited to a hope that God will "think of them." The king speculates on the inner workings of the mind of God, which as a pagan in this story, he can only guess at. We are thus ready for the next transition of meaning, when Jonah speaks yet again of what he knows (4:2):

כי ידעתי כי אתה אל חנון ורחום ארך אפים ורב חסד ונחם על הרעה

"for I <u>knew</u> that Thou are a gracious God, and compassionate, long-suffering and abundant in mercy, and repentest Thee of the evil." Jonah has a special knowledge of God - knowledge that comes not merely from his personal experience, but also from his tradition, in a formula of the "Attributes of God" that goes back to the encounters between Moses and God (72), and which was celebrated in various forms throughout the Biblical tradition (73). Thus here the root ידע takes on the peak of its meaning, the transcendent knowledge of the nature of God, obtained through revelation, and confirmed in the experience of Israel - and at the same time in the mouth of Jonah, that knowledge becomes absurd! Because it is spoken in the middle of Jonah's complaint about these very qualities of God, and, in addition, because of the ironic fact that but for this very patience and compassion of God, Jonah himself would not be alive to complain about them! Thus the prophet who can speak of the transcendental knowledge of God, lacks the simple, "human" knowledge of the sailors (1:10) about the significance of flight from God; and thus one of the circles of meaning is completed, as these two ideas interact afresh with each other.

When the verb returns for the last time, it is given a "neutral" context which allows all the meanings we have seen till now, as well as other dimensions, to reverberate with each other. God, in His final speech, characterises the people of Nineveh, and thus the pagan world, as (4:11):

..... העיר הגדולה אשר יש בה הרבה משתים עשרה רבו אדם
אשר לא ידע בין ימינו לשמאלו ובהמה רבה

"...that great city, wherein are more than twelve myriad persons that cannot discern between their right hand and their left, and also much cattle." The root ידע is used in the sense of distinguishing between two things, which gives it a quite new dimension in "Jonah". Nevertheless since it cannot "lose" the associations it already has, the complex of ideas is taken a stage further by the very "neutrality" of the context ("between left and right"), which cannot be meant in its literal sense (74). Two distinctions are thus presented: firstly, the difference between the pagans as a whole and Jonah - namely the knowledge the latter has of YHWH, with all its implications (and all the reservations about Jonah's real knowledge); secondly, the ability to distinguish between different things, presumably values like "good" and "evil" which are so prominent in the final chapter (75). Precisely this latter choice is demanded of Israel (76), and in their ignorance, the pagans are not just to be arbitrarily destroyed, but rather to be "pitied."

However one interprets this final usage, it is yet another part of the subtle way the author has drawn out the dimensions of meaning in a single root by varying the context and subject, thus allowing once again contrasting aspects of his characters to emerge, and deepening the nature of their interrelationship.

Movement and Counter-Movement

Until now, starting from the usage of individual verbal roots, we have examined certain interrelationships in the book. As we move on to study two further roots (הלך and עשה) in more detail, we can draw together the elements of a broader motif, a movement and counter-movement in the book, that is similarly underlined by the usage of individual words.

With הלך we enter, as well, the problem of where repetitions really have significance, and where they are merely there by chance - perhaps one of the key problems in this way of reading a narrative text. Since of the three "call words" to Jonah both קום and קרא have repeated themselves significantly (in the words of the captain of the crew, etc.) can one see similar significance in the repetitions of הלך in chapters 1 and 3?

We can break down the usages of הלך into certain clear units. There is the call itself (1:2), its repetition (3:2) and the first stage of its fulfillment by Jonah (3:3) - all three of which instances parallel the use of the other call words. In Chapter 1 it is used twice in relationship to the storm (1:11, 13 הולך) in phrases which we shall study further in a later section (77). Here it contributes to the sense of movement of the storm as it grows in fury. The other use here (1:7) is in the common idiomatic form לכו "come let us...," with regard the casting of lots. In Chapter 3 it appears twice in the form מהלך which is used both to describe the dimensions of Niniveh and the distance into it penetrated by Jonah. Without entering into the controversy about whether "three days' journey" refers to the diameter, circumference or the sum of all the streets, or into the archaeological evidence as to the size of Nineveh (78), the effect of this usage is to contrast the actual size of the city and the distance penetrated into it by Jonah - namely one third of the way (79).

At first glance we have here a miscellaneous set of usages not clearly interrelated, but we can say at least that yet again despite this variety, the root is restricted to Chapters 1 and 3. This in turn suggests that, as with the other call words, the root הלך remains "in the air" until the actual word of God is fulfilled, after which the word is no longer "required." We can note furthermore that whereas in Chapter 3 all four usages relate directly to Jonah and his "walking" to fulfil his mission, in Chapter 1 the second three usages relate to "others" (the sailors' words, the growing storm) - both of which events are caused by Jonah's initial flight. It seems as if the author is trying yet again to show that if God's word is not fulfilled directly, a partial or "distorted" version of it nevertheless begins to act in the world, partly as an echo to remind Jonah of his call, partly as a source of trouble (for himself and others). Thus just as God treats Jonah indirectly through various natural agents (wind, fish, plant, etc.) (80), so His "word," with an independent existence of its own, continues to trouble the reluctant prophet. Certainly this accords with the use of הטיל (81) we have seen above, and also the changing meaning of קרא (82) and the formal repetition of קום (83). In view of this we would conclude that the repetition of all three call words is part of an intentional design of the author, and that they relate to the motif that God's word, once expressed, remains present, waiting until it is fulfilled, creating secondary effects if it is not (84). Furthermore we can see that they are part of a movement in the book which sets the omnipotence of God over against the powerlessness of man to disobey Him.

As we move on to examine עשה we meet again the problem of a word with a very general meaning, which seems to serve various unrelated purposes in the book.

Its first occurrence is in Jonah's description of his God in 1:9, culminating in:

אשר עשה את הים ואת היבשה

"...who hath made the sea and the dry land." In the context of the storm, the meaning is clear that YHWH is the all-powerful controller of the land and sea, who is acting, through the storm, against his prophet. To this powerful God the sailors pray, acknowledging His omnipotence and their utter helplessness in His hands (1:14):

כי אתה ה' כל אשר חפצת עשית

"...for Thou, O YHWH, hast done as it pleased Thee." Sandwiched between these two exclamations of the might of God, come two human "deeds": the shocked cry of the sailors to Jonah (1:10): מה זאת עשית "What is this that thou hast done?", and their bewildered question: מה נעשה לך "What shall we do unto thee?". Both cases imply the impotence of man against the background of divine acts: How could Jonah have tried to flee from his God? What can be done to rectify the situation? (85)

We have already examined above (86) the play on עשה which occurs in Chapter 3, where, around the pivotal point of "turning" from their evil deeds, God is led to repent from the evil He said He would do "and He did it not" (3:10). With this verse we have the culmination of the countermovement which began with the "belief" of the Ninevites in God (87). Despite the omnipotence of God, so strongly underlined in the narrative till now, man can exert influence upon God, and lead Him to change His mind - not through flight from God's word, which only leads to confusion and ultimately destruction, but through "Teshuvah," "turning" from evil, back to God.

Yet עשה recurs once more in a sort of epilogue to this episode, when it is used to describe Jonah's "making" of a booth (4:5). If we take this usage in connection with the root דבר which we have examined above (88), we can see that it fits again with the pattern of Jonah's wilfulness in setting his "word" against that of God. Thus both the theme of Jonah's quarrel with God, and that of the relative power of man and God, expressed through the root עשה , enter their final resolution.

An interesting confirmation of this interpretation of the movement and countermovement, comes through examining the uses of the infinitive in the book (89). A useful starting point is the observation by Good (90) that whereas the infinitive is used in Jonah's unsuccessful attempt "to flee" (1:3), when he rises up and "goes" (3:3), the "co-ordinate finite verb" is used. Though Good has not followed this through, it can be seen that all the acts performed by men, which are introduced by the infinitive, turn out to be unsuccessful; however, when the infinitive is used for an act by God, it succeeds. In 1:3, Jonah goes down into the ship "to come" with them to Tarshish - but never arrives. In 1:5, the sailors try to lighten the boat and thus save themselves, but this is ineffective. In 1:13, they try to return to the dry land, but cannot. In 3:4, Jonah begins to come into the city, and the use of the verb "to begin" in addition to the infinitive, reinforces the impression that he "only just" entered it (91), and thus did not succeed in going the whole way that was intended. In 4:2, Jonah recalls his failed attempt to flee.

In contrast the things that God ordains (using the infinitive) succeed. In 2/1, YHWH prepared a great fish to swallow Jonah. In 4:6, the gourd grows over Jonah's head to shade him and to deliver him from his evil. (In the former intention God is successful, in the latter case we are left with the question mark at the end of the book). But the one case where an infinitive is used about an action of God that "fails," it is in association with precisely this focal point of repentance (3:10b) "And God repented of the evil which He said to do to them; and He did it not." Only God has the power to break the rules by which events (and, so to speak, the language which describes these events) are governed. To the further implications of this movement and countermovement we shall return in the Analysis of Themes (92).

The Growing Phrase

Till now we have paid attention to the usage of isolated words. As a next step we will examine how similar techniques of the author are applied to larger units, namely whole phrases.

The author's economy of language and of vocabulary, as we have already seen, rather than limiting him, has in fact opened up reverberations between the various repetitions of words. When we come to deal with phrases, a further dimension becomes apparent. The repetition of an identical phrase after an interval enables us to examine the same events in a new way, in the light of the intervening experience. Thus the Jonah who hears God's almost identical command in Chapter 3, is different from the Jonah who heard it in 1:1. Though the words are the same, his response is different (93).

A particular feature of "Jonah" is the use of the "growing phrase," i.e., a phrase which is repeated with the addition of a further word or element to it. The significance lies in the added meaning given by the extra element, in addition to the intervening events. Though the fact of such repe-

titions as a stylistic device has long been recognised (94), it is only re-
latively recently that the effect it produces has been studied (95).

A good account of the developing fear of the sailors comes from Fränkel (96), who brings together the three phrases:

1:5 וייראו המלחים

1:10 וייראו האנשים יראה גדולה

1:16 וייראו האנשים יראה גדולה את ה'

"In the form of writing is reflected its content. The sentences which en-
large and go onward, each one of which adds to the previous, emphasises
the change which began in the inner life of the men. When the storm breaks
out they react with וייראו ; when they hear of Jonah's flight from before
the Lord their fear increases to יראה גדולה; and when the sea ceases
from its raging their fear rises till: יראה גדולה את ה'. Note that the fear of
the men at the hour they are delivered from death is greater than when
death comes upon them."

To this Cohn adds the example of the growing phrase concerning the
storm:

1:4 ויהי סער גדול בים

1:11 כי הים הולך וסער

1:13 כי הים הולך וסער עליהם

"As Jonah runs away from God and the sailors come closer to God, the
storm rises further (1:6, 11, 13). The leitmotifs show the outer and inner dynamic in different directions" (97). One can add to this the specific
addition of עליהם . In the intervening verse Jonah tells them to throw him
overboard because he knows that בשלי הסער הגדול הזה עליכם "because of me
this great storm is upon you." i.e., that the storm is specifically of his
causing, and it is aimed against them. Nevertheless rather than throw
Jonah overboard, they try to return to dry land. But against this well-
intentioned initiative the storm grows worse - עליהם "against them," so
that they are forced unwillingly to comply with Jonah's wishes.

The concept of the "growing phrase" helps us to understand a further
exegetical problem of the book, the phrase in 3:3: ונינוה היתה עיר גדולה לאלהים
"Now Nineveh was an exceeding great city (before God)." Here the term
לאלהים has been translated as if a form of hyperbole is intended - even
by God's reckoning it would be a great city (98). Yet if one traces the
"growing" designations of Nineveh, the inner logic of this phrase becomes
apparant.

1:2, 3:2 קום לך אל נינוה העיר הגדולה

3:3 ונינוה היתה עיר גדולה לאלהים

4:11 ואני לא אחוס על נינוה העיר הגדולה אשר יש בה

הרבה משתים עשרה רבו אדם .....

At first we only know of Nineveh's size and its wickedness that has risen
to God - perhaps because at the beginning these are the only matters of
direct concern to Jonah. But when in Chapter 3 he comes to the city, then

it is revealed as being a great city "to God." As yet we do not know whether this only concerns its evil and its imminent punishment, or implies a fuller relationship to God. But in Chapter 4, with God's question, the fullness of the implications both of its relationship to God, and even its size, is spelled out - the myriads who do not know their right from their left and so much cattle (99).

A fourth example can be found in the final chapter. Twice "God" (100) questions Jonah. To understand fully the nature of the change in phrase here, one must also append to both the identical preceding statement of Jonah:

4:3-4   כי טוב מותי מחיי.   ויאמר ה' ההיטב חרה לך

4/8-9   ויאמר טוב מותי מחיי.   ויאמר אלהים אל יונה
ההיטב חרה לך על הקיקיון.
ויאמר היטב חרה לי עד מות

(4:3-4) "'... for it is better for me to die than to live.' And YHWH said: 'Is it well for you to be angry?'" (4:8-9) "And he said: 'It is better for me to die than to live.' And God said to Jonah: 'Is it well for you to be angry over the gourd?' And he said: 'It is well for me to be angry even to death!'"

Between the two statements in verses 4 and 9 stands the episode of the gourd. Jonah's first request to die is the direct result of his anger to the saving of Nineveh. The second follows his discomfort beneath the gourd. Does he well to be angry that Nineveh is not destroyed?; does he well to be identically angry that the gourd is destroyed? The common point here is Jonah's self-centredness, for both events are not for him significant in themselves (the suffering the Ninevites have been spared; the "suffering" of the destroyed gourd) but only in so far as they affect Jonah's personal desires or comfort (101). The addition of "the gourd" here, in verse 9, underlines the irony of the repetition of God's question. Though the phrase has grown in its questioning of the extent of Jonah's concern for the world about him, its irony lies in the awareness that Jonah's concern has in fact "diminished" from a "psychological" concern about Nineveh to a purely "physical" concern about the gourd (102). As in the case of Chapter 1, "the leitmotifs show the outer and inner dynamic in different directions" (103). Jonah's reply in verse 9 is significant for the absence of any mention of the gourd (104).

The Changing Names of God

There is a further element of Biblical narrative technique which should be considered before closing this chapter - namely the importance attached to the naming of people and things, and to changes in these designations (105). Of immediate concern here is the varying usage of names for God. Three main lines of approach to this problem can be seen in the literature:

i. The attempt to discover behind the text different Yahwist and Elohist sources (106) has been abandoned (107), largely because of the recognition of the essential unity of the work (108).

ii. The contrary assumption (109) that to the author's text a later scribe or copyist, embarrassed by the use of the name YHWH, corrected to Elohim where he could, or appended Elohim (e.g., 4:6), takes no account of the systematic nature of the usages of the names. Neither, of course, does the desperate resort to "Promiscue-Gebrauch der Gottesnamen" (110).

iii. Rudolph (111) cites Boman (112) as the first to make a distinction between the meaning of the different names of God as giving a clue to their usage (YHWH as the merciful God, Elohim as the trans-cendent God), and this has been the most fruitful, if not yet fully worked out, line of approach (113).

We would suggest that some of the problems of the usage of the divine names disappear when it is recognised that two distinct systems are being used: one employed in Chapters 1-3, the second being confined to Chapter 4 (with the exception of 2:1). A brief survey of the usages of the names will be helpful (114).

It is the word of YHWH which comes to Jonah in 1:1, and hence it is from "before the presence of" YHWH that he flees in 1:3 (the name being repeated in this verse). In 1:4, YHWH hurls the great wind onto the sea. In 1:5, however, the second name appears - each sailor cries to his "Elohim," and the captain of the crew (1:6) asks Jonah to cry to "your Elohim." In the second part of 1:6, the third designation appears: HaElohim That it is not merely a variation on "Elohim" will become apparent later (115). The phrase of the captain "perhaps 'HaElohim' will think of us," has its parallel, of course, in Chapter 3 (verse 9) when the king of Nineveh says: "Who knoweth whether 'HaElohim' will not turn and repent." In 1:9, Jonah confesses the name of "YHWH, Elohey haššamayim," and the sailors in 1:10 recognise that he is fleeing from "before the presence of" YHWH. In 1:14, they call to YHWH, ask YHWH not to hold them guilty, and bring a good quotation from Jonah's tradition (116), to the effect that YHWH does what He desires. When the sea is calm, they fear YHWH and offer sacrifices to YHWH.

It is YHWH (2:1) who appoints the fish to swallow Jonah and it is YHWH, his Elohim, to whom Jonah prays: mentioning His name in verse 4, and again (as YHWH, my "Elohim"), in verse 7. In verse 8, he remembers YHWH and in verse 10 he ends with the triumphant: "Salvation is of YHWH!" YHWH speaks to the fish and it vomits Jonah out.

YHWH speaks again to Jonah in 3:1, and he goes (verse 3) "according to the word of YHWH." We are also informed here that Nineveh is a great city to "Elohim," and it is in "Elohim" that the people of Nineveh believe (verse 5). The king of Nineveh tells the people to call to Elohim (verse 8), but significantly it is "HaElohim" (117) who might turn and repent (verse 9), and it is indeed "HaElohim" who sees and then repents (verse 10 twice).

Until now one can discern a quite clear system which is operating throughout these three chapters, which we may summarise as follows:

YHWH is the God of Israel (118), who is also the God of the heavens, the
supreme God.

Each sailor, and the people of Nineveh, has a "local" god, or local concept of god, to which he prays: Elohim

The captain of the ship, and the king of Nineveh, perhaps as more sophisticated people and as leaders of the pagan world, recognise the actual existence of a "supreme" God, and they can go so far as to identify Him as
"HaElohim" (119). The sailors come to recognise this supreme God as
YHWH (120), and presumably convert. The Ninevites "merely" repent of
their evil ways, having been taught by the king that the supreme God, "Ha-
Elohim," wishes this, but they make no further identification with YHWH
(121).

However, with Chapter 4, we enter into a quite new system of names, which
would at first sight upset the schema given above. It is to YHWH that the
angry Jonah prays (4:2), addressing Him as YHWH and describing His attributes, and asking YHWH to take his life (verse 3). YHWH answers in verse
4 by asking if his anger is "good." In verse 6, it is YHWH Elohim who
appoints the gourd; it is HaElohim in verse 7 who appoints the worm; and
Elohim (verse 8) who appoints the East Wind. (Four times the verb וימן
is used, and four times with a different name of God.) To conclude, it is
Elohim (in verse 9) who asks Jonah whether his anger is good (a fact of
great significance since it was YHWH who asked the question previously
in verse 4); and YHWH who poses the final question to Jonah in verse 10.

We must now attempt to explain this sudden interchange of names in Chapter 4; and it must be clear from the systematic way that these changes are
made (four different names with וימן ; the same question posed by YHWH
and later Elohim), that this is no mere accidental (or "promiscuous")
swapping of synonymous designations, but must have a significance within the chapter and the book as a whole.

The answer seems to lie in the statements of Jonah himself, for it is he
who sets up the definitions of God with which the various chapters deal. By
designating God as "YHWH, Elohey Haššamayim," he gives a definition of
the supreme God of the universe who is also Israel's God - a definition which
explains the names used by Jonah, the sailors, the Ninevites and their leaders (the captain and the king) throughout the first three chapters (122).
And all the usages are consistent with this definition within these three
chapters. However in Chapter 4, Jonah brings another theological consideration: namely the attributes of mercy and compassion that represent
the aspect of God with which he has his particular quarrel. And therefore
it is within the context of this definition that the various names employed,
and their interchange, must be considered.

THE CHANGING NAMES OF GOD

In the first part of the chapter, the initial question is posed by YHWH, whom Jonah has berated as being too compassionate When God appoints the worm to strike the plant and the scorching wind, so that the sun strikes Jonah's head, it is variations on Elohim/HaElohim which predominate. With the final question, which contrasts Jonah's selfishness with the compassion of God, we return again to the name YHWH. Thus we can say that the aspect of God as compassionate, merciful and long-suffering at the beginning and end of the chapter, and in Jonah's definition, are all subsumed under the name YHWH. Whereas the aspect of God which disciplines, and perhaps, to some extent, punishes, Jonah, is subsumed under variations of the name "Elohim." This system is consistent with the change in name in the repeated question about Jonah's anger: it is YHWH who speaks to Jonah's petulant request to die, giving the prophet still the chance to admit that his anger is "bad"; and it is Elohim, after introducing the didactic device of the gourd, who asks him the same question the second time, extending it ironically to his concern about the gourd.

If we now examine in detail the four names associated with וימן , the precision of this system is confirmed:

2:1 וימן ה' דג גדול לבלע את יונה
4:6 וימן ה' אלהים קיקיון ..... להיות צל על ראשו להציל לו מרעתו
4:7 וימן האלהים תולעה ..... ותך את הקיקיון
4:8 וימן אלהים רוח קדים חרישית ותך השמש על ראש יונה

And YHWH appointed a great fish to swallow Jonah. (2:1) And YHWH Elohim appointed a gourd...that it might be a shade over his head, to deliver him from his evil. (4:6) And HaElohim appointed a worm...and it smote the gourd. (4:7) And Elohim appointed a vehement East wind; and the sun smote his head.... (4:8)

The fish that saves Jonah's life, and gives him another chance to repent and fulfil his mission, is sent by YHWH (123).

The gourd which has two purposes (emphasised by the word-play on צל / להציל) (124) a. to be a shade over his head, and b. to deliver him from his evil, exemplifies precisely the change-over in God's dealings with Jonah, and thus, quite consistently, employs the two names: "YHWH" brings the gourd to provide a shade over his head; "Elohim" brings the gourd to begin the process of instructing Jonah, to "deliver him from his evil" (125).

Consequently the worm which strikes the gourd, and the East wind, which brings discomfort to Jonah are both appointed by variations on the name Elohim (126).

It is God as YHWH whose compassion extends to all His creature and works. It is God as Elohim who can bring a painful physical lesson and a testing to His prophet - paradoxically in order to lead him to an understanding of, and participation in, precisely this compassion of God (127). That the significance behind the change of names is to draw Jonah out from his own self-centredness to a greater sensitivity to others is shown in general by the

CHAPTER I - ANALYSIS OF LANGUAGE

first of the "Elohim" phrases (4:6) "to deliver him from his evil," and
more specifically by the second question: (verse 9) "Is it well for you to
be angry over the gourd?" - where Jonah should feel pity for the gourd
which has been destroyed yet really feels only pity for himself (128). Thus
the author plays with the two names, both of which are nevertheless subsumed under the definition of God's compassionate nature: YHWH's compassion that has no limits; Elohim who teaches His creatures to understand
and to share in this compassion (129).

It can be argued against the interpretation offered here that rather than
two separate systems, a single one should be found which covers the whole
book. However it must be pointed out that the book divides consistently
along the basis of Chapters 1-3 which deal with all of Jonah's experiences
with the pagan world, and Chapter 4 which deals exclusively with his private argument with God. This 1-3/4 division is further strengthened by
the key words which are restricted to these chapters (e.g., the "call" words
קרא הלך קום, and also שוב of Chapters 1-3; טוב and מות in Chapter 4)
(130). Likewise just as Chapters 1-3 are determined by the initiative of
God in calling His prophet, so Chapter 4 is initiated and determined by the
prayer (the "word") of the prophet (131). God's call to outer action (and
the question of the "repentance" of the world at large) determines the meaning of names in Chapters 1-3; man's demand for inner satisfaction (and the
question of the "repentance" of the individual) determines the exploration
of the inner significance of the names of God in Chapter 4.

The full significance of the use of וימן can now be appreciated:

i.   It affirms that all the names of God used in the book refer ultimately
       to the same God: Jonah's "YHWH, Elohey Haššamayim," who made
       the sea and the dry land, and who can command the fish of the sea,
       the plants, the creatures that creep through the earth, the winds
       (c.f. 1:4 and 4:8); He is YHWH the compassionate and long-suffering
       God who saves his prophet from the sea to give him a further chance
       to repent and obey; He is Elohim who firmly disciplines His prophet
       to teach him a lesson in compassion;

ii.   It points to the same significance of all four "miracles," whether
       they are to be understood as the wonder of God's intervention in the
       world on behalf of His faithful (132), or as a device of the author to
       demythologise his miracles by stressing their similar, parabolic
       nature (133);

iii.   At the same time it allows exactly this distinguishing of the two
       aspects of God's dealing with Jonah by emphasising a common verb
       with different associated names as its subject.

A further objection may be raised about one specific usages of the divine
names: When Jonah prays to "YHWH, my Elohim" (2:7), it may be objected
that he does not conceive of God as a "private god" (as does the captain
of the ship in addressing Jonah - 1:6) However we shall see how this usage

THE CHANGING NAMES OF GOD

conforms with the description of Jonah's prayer in 2:2 - to YHWH, his Elohim (134). Furthermore one can argue that the usage here is subsumed to the system, though Jonah's understanding of God is different, just as "HaElohim" actually responds to the repentance of the Ninevites in 3:10, even though YHWH is meant (135).

To sum up: The problem of the changes of the divine name in the book can be resolved if it is recognised that two systems are being used by the author. In Chapters 1-3, YHWH is the "God of the heavens," who is also Israel's God; the sailors and Ninevites worship their own "private" Elohim; only the captain and king recognise in these "private" gods, HaElohim, the supreme God, ultimately identified by the converting sailors as YHWH, but not so identified by the Ninevites. In Chapter 4, the two-fold distinction between YHWH on one side and Elohim/HaElohim on the other marks the difference between two aspects of God's attribute of mercy: YHWH whose mercy is boundless; Elohim/HaElohim who must be strict in order to teach men to understand and share in the compassion of God.*

*An almost identical conclusion has been reached independently by Dr Aryeh Strikovsky (see p.170 below, for bibliographical details).

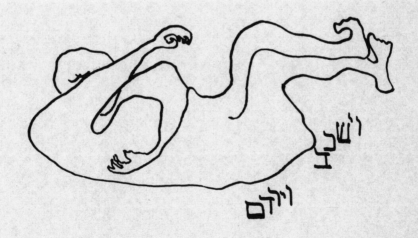

Chapter II

ANALYSIS OF THE "PSALM"

The "Psalm" which appears in the second chapter of "Jonah" (verses 3-10) provides exegetical problems on many levels. Most commentators have agreed that it is a secondary intrusion into the book, usually on the grounds that its content does not seem appropriate to its situation in the story for various reasons. That Jonah could compose a "psalm" in the belly of the fish is unlikely enough, but why was it not a confession of guilt or a plea to be released instead of this song of thanksgiving uttered while still in distress!(1) It has also been ruled out on structural grounds (2); on the basis that it does not describe his actual situation (3); as psychologically inappropriate (4).

Traditionally it has been defended as being in the right place, (5) though sometimes by resorting to somewhat desperate measures, (6) and some degree of criticism has been levelled against Jonah for the form of prayer (7). Though a number of conservative scholars have tried to show its integrity within the book, (8) the trend has been against them, with, however, a few recent exceptions (9).

The "psalm" is thus generally conceived of as a later insertion, the interpolator feeling the need to insert the "prayer" which Jonah is said to have prayed inside the fish (10). It would thus be analogous to the prayers ascribed to Hannah (I Sam 2:1-10) and Hezekiah (Isaiah 38:9-20) (11).

The nature of the "psalm" and its similarity in phraseology to others in the Psalter, has pointed to a cultic origin. Gunkel (12) classifies it as a "Dankpsalm." Though the customary "introductory praise" is missing, it continues with the usual account of the experience of the worshipper (addressed both to the listeners and to God). It is followed by three items, this form "finding its most concentrated expression in Jonah 2:3:

(a) 'In mine <u>affliction</u> (b) I <u>cried</u> unto YHWH (c) and He heard me.'" (13)

The form continues with the "confession" to God as saviour from distress, and a final reference to the thank-offering itself, e.g., Jonah 2:10.

It is clear from the structure of the "psalm" that it is designed to exist as an independent unit, indeed analogous to other thanksgiving psalms. However its placing at this point within the Book of Jonah must give it an additional level of meaning within this specific context. The analysis of the "psalm" will, therefore, examine the following problems:

    a. Construction and Authorship.
    b. Quotations from the Psalter in the "Psalm."
    c. The Meaning of the "Psalm" by Itself and Within the Book.

Construction and Authorship

The general consensus that the "psalm" is an addition, together with its similarity to others, have distracted attention from its unique character- istics. A close reading of the text reveals certain stylistic features which it has in common with the narrative parts of the book, and which distin- guish it in significant ways from other thanksgiving psalms.

"The Growing Phrase" - Attention has already been drawn to the technique of the "growing phrase" (14). An analogous technique can be demonstrated twice in the "psalm." The word יסבבני occurs twice (verses 4, 6), each time with a different subject:
(verse 4) And the flood was round about me   ונהר יסבבני
(verse 6) The deep was round about me   תהום יסבבני
In the context (a description of a progressive descent into the depths of the water), the repetition of the word emphasises the downward direction in which Jonah goes: at first the "flood," the currents on the surface of the sea surround him; (5) and then "tehom," the deep surrounds him.

The second phrase which is repeated is אל היכל קדשך which appears in ver- ses 5 and 9:

אך אוסיף להביט אל היכל קדשך (5
אך אוסיף להביט אל היכל קדשך (9

(verse 5) Yet I will look again toward Thy holy temple.
(verse 9) And my prayer came in unto Thee, into Thy holy temple.

Here the direction of movement is, so to speak, reversed: at first he can only look towards "Thy holy temple," then later his prayer comes to "Thy holy temple" (16).

There is thus a perfect balance between his physical descent and his "spirit- ual" ascent, similar in fact to the two-way movement in the first chapter of the book, also illustrated by the use of the "growing" phrase, as the storm rises higher, the sailors come closer to God (17).

We thus have a technique common to the "psalm" and the rest of the book. But we must also note that a "two-way" direction expressed in this form occurs in none other of the thanksgiving psalms, though the technique of the repetition of a word or phrase within a psalm occurs commonly as a liturgical device (18) or to convey a further dimension of meaning (19).

Narrative Technique - As striking is a second feature that is different from all such psalm material relating to symbolic descriptions of "distress": descent into "sheol," "the deep," etc. The stages of descent in "Jonah" are described with almost "geographical" exactitude: at first the "flood," the breakers and waves pass over him; he descends further to the base of the mountains till the very earth closes over him. Every other such description in the Psalter consists only of a series of synonymous phrases (20), any of which are interchangeable, but no other consecutive descent is described.

The significance of this is two-fold. Once again it demonstrates the unique-
ness of this "psalm" and the unlikelihood of it being taken from a standard collection of such material. Secondly it displays essentially a narrative
technique that has organised the symbolic terminology of the "underworld"
(21) into a coherent pattern of the continuing descent,(22) and is thus stylistically the same as the form chosen by the author for the book as a
whole.

It is now possible to examine the overall structure of the "psalm" and
consider the third factor that enters into this narrative pattern. For the
moment we can put aside the introductory formula of verse 3 and the
closing formula of verse 10, together with the "moral" inserted in verse
9. (See Diagram 2, page 42.)

As the diagram shows, the core of the "psalm" moves between three separate elements: the act of God (to cast the speaker into the depths and
to draw him up); the physical situation of the speaker as he sinks; and
his inner state which "rises." The act of God (a throwing down and a
raising up) exactly parallels the outer and inner movement within the
speaker. This picture of God as the inaugurator of events, which must
be acted out by man, is thematically consistent with the image of God
emphasised throughout the book, (23) and is thus further evidence of
the same authorship.

One can also see clearly by separating off the verses describing the
inner state of the speaker the change which takes place within him. Two
sentences express his inner situation (verses 5, 8). The first begins
with an emphatic "I": "I said: 'I am cast out from before Thine eyes.'"
It continues: "Yet I will look again toward Thy holy temple." The con-
junctive אך (24) conveys two possible senses to the latter phrase - a
repentant expression of hope for a future return to God; or a stubborn
refusal to accept God's dismissal. Since it has been God who cast the
speaker out, and since no positive response is given by God to this statement, other than allowing a continuation of the descent, the latter meaning is the most probable - the emphatic "I" of the speaker sets itself in
the centre of the stage. This is borne out by the second sentence, when,
after the earth has closed its bars over him, and no human way out is
possible, God has suddenly responded, intervening to raise up the speaker. In the new sentence the verbal construction is totally different. In
place of the "I," the speaker speaks of himself in the third person, in
a construction which conveys the sense of disembodiment: בהתעטף עלי נפשי
"When my soul fainted within me." This is followed by: "YHWH I remembered" את ה' זכרתי where the word order puts the emphasis upon
YHWH and not the "I remembered" of the speaker. And in place of the
"Yet I will look again toward Thy holy temple," the prayer, as if totally detached from its owner, comes "in unto Thee, into Thy holy temple."

ותבוא אליך תפלתי אל היכל קדשך (With the recurrence of ואני in
the last verse of thanksgiving, the "I" of the speaker is "reconstituted"

Diagram 2

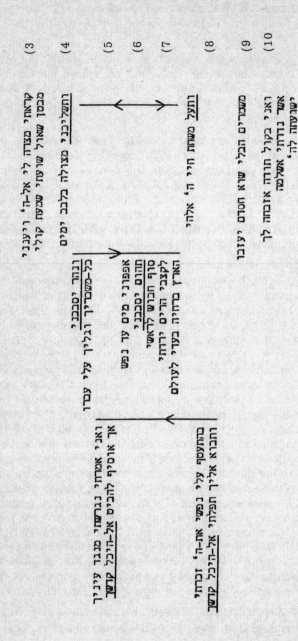

CHAPTER II – ANALYSIS OF THE "PSALM"

after his experience, and fully restored he comes to express his gratitude.)

To sum up, we have noted two stylistic features common to the psalm and
the narrative parts of the book, as well as two common thematic ideas (the
role of God and the selfwilled individual who must submit his will to God's).
It is therefore our contention that the "psalm" was indeed composed by the
author of the book and incorporated by him at this point. Further evidence
will be brought at each stage of the remainder of this analysis.

It remains for this section only to show how by the use of key words the
"psalm" is linked to certain underlying themes of the book and more firmly incorporated (25). The subtlety of the author's method can be seen immediately from a consideration of the names by which the speaker addresses God in the "psalm." In verse 7 comes the climactic:

ותעל משחת חיי ה' אלהי   "Yet Thou hast brought up my life from the
pit, <u>YHWH my God</u>!" This coincides with the appellation used by Jonah in
the sentence immediately preceding the prayer (2:2):

ויתפלל יונה אל ה' אלהיו ממעי הדגה

"Then Jonah prayed unto <u>YHWH, his God</u> out of the fish's belly." But the
significance of the association of these two "personal" descriptions of God
only becomes apparent when contrasted with Jonah's appellation of God
the next time he prays (4:2) where "YHWH" stands quite alone; for the Jonah who prays out of fear and distress to "YHWH, <u>his</u> God" is in quite a
different mood when he angrily asks "YHWH" to take his life from him!

Cohn (26) has pointed out how the use of קראתי (I called out) (2:3) comes
here at a significant point in the book. God has told Jonah to "call" against
Nineveh (1:2), but Jonah was silent; the captain of the ship bids him to
"call" (1:6), but Jonah remains silent. The sailors also "call" (1:14), and
now at last it is Jonah's turn to "call" and restore his connection with God.

Complementary to this is the close of Jonah's prayer:

ואני בקול תודה אזבחה לך אשר נדרחי אשלמה

"But I will sacrifice unto Thee with the voice of thanksgiving; that which
I have vowed I will pay." This brings us into connection again with the
sailors who have also made vows on being saved (1:16):

וייראו האנשים יראה גדולה את ה' ויזבחו זבח לה' וידרו נדרים

"Then the men feared YHWH exceedingly; and they offered a sacrifice unto YHWH, and made vows."

The use of ירדחי "I went down" in verse 7 is a key word in the description
of Jonah's symbolic descent. It is contrasted within the "psalm" by God's
act on drawing the speaker up (verse 7)   ותעל משחת חיי ה' אלהי
"Yet Thou hast brought up my life from the pit, YHWH my God" (27).

Thus certain key words and phrases have been used as one device for integ-
rating the "psalm" into the book. The major examination of its meaning

and the purpose it fulfils within the book as a whole will be discussed in the third section. First, however, we must deal with the appearance in the "psalm" of phrases identical with, or similar to, phrases in the Psalms.

Quotations from the Psalter in the "Psalm"

The similarity between phrases in Jonah 2:3-10 and phrases in the psalms has long been recognised (28). But opinions as to the significance of this range from considering the Jonah "psalm" as a mosaic of psalm fragments (either remembered and composed by Jonah in the fish, or more probably composed by the author or interpolator) to the suggestion that the composer of the "psalm" merely used a generally available vocabulary and that no specific connection with other psalms was intended (29). Even if one accepts the possibility of a deliberate borrowing from the psalter, it is difficult to prove the dependence of one text on the other. We shall examine this general problem in more detail in the Analysis of Quotations (30), but suggest here a possible approach to the problem immediately before us.

Three methods are methodologically possible. One can examine each apparent quotation and, where possible, show the dependence upon a source in the book of Psalms. If a number of such examples prove to be verifiable quotations, then the cumulative evidence will strongly suggest that all are indeed selected by the author in this way. Alternatively one can begin with an analysis of the "psalm" and examine the function such quoted material would play within it: i.e., try to discover the dominating themes to which the incorporated material must have been subsumed - all quotations must then be shown to fit into this pattern. The third possibility is perhaps the most helpful from the point of view of organising our material in a coherent manner - namely to begin with demonstrating such passages as can be proven to be quotations, and then examining the rest in the light of an overall theory.

(i) The most obvious place to start is with verse 4b of the "psalm" which is identical with Psalm 42:8b: כל משבריך וגליך עלי עברו
"All Thy waves and Thy billows passed over me."
The phrase fits perfectly into the "geographical" setting of the "psalm": in the heart of the seas, the floods surround him, waves and billows pass over his head. However, of all the elements which cover the speaker (floods, waters, the deep, reeds, the earth), this is the only one which has a suffix ascribing it to God. Thus one can argue that the author took this phrase from the Psalm because it was descriptively appropriate, but was unable to amend it (by removing the suffixes) without destroying the rhythm, (31) and perhaps, too, its familiar echoes. Had he made his own coinage, it would have been consistent with the form of the other phrases.

(ii) There are two phrases which are similar to phrases at two places in Psalm 31, a feature which itself makes "borrowing" more likely. Furthermore, the changes in both "quotations" are significant in relationship to the context from which they come. Jonah 2:5a reads:

ואני אמרחי נגרשחי מנגד עיניך (אַך אוסיף להביט אל היכל קדשך)

"And I said: 'I am cast out from before Thine eyes'; (yet I will look again toward Thy holy temple)."
Psalm 31:23 reads:

ואני אמרחי בחפזי נגרזחי מנגד עיניך (אָכן שמעת קול חחנוני בשועי אליך)

"As for me, I said in my haste: 'I am cut off from before Thine eyes'; (Nevertheless Thou heardest the voice of my supplications when I cried unto Thee)."

We have explained above (32) that the phrase "I said: 'I am cast out from before Thine eyes...'" is so constructed (in contrast with the later statement in verse 8 of the "psalm") that it emphasises the "I" of the speaker. Since this is a continuing "psychological" state of the speaker, which will only be changed after the full effects of his "descent," it would be consistent with adapting the "quotation" to remove the word בחפזי " in my haste," since it would cloud the significance of the change which takes place. Likewise the unusual form נגרזחי could have been amendet to נגרשחי either to make an obscure word clearer (33), or precisely because of the change to draw attention to the original text. In its "amended" form the phrase fits perfectly adequately into the context of the "psalm." What is significant, however, is the continuation of the sentence in both contexts. Psalm 31 continues with אכן שמעת (Nevertheless Thou...) and an expression of gratitude to God who, despite rejecting the speaker, has listened to his cry. Conversely, the speaker in the "psalm" continues with אך אוסיף (yet I...) and is himself very firmly the subject of what follows. We have already seen how this placing of himself in the centre of the stage is significant for this part of the development of the "psalm," thus the echo of Psalm 31 and its "nevertheless....," but with a quite different continuation, heightens the contrast between the speaker in the original passage and the speaker in our "psalm" - and thus further emphasises the change that will take place in him.

No less significant is the second "quotation" from Psalm 31. Jonah 2:9 contains the quite unexpected:

משמרים הבלי שוא חסדם יעזבו

"They that regard lying vanities forsake their own mercy."
Nothing in the context so far has led us to expect this statement, and much ingenuity has been used by commentators to explain to whom the speaker is referring, and what indeed he means. The phrase in Psalm 31:7 reads:

שנאחי השמרים הבלי שוא ואני אל ה' בטחחי

"I hate them that regard lying vanities; but I trust in YHWH." That the author wished this association to be made is implied in his use of the unusual form משמרים (34), the only instance of the Piel of the root שמר. One is forced to compare this verse with its original source, of only because of this strange change of verb form. What is immediately apparent

QUOTATIONS FROM THE PSALTER

is that the Jonah version lacks שנאתי "I hate"; and in place of the Psalm's contrasting "but I trust in YHWH," the Jonah verse continues by describing the fate of "those that regard lying vanities," namely that they "forsake their own mercy." (The contrasting "but I" reappears in the next verse of the "psalm": "But I will sacrifice unto Thee....")

This statement by the speaker coming at this point in the "psalm" must be a summation of his experience and the lesson he has learned from it (35). Since there has been no mention of the reason for God casting the speaker away in the first place, we may assume that somewhere in this statement lies the solution also to that problem. Yet the sentence by itself, a generalised impersonal statement about the fate of those who "regard lying vanities" (presumably idolaters from the parallelism of its context in Psalm 31:7) (36), tells us nothing. Methodologically we can argue that since the sentence surprises us by its sudden appearance, and puzzles us by having no obvious relationship to the experience described in the "psalm," we are forced to go to the only other place where an answer might lie (to which we are also led by the unusual verbal form), namely the original source of the phrase with which we are familiar from our tradition, namely Psalm 31. And here we do have a clue in the form of a statement in the first person: "I hate," which is significantly absent in our "psalm." We are thus led to conclude that the speaker in our "psalm" no longer hates the worshippers of idols but accepts instead that if they continue to regard their idols (the Piel form suggesting a repeated action or a more intense form of attachment), then they will ultimately exhaust the mercy which is bestowed upon them by God, they will forsake their חסד (37). Thus the speaker has come to accept a more tolerant, though still rather grudging, view of idolaters, and in a wide sense, presumably other nations. Without such a cross-reference, which the author clearly intended, there would be no way within the context of the "psalm" as it exists as a unity by itself, to understand the meaning.

We have thus demonstrated two instances of quotations from the same Psalm where the use of the quotation (with its quite specific emendations) adds a further dimension of meaning, or makes comprehensible what would not otherwise be. We shall see later how these same phrases acquire further meaning when seen in their context of the book as a whole (38).

With these examples behind us, we can now continue to examine the other parallel phrases on the assumption that they too are quotations. Our task now is to show the significance that lies in the selection of phrase and the emendation the author has made, bearing in mind that this can be no more than a hypothetical retracing of the author's steps.

(iii) The "psalm" begins in verse 3:

קראתי מצרה לי אל ה׳ ויענני

"I called out of mine affliction unto YHWH, and He answered me."
Though this is a common form of opening (39), the nearest parallel to
it is Psalm 120:1:

אל ה' בצרתה לי קראתי ויענני

"Unto YHWH in my distress I called, and He answered me." The most striking difference here is the change in word order. Whereas the Psalm begins with the name of YHWH to whom, in his distress the speaker called, the version in "Jonah" begins with the speaker himself: "I called" out of mine affliction to YHWH. The significance lies again in the emphasis upon the speaker who becomes the central dominating figure in the "psalm," for whom God, the inaugurator of events, is nevertheless given a secondary place.

The use of מן in מצרה לי in place of ב (בצרתה לי) fits in with the three-fold usage of the former preposition which strongly affirms that this was indeed the prayer he recited <u>from</u> the belly of the fish:

מבטן שאול – מצרה לי – ממעי הדגה

The structure of the second part of the sentence is determined by the in-clusion of מבטן שאול , a coinage of the author which suggests the belly of the fish. Thus the source of the remaining words which also belong to the usual introductory sentence (40), cannot be accurately identified.

(iv) To the first part of verse 4:

ותשליכני מצולה בלבב ימים

"For Thou didst cast me into the depth, in the heart of the seas," there is no direct parallel, and one can only note that ותשליכני occurs once in relation to God's act (41), and that מצולה is part of the terminology of the sea and netherworld (42). Conversely the phrase בלבב ימים in this exact form is unique to Jonah (43).

We have already discussed the significance of ונהר יסבבני in relation-ship to ההום יסבבני (44) and these are both coinages of the author with a clear role to play in the "psalm" as a whole.

(v) The phrase in verse 6:

אפפוני מים עד נפש

"The waters compassed me about even to my soul" appears to be a compos-ite one put together by the author. This is harder to prove without know-ing the extra-Biblical usage of words, however, if we remain with the hypothesis that the author tried to utilize phrases from within the Bible itself, we must note that אפפוני only occurs otherwise in combination with הבלי מות or משברי מות (the cords, or waves, of death) (45). Though either of these might seem appropriate to our "psalm," the word מות "death," would be out of place here as it seems to be a key word restricted to the last chapter. Although Jonah has approached a symbolic death with the "tardema," and has implied that he wishes to die by being cast over-board, it could still be too soon in the writer's purpose to spell out the prophet's wish, for it would destroy the tension of the argument with God in Chapter 4. If this is so, then he appears to have brought in its place the phrase from Psalm 69:2: מים עד נפש
"Waters...even to my soul" (46).

QUOTATIONS FROM THE PSALTER

(vi) In verse 7, after a whole string of phrases which are unique to the "psalm," comes the sudden response of God

ותעל משחת חיי ה' אלהי

"Yet Thou hast brought up my life from the pit, O YHWH, my God." Once again, with so limited a phrase it is difficult to be certain whether this too is an amended quotation or a new coinage. If the former, it probably comes from Psalm 103:4: הגואל משחת חייכי "Who redeemeth thy life from the pit." The change from עלה to גאל being explained, as above (47), by the use of עלה as a key word both within the Psalm and in relation to the book as a whole.

(vii) We are no more certain ground again in the next verse with the phrase "When my soul fainted within me."

בהתעטף עלי נפשי

The only other parallel uses of the rare verb עטף (48) occur in Psalm 142:4: "When my spirit fainteth within me..." בהתעטף עלי רוחי and Psalm 143:4: "And my spirit fainteth within me..." ותתעטף עלי רוחי The rareness of the verb and the similarity of phrase suggests strongly that we have here a quotation, and the author has been forced to replace רוחי with נפשי as the latter is also a key word within the "psalm" itself (verse 6) and the rest of the book (1:14; 4:3, 8) (49).

(viii) To the last verse there is no exact parallel:

ואני בקול תודה אזבחה לך
אשר נדרתי אשלמה
וישועתה לה'

"But I will sacrifice unto Thee with the voice of thanksgiving; that which I have vowed I will pay. Salvation is of YHWH " The closest to verse 10a is Psalm 116:17a: (50)

לך אזבחה זבח תודה ובשם ה' אקרא

"To Thee will I offer the sacrifice of thanksgiving, and will call upon the name of YHWH." The reappearance of ואני at this point in the "psalm" serves a number of functions. Firstly it restores the contrast between the fate of the speaker and that of the idolaters which was present in Psalm 31:7, as mentioned above (51). Furthermore it comes as a point of resolution within the "psalm"; the speaker is restored to his "wholeness" after the "disembodiement" of verse 8; and also one hears again his complaint in verse 5, happily contrasted with his new situation of thanksgiving (52). Nevertheless it is interesting to note once again the difference in word order between our verse here and Psalm 116 - the לך אזבחה (to Thee will I sacrifice) of the latter has a quite different emphasis from אזבחה לך (I will sacrifice to Thee) of the former. Even if the comparison of verses here must be speculative, one can nevertheless note that the sequence of subject and object remains consistent throughout the "psalm" - the speaker sets himself firmly in the centre, except for the dramatic change in verse 8.

It remains only to note that the closest parallel to the closing phrase ישועתה לה' "Salvation is of YHWH!" occurs in Psalm 3:9:

CHAPTER II - ANALYSIS OF THE "PSALM"

לה' הישועה על עמך ברכתך סלה

"Salvation belongeth unto YHWH; Thy blessing be upon Thy people." The inverted order in the "psalm" makes the name of YHWH the final word, so that fittingly the Psalm begins with the "I called" of the speaker, but ends with the name of God.

The best way to sum up the effect of these quotes is to show where they play a part within the "psalm" and where not. (See Diagram 3, page 50.)

The familiar frame of reference and customary terminology continue until verse 6a, and then suddenly in this second stage of descent, all familiarity ceases:

> The deep was round about me;
> The weeds were wrapped about my head.
> I went down to the bottoms of the mountains;
> The earth with her bars closed upon me forever.

At this point both stylistically (the narrative form) and from the point of view of what is described, the author breaks into new territory, where the terminology of his tradition is no longer used, and perhaps can no longer be used (53). In parallel to the situation he describes, the sudden change from familiar to unfamiliar language takes one into the depths of a frightening new world, far from God, where only the sudden intervention of God Himself can restore the lost soul.

To sum up what we have seen from the use of quotations: in constructing the "psalm," the author has apparently taken where possible familiar phrases from his tradition. On occasion he has amended them either to fit in better with key words or ideas in the book as a whole, or because of the necessary contrast between the source of the quote and the usage of the phrase in the "psalm." At certain points, notably in the description of the latter part of the speaker's descent, he has turned away from traditional terminology and created his own description. In the next section we shall examine the significance of the latter, and the overall effect of this construction.

The Meaning of the "Psalm" by Itself And Within the Book

If we now recapitulate what we have seen of the "psalm" construction, we can understand how it would function as an independent unit.

The speaker opens with the usual formula describing the overall situation: "I cried to God and He heard me." Only the echo of Psalm 120:1 gives us a hint already that the self-centredness of the speaker is a central element. Then he moves into the detailed account of what happened, using however both familiar and unfamiliar language, switching at first between the author's own coinages בלבב ימים , ונהר יסבבני , and echoes from familiar liturgical passages:

Diagram 3

1.	
אל ה' בצרתה לי קראתי ויענני	(3) קראתי מצדה לי אל ה' ויענני
2.	
שמעה קול (תחנוני) בשועי אליך	מבטן שאול שועתי שמעת קולי
4. 3.	
... וחשליכני ... מצולה ...	(4) ותשליכני מצולה בלבב ימים
	ונהר יסבבני
5.	
כל משבריך וגליך עלי עברו	כל משבריך וגליך עלי עברו
6.	
ואני אמרתי בחפזי נגרזתי מנגד עיניך	(5) ואני אמרתי נגרשתי מנגד עיניך
7.	
אכן ..... אל היכל קדשך	אך אוסיף להביט אל היכל קדשך
9. 8.	
אפפוני ..... מים עד נפש	(6) אפפוני מים עד נפש
	תהום יסבבני
	סוף חבוש לראשי
	(7) לקצבי הרים ירדתי
	הארץ ברחיה בעדי לעולם
	ותעל משחת חיי ה' אלהי
10.	
הגואל משחת חייכי	(8) בהתעטף עלי נפשי את ה' זכרתי
11.	
בהתעטף עלי רוחי ..... זכרתי	ותבוא אליך תפלתי אל היכל קדשך
12.	
תבוא לפניך תפלתי	(9) משמרים הבלי שוא חסדם יעזבו
13.	
(השמרים) הבלי שוא	(10) ואני בקול תודה אזבחה לך
14.	
לך אזבחה זבח תודה	אשר נדרתי אשלמה
15.	
נדרי לה' אשלם	ישועתה לה'
16.	
לה' הישועה	

---

1. Psalm 120:1
2. Psalm 31:23b; 116:1; 145:19
3. Psalm 120:11
4. Psalm 69:3, 16
5. Psalm 42:8
6. Psalm 31:23a
7. Psalm 5:8; 138:2
8. II Sam 22:5; Psalm 18:5; 116:3

9. Psalm 69:2
10. Psalm 103:4
11. Psalm 143:4-5; 142:4
12. Psalm 88:3; 102:2
13. Psalm 31:7
14. Psalm 116:17; 50:14
15. Psalm 116:16, 18; 22:6; 50:14; 56:13, II Sam 15:7
16. Psalm 3:9.

God acts, the speaker's physical situation changes, and he responds. But his response is too self-centred and not appropriate, so he sinks further into the underworld. Now the language becomes totally unfamiliar, and as it progresses an oppressive feeling of claustrophobia, of utter helplessness, grows and closes in upon the speaker: the reeds wrap about his head, he sinks down and down to the bottoms of the mountains, the earth, like bars, closes over him. And at the moment of greatest darkness and despair, when no human action can release him, God breaks through all these suffocating layers, and draws his life out to safety. And then only does he respond, almost as a disembodied soul, without his human arrogance, utterly dependent upon, and secondary to, God. And from his experience he brings the lesson, that those who continually go after vanities, worthless things, (whether other gods or perhaps their own self-centredness) will one day lose the חסד of God. And he closes with the appropriate formula prior to his bringing of an offering, and the ringing affirmation "Salvation is of YHWH!" As noted above, the first word belongs to the speaker, "I called," but the last word is the name of God.

It is a remarkable creation, both evoking traditional forms of such address to God, yet, precisely because of its narrative effect, its development of the layers through which the speaker sinks, and its sudden breaking away at a critical moment from familiar terminology, it gives a whole new dimension to the form. The significance of this change from familiar to unfamiliar is further evidence of the authorship of the "psalm" by the author of the book, because it expresses in this structure yet another key theme running through the book. Jonah is told to go from the familiar out to the unfamiliar, to the alien; from "mine own country" (4:2) to the enemy Nineveh. All the terminology that formerly belonged exclusively to Israel comes now from the mouth of strangers (54): the Ninevites who "believe" in God and can hope that He will change His decree against them; the sailors who know that "Thou hast done as it pleased Thee." The prophet himself must step beyond a pious recapitulation of God's qualities of compassion to a realisation of their new, wider significance. Once again in this play between traditional and new language, between a familiar form of thanksgiving and an unfamiliar style, the form of the writing echoes and underlines its content.

What happens, however, to the "psalm" when we place it into the book of Jonah as a whole? This in turn leads us to ask three further questions: Why did the author feel the need to insert a "psalm" at all? Why of this particular type of thanksgiving which seems inappropriate to the prophet's situation? Why did he insert it at this point of the book? (55)

If there was no "psalm," we would be faced with the following problem. After three days and nights in the belly of the fish, Jonah finally prayed. His prayer was acceptable to God in that Jonah was released by the fish and restored to dry land. But though it is consequent after his being

THE MEANING OF THE "PSALM"   51 swallowed that the fish would vomit him out, there is also a suggestion of malicious humour in this picture of the prophet being disgorged in so undignified a fashion, and certainly more than a hint of scorn and disgust if one examines the usage of the root קיא (56). And why must God's word come a second time to him (3:2) (57) if it was already clear from Jonah's prayer that he was ready to accept the mission? And why, too, was he no longer to cry over Nineveh general prophetic words of rebuke, but only the words God put in his mouth?

The answer to these questions must lie in the words of his prayer, so the author was obliged to provide it.

Why choose the form of a thanksgiving psalm? The author has one partic- ular device which one can note throughout the book. He puts into Jonah's mouth certain pious affirmations, that stem from his tradition, yet each comes out in a peculiarly ironic way in its context in the book. The de- scription of God as He who "hath made the sea and the dry land" is ironic since Jonah has fled to the sea to escape His mission. The citing of the magnificent attributes of God, of patience and compassion and mercy, in Chapter 4, is ironic because Jonah hurls these at God in his anger: "I knew You were much too merciful and compassionate... and that is why I fled!" His prayer in Chapter 4 begins with the pious formulation "I pray Thee, O YHWH...." (like the prayer of the sailors in 1:14) (58), only to be interrupted by his long complaint and self-justification, before return- ing to the stereotyped request: "therefore now, O YHWH, take, I beseech Thee, my life from me." So Jonah inside the fish recites his pious Psalm of Thanksgiving in anticipation (59) of being restored to dry land, and in confession of his dependence upon God. Nevertheless we must expect this "psalm" also to have its ironic element to it, in keeping with Jonah's other resorts to piety; and the element is not hard to find, for where in Jonah's words is any mention of the mission he was supposed to fulfil? Where is his repentance for fleeing from God? (60) The whole "psalm" is entirely restricted to the current situation in which the prophet finds himself, with no allusion to any preceding event. Piously he begins: "I called out of mine affliction unto YHWH...," but why is he in affliction? Only be- cause of something that God has done! "For Thou didst cast me into the depth, in the heart of the seas...." Nevertheless, as we have shown, the speaker undergoes an inner development through the course of the "psalm," but now we can recognise the irony even of this. Jonah sees his prayer as an appropriate, dutiful thanksgiving one - he acknowledges that God has saved him, and describes with due humility his loss of self-centredness. The statement about "those who regard lying vanities" could also be a pious affirmation, as it stands in the inner structure of the "psalm," (Jo- nah, too, no longer hates), and he ends with an appropriate vow (61). Yet precisely because no mention is made of the mission he failed to fulfil, the reader can see throughout the inadequacy of his confession (62), the spitefulness of the "lying vanities" remark as it must apply to Nineveh, ("I know they will repent now, but they cannot keep it up for long!"), and the careful assumption that the arrival of his prayer at "Thy holy temple" and the offering of a sacrifice is the end of the whole matter. So Jonah, to his own satisfaction, has reconciled himself to God. Naturally Jonah cannot see, as can the reader throughout the book, the inadequacy of his responses (what they really are in comparison with what he thinks they are) up to the very last question of the book. The author has even emphasised the incongruity of Jonah's closing words by the sequel to his prayer. Jonah reaches his climactic affirmation: "Salvation is of YHWH!" - and indeed in response YHWH spoke to the fish - and it vomited Jonah out!

Yet having noted the ironic effect of all Jonah's pious affirmations, we must also show that the author, as an excellent "midrashist" (63) has presented three theological propositions in a highly diverting and memorable way:

Who is the God of Israel? He is YHWH, the God of heaven, who hath made the sea and the dry land."

What is His nature? He is "a gracious God, and compassionate, long-suffering, and abundant in mercy and repents of evil."

What is man's relationship to Him? "I called out of mine affliction to YHWH and He answered me" "For Thou didst cast me into the depths... yet Thou hast brought up my life from the pit, YHWH my God." "But I will sacrifice unto Thee with the voice of thanksgiving."

One can add to this that the "psalm" is also a necessary complement to the actions of the prophet described in the book. If one had only an account of his behaviour it would be almost impossible to take Jonah seriously, and remarkably difficult to understand why God bothers with him. Yet for all his selfishness and absurdity, even Jonah has an inner life; he is capable of crying to God and of a limited degree of change in response to God's command and teaching.

From examining the overall structure of the book, however, we get the clearest view of the role of the "psalm" at this point (64). The book is divided into two almost equal, parallel sections (Chapter 1-2, 3-4) in each of which the same pattern is followed:

God speaks - the twice-repeated command to Jonah.
Jonah responds - he runs away/he obeys.

A series of events follow involving others - sailors/Ninevites.

God brings a dramatic resolution - the storm ceases, the fish comes/ Nineveh is forgiven.

Jonah brings his own reaction and interpretation of events - the prayers in Chapters 2 and 4.

God says the last word - to the fish/the question to Jonah.

THE MEANING OF THE "PSALM"

Summary

1. We have demonstrated through stylistic and thematic analogies, as well as the use of key words, that the "psalm" was also composed by the author of the book and included by him.

2. We have shown how in constructing the "psalm" the author took phrases from certain Psalms, thus giving a familiar framework against which to contrast his own original material, and to enable certain echoes from the original context to come through. One can already say at this point, in further confirmation of the single authorship of the book, that the same technique will be shown to have been employed in the "quotations" of material in the rest of the book (65).

3. We have shown that the apparent "inappropriateness" of the "psalm" disappears if one recognises the ironic purpose it fulfils in the book, like the other pious citations and prayers of Jonah. Furthermore it is part of a series of theological statements which the author has conveyed by this "inverted" technique. It is also quite consistent in its inner problematic with the character ascribed to Jonah throughout the book.

4. Finally it fits into this part of the book, closing the first half, and hinting forward to the final "parallel" chapter when the still unanswered problem of the reason for Jonah's flight will be resolved.

The remaining evidence for the "psalm" being intended from the beginning as an integral part of the book will be given in the Analysis of Structure.

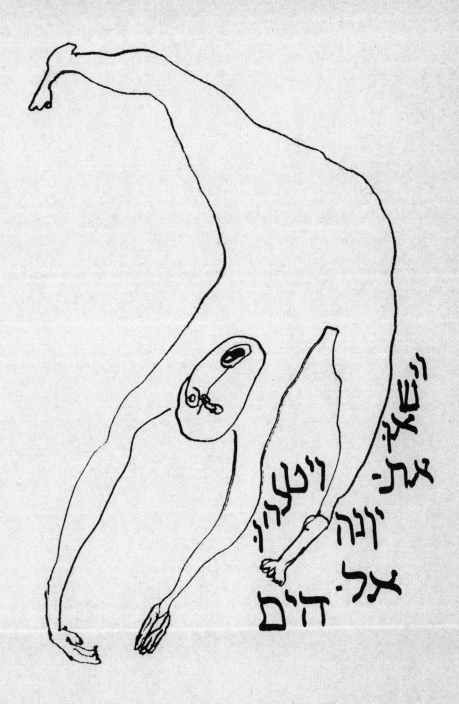

Chapter III

ANALYSIS OF STRUCTURE

The structure of the book is, at first glance, deceptively simple. It divides neatly down the middle. Chapter 1-2 deal with the first call to Jonah, his attempted flight and forced return, his reaction to these events; Chapters 3-4 deal with the second call, the successful mission to Nineveh, Jonah's reaction to it and God's lesson and final question. We have already noted that such an analysis of structure enables us to see a useful parallel between Chapters 2 and 4, whereby the "psalm" and the final discussion with God, both serve to reveal the inner workings of Jonah's mind (1).

On such an analysis we can recognise certain clear units:

1:1 - 1:16	The first call - flight. Sailors.
2:1	Transition
2:2 - 2:11	Prayer - "discussion" with God.
3:1 - 3:10	The second call - obedience. Nineveh.
4:1	Transition
4:2 - 4:11	Prayer - "discussion" with God.

We have already noted the repetition of the "call" of 1:1-3 in 3:1-3, with its similarity and significant differences (2). We can note also the relationship of the introduction to the two prayers of Jonah in 2:2 and 4:2

2:2 ויתפלל יונה אל ה' אלהיו ממעי הדגה ויאמר .....

4:2 ויתפלל אל ה' ויאמר .....

As we have noted (3), Jonah in distress prays to "YHWH, <u>his</u> God"; the angry Jonah in Chapter 4 prays to "YHWH." Even the brevity of the second introductory formula is suggestive of his impatience and anger.

The two transitional sentences (4) serve to bring the focus of attention back to Jonah after dealing with the sailors (1:16) and Ninevites (3:10).

Lohfink (5) has noted that the language comes to a standstill at the end of 1:16 to show that we have reached the end:

וייראו האנשים יראה גדולה את ה'

ויזבחו זבח לה'

וידרו נדרים

A similar closing sequence, though less obviously graded, occurs at the end of 3:10:

וירא האלהים את מעשיהם

כי שבו מדרכם הרעה

וינחם האלהים על הרעה
אשר דבר לעשות להם

ולא עשה

A second division of the book, however, has also been noted (6). Namely, Chapters 1-3, in which God deals with the pagan world, and in which a particular scheme is used to designate the names of God; and Chapter 4, a sort of inner dialogue between God and Jonah/Israel, in which a further dimension of the attributes and names of God is revealed.

Concentric Structures

A significant step in the development of analysis of the construction of the book came with the work of Lohfink (7) on the structure of Chapter 1 - work which was taken up by Keller (8), Pesch (9), Landes (10), Trible (11), and Cohn (12).

As Diagram 4a (13) shows, a recognition of the concentric structure of Chapter 1 allows certain interesting parallels to be seen more clearly.

1/I Show the beginning and end of the storm. The wind is hurled onto the sea, Jonah is hurled into the sea.

2/II Show the prayers of the sailors, at first to their gods, but then finally to YHWH.

3/III Show the parallel attempts of the sailors to save themselves through technical methods.

4/IV Set in parallel the speeches of the captain and of Jonah - here the more formal parallelism breaks down, though a relationship of Jonah to the captain is suggested, similar to the relationship of Jonah to the king of Nineveh.

5, 7/VII, V Show the two sets of statements of the sailors (14). 1/C/I Contain the three places where the "growing phrase" of the fear of the sailors appears.

As Rudolph rightly remarks (15), there are problems to this analysis, notably the necessary omission of 1:16b to maintain the pattern. But the "mathematical ambitions" of the author are clearly present, even if they are not followed through with the rigid, symmetrical exactitude that Rudolph seems to demand (16).

Curiously, although attempts were made to apply a similar analysis to other parts of the book (17), no one followed the lead suggested by Keller (18) in examining the symmetrical structure of Chapter 4. Diagram 4b shows the concentric structure of the chapter with its interesting balance between words and deeds. Jonah chooses the "weapons" for his duel with God (19). In 1 he speaks, in 2 God speaks; in 3 Jonah acts, in 4 God acts. In IV Jonah speaks, and the two speak alternately till the end. The formality of the symmetry can be shown from the curious detail that Jonah's first speech consists of 39 words (30 if the Maqqephs are taken into consideration); God's closing speech also consists of 39 words (30 with

Diagram 4a

1)	4,5a	Narrative - Fear
2)	5b	Prayer of Sailors
3)	5c,6a	Narrative
4)	6b	Speech of Captain
5)	7a	Speech of Sailors
6)	7b	Narrative
7)	8	Speech of Sailors
C)	9,10a	Proclamation by Jonah - Fear
VII)	10b	Speech of Sailors
VI)	10c	Narrative
V)	11	Speech of Sailors
IV)	12	Speech of Jonah
III)	13	Narrative
II)	14	Prayer of Sailors
I)	15,16a	Narrative - Fear

Diagram 4b

1)	2,3	Speech of Jonah
2)	4	Speech of God
3)	5	Act of Jonah
4)	6a,b	Act of God
5)	6c	Jonah happy
C)	7,8a	Act of God
V)	8b	Jonah "unhappy"
IV)	8b	Speech of Jonah
III)	9a	Speech of God
II)	9b	Speech of Jonah
I)	10,11	Speech of God

the Maqqephs). In 2 God replies with three words; in II Jonah's closing remarks to the book consist of 3 words (5 without the Maqqephs). In 2 God asks the question:
"Is it well for you to be angry?"
In II Jonah finally answers:
"It is well for me to be angry even to death."

The Problem of 4:5

In the light of this analysis we can also review the vexed question of the positioning of 4:5 (20). If Jonah already knows that God has forgiven Nineveh, as the sequence of events hows, then why does he now sit outside the city waiting to see what will happen in it? The argument usually runs as follows: although the verse does not make sense at this point, it would fit if it came immediately after Jonah's proclamation in Nineveh in 3:4, before he knew God's response. Therefore logically it should belong there. How came it to be in its current place? Either because of some mistaken amendment of a later editor, or because the author has deliberately delayed telling us about Jonah's movements till he has finished relating the reaction of Nineveh to God's message, in which case we are still to understand the events in 4:5 as following 3:4. This explanation seems to deal with a further problem, the apparent double source of shade on Jonah's head. If in 4:5 he has already built a booth, what purpose does the gourd serve in being "a shade over his head?" The argument usually runs that by putting the booth back to 3:4, a sufficient distance lies between the two sources of shade so that "no problem of contiguity arises" (21).

To deal with these two problems in reverse order: the placing of the booth in 3:4 in no way removes the fact that two sources of shade are being described and must be explained. However if we examine the problem in the light of the structure of Chapter 4, it becomes clear that the act of Jonah in leaving the city is a direct answer to God's question whether Jonah is right to be angry. It is not a reply in words but in deeds. One element in this answer is the building of the booth and his general concern with his comfort (22). When God in turn replies, also by a deed instead of a word, it is to take up the issue of Jonah's comfort and make his shade even more adequate (23). Symbolically God is saying: You are more concerned with your comfort than the destruction of a city full of people - very well, let us see what the implications of your concern are. Jonah then goes on to experience both the comfort which makes him rejoice, and the pain of destruction when the gourd withers. Thus just as Jonah's flight to sea led God to "answer" him in his own "language," by means of a storm at sea, so here too God allows Jonah's choice of action to dictate His method of reply. Once this is recognised then the full significance of the choice of the gourd as a means of teaching Jonah a lesson becomes apparent.

Diagram 5

Divisions of the Book

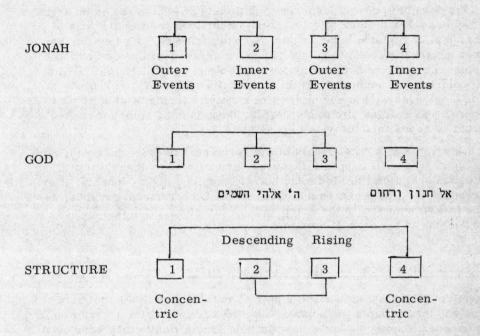

To return to the first part of the problem: what does Jonah expect still to happen in Nineveh? (24) We shall see below the possible attempts to interpret what Jonah expects to see (25), but here we would point out two matters. Firstly, as noted already (26), the verb "see" is used both of God and of Jonah, so that in line with other similar comparisons between God and Jonah through the use of the same verb, the two protagonists are set in opposition to each other: what God has seen, what Jonah wants to see. This does not prove the correct positioning of 4:5 (as the same argument would hold if it came after 3:4), but underlines the implications of this description of Jonah's behaviour. Secondly, the major objection that it is not logical for Jonah to go against the expressed will of God and expect something else to happen, ignores Jonah's equally "illogical" flight "from before the presence of YHWH" in the first place. It is precisely his self-contredness, his seeing the world only in terms of what he wants to happen, that enables him to act despite "knowing" on some other level that what he hopes to achieve is impossible (27).

It is thus clear that both elements of the "problem" of 4:5 - the booth, and the "seeing" what will happen in Nineveh, are related to Jonah's initial flight to sea - in dictating God's method of teaching, and in Jonah's "illogical" response to God's expressly stated word. On structural grounds, as well as in conformity with the inner logic of the story, 4:5 should be retained here as in its correct position.

The Stepwise Structure of Chapters Two and Three

The question of the structure of Chapter 3 naturally follows, but as we have noted, the attempts to compare Chapter 2 with Chapter 1, or to build a pattern over Chapters 3 and 4 have failed. The difficulty may have been ultimately a psychological one, due to the apparent intrusion of the "psalm," which necessitated regarding the book as actually built around three chapters. When the "psalm" is recognised as a fully integrated part of the book, and its structure is also analysed, a very obvious pattern emerges. For the key to understanding Chapter 3 already lies at hand in the recognition of the construction of the book as a whole. (See Diagram 5, page 59.) The form of Chapters 1 and 4 are similar (28), and so are the forms of Chapters 2 and 3. Moreover, these two central chapters are constructed to be mirror images of each other. The general relationship between them can be clearly expressed in the general formula that whereas Jonah (in Chapter 2) descends in a step-wise manner into the depths (both geographical and spiritual), the people of Nineveh rise in a step-wise manner to the heights (29). The formal nature of the constructions in both cases will become apparent from an examination of Diagram 6 (page 61).

The construction of Chapter 3 can be seen as follows (30): In verse 4, God's proclamation is made: "Yet forty days and Nineveh shall be overthrown." The first response (A) (verse 5) is that the people of Nineveh (key word for

Diagram 6

10

     which He said He would do unto them
      and He did it not.
    and God repented of the evil
  that they turned from their evil way
 And God saw their works
        that we perish not?"
      and turn away from His fierce anger
    Who knoweth whether God will not turn and repent
      and from the violence that is in their hands.
    yea, let them turn everyone from his evil way,
      and let them cry mightily unto God
        (both man and beast)
      but let them be covered with sackcloth
        nor drink water
        let them not feed
 "Let neither man nor beast, herd nor flock, taste anything
  (by the decree of the king and his nobles), saying:
    and published through Nineveh
  And he caused it to be proclaimed

7

      and sat in ashes.
    and covered him with sackcloth
     and laid his robe from him
     and he arose from his throne
 And the tidings reached the king of Nineveh

6

      (from the greatest of them even to the least).
       and put on sackcloth
     and they proclaimed a fast

5

 And the people of Nineveh believed in God

4b

 "Yet forty days and Nineveh will be overthrown."

C

For Thou didst cast me into the depth
 in the heart of the seas.

B

And the flood was round about me
 all Thy waves and Thy billows passed over me.

A

And I said: "I am cast out from before Thine eyes
 yet will I look again toward Thy holy temple,

B

The waters compassed me about, even to the soul
 the deep was round about me.
the weeds were wrapped about my head.
I went down to the bottoms of the mountains
 the earth with her bars closed upon me forever

C

Yet hast Thou brought up my life from the pit,
 YHWH my God

the separation off of each separate section, as is "sackcloth"), believed in God and acted accordingly. The second response (B) (verse 6) is the personal one of the king of Nineveh on hearing the news - he too reacted in a penitent manner, thus the spiritual reaction continues to ascend. The third response (C) (verses 7-9) is the decree of the king (published throughout Nineveh), proclaiming a succession of penitent actions reaching their climax with "let them turn everyone from their evil way and from the violence that is in their hands." At this climactic point in the ascent (3:10), God responds on seeing that "they turned from their evil way." Thus we have an initial move by God (Jonah's proclamation); a first stage of response - by the people of Nineveh; a second stage of response - the personal action of the king; a third stage of response - the proclamation of further action; and, at the climactic point, God's intervention to round off the episode.

If we now turn to the "psalm" and the actions of Jonah, we see that it, too, begins with God's action (2:4) "For Thou didst cast me into the depths." Jonah's response is not one of penitence, so response A is the first stage of his sinking beneath the waves (verse 4b). Response B is his personal reaction (verse 5) in exact parallel (and contrast - as we have analysed in studying the "psalm") (31) to the personal reaction of the king of Nineveh (32). Response C is thus a continuation of his descent (verses 6-7b), for, as we have already seen, his personal reaction was not the correct one. Yet when he reaches the lowest point of his descent, it is once again God who intervenes (verse 7c) "Yet Thou hast brought up my life from the pit, YHWH my God."

The recognition of this "mirror image" parallelism between Chapters 2 and 3 seems to be conclusive evidence that the "psalm" was from the very outset an integral part of the author's composition (33).

By recognising this structure, we are now in a position to resolve two textual problems that could not otherwise be explained. As a foreword to this, one should note the exact balancing of the two sides of the mirror image, and particularly that section C in each case is twice as long as Section A, thus giving to the "psalm" the feeling of an endless, accelerating descent, to the actions of the Ninevites a limitless, accelerating rise.

We have already noted in our discussion of the "psalm" (34) the strange feature that the author uses quotations and reminiscences from his tradition up to a certain point (verse 6b) and then all the imagery of the last part of his descent is the author's own coinage. We have suggested that this implies that just as Jonah must break out of his traditional attitudes to face a new situation, so the use of unfamiliar language at this point in the "psalm" underlines the unfamiliarity of the situation. We have a significant confirmation of this interpretation if we now examine the "mirror image" of Jonah's descent, the "rise" of the Ninevites. Which brings us to our second textual problem, the apparent redundance of the first part of the king's edict. The repentant Ninevites (3:5) proclaim a fast and put

CHAPTER III - ANALYSIS OF STRUCTURE

on sackcloth. The king himself puts on sackcloth (verse 6). In his proclamation he begins by ordering a fast (for man and beast) and also the
wearing of sackcloth (verses 7-8a), measures which extend these actions
to the beasts, but are already redundant. Yet if we examine these actions
in the light of the "mirror image" in Jonah, they fulfil the same role as
the author's use of traditional terminology up to a certain key point in the
"psalm" - the people of Nineveh react in their traditional manner (fast and
sackcloth), as does the king at the beginning of his proclamation. But precisely at the point where Jonah plummets down into a new, unknown, and
"untraditional" depth in the sea (in the middle of response C), the king of
Nineveh bursts upwards into a new dimension of penitence for his pagan
people: "and let them cry mightily unto God; yea, let them turn every one
from his evil way, and from the violence that is in their hands. Who knows
...?" Significantly it is precisely in response to this breakthrough to a
new height that God responds (verse 10): "And God saw their works that
they turned from their evil way..."

We shall return to the meaning expressed in the structure and content of
these two chapters when we sum up all our material later. However, it
is clear already that the theme of venturing out from a traditional situation
into a new one, willingly or unwillingly, is one key to the understanding of
the book.

ויאמר
יהוה לדג
ויקא את
יונה אל־היבשה:

Chapter IV

ANALYSIS OF QUOTATIONS

Since the work of Feuillet (1) general recognition has been given to the
use of quotations throughout the Book of Jonah, though earlier commentators had already remarked on certain connections with the other books (2).
The two most obvious relationships which have been established are with
episodes in the life of Elijah (I Kings 19) and Jeremiah (especially Chapter
26 and 36).

However, despite the certainty (3) with which it is accepted that the
author of Jonah deliberately made use of quotations from earlier sources,
there is no clear methodological basis to these assertions; and whereas
in some cases no doubts need be entertained, other alleged borrowing are
far from proven - notably in the relationship between "Jonah" and Ezekiel.
In this section we will attempt to analyse the techniques used by the author
in his use of quotations and apply these findings to more problematic cases.

The first distinction to be made in analysis is to determine when we have
a "quotation," and when a "reminiscence" (4). No one familiar with the
Bible can read about Nineveh and the word נהפכת without at once thinking
of the overthrow of Sodom and Gomorrah (5). And an examination of the
concordance will reveal that except for one reference to the fear of the
king of Ammon that David will overthrow his city (II Samuel 10:3; I Chron
19:3), all other usages of this verb with regard to a city refer directly to,
or use the analogy of, Sodom and Gomorrah (6). Similarly one cannot help
but contrast the attitude of Jonah to the threatened overthrow of the city to
that of Abraham (7). Such an evocation we must term a "reminiscence"
since no direct quotation is involved; yet this evocation is as physically
present in the associations produced by the book as any direct quotation.

Likewise, as Orlinsky points out: "Interestingly, the terms used in Jonah
for the transgressions by the Ninevites, ra'ah (1:2; 3:8) and hamas (3:8)
are the same as those employed in Genesis 6:5, 11, 13 for the generation
that was responsible for God's decision to bring the Flood upon the earth"
(8). Thus one can say that the reminiscence of the "generation of the flood"
and of "Sodom and Gomorrah" fills out for us the significance of the evil
of Nineveh by giving it these "historical" associations. Conversely the
description of the fate of Nineveh forces us to reconsider our attitudes
(or at least God's attitude) to these aforementioned events.

A third example will show a further aspect of the problem. We have noted
often the precision with which words are used by the author, and the significance that must be attached to repetitions. What do we make, therefore,
of the word יבשה which comes three times in the first two chapters:
1:9, 13; 2:11. That it stands here in contrast to the yam sea, is clear
from its usage in Jonah's affirmation that YHWH has made "the sea and

the dry land"; Likewise the sailors fail to bring Jonah back to "dry land" because the sea became more and more tempestuous against them. Yet the significance cannot lie in any mythological struggle between God and the waters, because we are explicitly told that God was responsible for the storm, and anyway He "made the sea and dry land" (1:9), a phrase which automatically evokes Psalm 95:5:

אשר לו הים והוא עשהו ויבשת ידיו יצרו

"The sea is His and He made it; and His hands formed the dry land." Behind both statements stands also the creation story (Genesis 1:9-10):

ויאמר אלהים יקוו המים מתחת השמים אל מקום אחד ותראה היבשה ויהי כן
ויקרא אלהים ליבשה ארץ ולמקוה המים קרא ימים וירא אלהים כי טוב

"And God said: 'Let the waters under the heaven be gathered together unto one place, and let the <u>dry land</u> appear.' And it was so. And God called the <u>dry land</u>, Earth...."

Yet Biblical tradition knows another יבשה which is no less significant a reminiscence within the framework of our book. The <u>dry land</u> on which the children of Israel walked as they passed through the Reed Sea (and later the Jordan) is repeatedly emphasised as evidence of the protection of God for His people, the "dry land" upon which they may walk in safety (9). Which "dry land" is being evoked here by the threefold repetition, Creation or Exodus? Or are they both?

Clearly no decision on this matter can be made merely on the basis of the repetition of a single word; it will therefore be necessary to make a thorough study of all such "evocative" words and situations, against a background of whatever can be established as genuine quotation; and then fit this material into an overall understanding of the book itself, before proper conclusions can be drawn.

This leads us to the methodological problem of establishing where a quotation from another Biblical text is being used. We have demonstrated in the section dealing with the "psalm" certain techniques for dealing with this problem, but it is perhaps now the appropriate place to make a note of the underlying problems. When a phrase or sentence appears in two places in the Bible, it is possible that A quotes B, or that B quotes A, or that both have used independently a third source C. A further possibility is that a later editor has inserted the same phrase into both texts (10). In some cases an independent fact, such as the relative dating of the two passages, can determine the possible historical relationship between the two usages: the earlier text can hardly be citing the later, though the possibility of an insertion by a later editor cannot always be ruled out. One is thus forced to a very careful assessment of the contexts of both phrases to see if there is perhaps a logical relationship between the usages in both places, preferably where it can be demonstrated that the interpretation of one can only be made when the existence of the "original" is presupposed. In this latter case, it is helpful if the context of the "quote" offers other clues (for example a second "quote" or similar theme) that lead us back to the same source. In addition we may consider the stylistic characteristics of both authors and assess the texts before us in relationship to their usual techniques. The place of the "quotation" within the overall context (whether it is an isolated phrase or fits into a consistent pattern of ideas) is an additional guide. We shall have recourse to all these methods in the analysis ahead, and will deal with them in more detail in the appropriate place.

To begin with we shall examine passages where there is some certainty that Jonah is quoting an earlier source, and see what principles underlie his technique. We will then apply these principles to certain problematic passages as a way of testing our analysis. When the extent of quotations has been assessed we will bring together in a further section the material obtained so far, in an attempt to assess the purposes behind the author's work.

"Tardemah" and Elijah

In 1:5 and 6 there appears the root r-d-m. It is a rare root appearing only eleven other times in the Bible (11). The fact of its repetition in this story (as nowhere else in the Bible); plus the curious fact that the captain of the crew can distinguish a "Tardemah" from normal sleep, implies that the author wishes to emphasise this word. It is therefore valid to ask what specific meaning does he wish to impart by the use of this word, and can the answer to this question be found within the text of the book alone.

If we examine the narrative contexts in which this word appears in the Bible, we learn certain of the ideas that cluster around it. It is the sleep that falls upon Adam when Eve is created (Genesis 2:21) - hence it is a sleep that lies beyond the pain threshold, and is associated with creation. It is the sleep that falls upon Abraham (Genesis 15:12) at the "covenant between the pieces," when a prophecy about the future is given to him. It is the stage of "sleep" just prior to death that comes to Sisera at the hands of Jael (Judges 4:21), and the deep sleep that falls upon Saul and his encampment when David steals his spear and cruse of water. Thus far we can see two broad associations with the word - the deep sleep beyond rousing which is close to death; and a sleep in which revelation (in the form of prophecy or creation) takes place. The former meaning can be seen in Proverbs 10:5; 19:15; Psalm 76:7; and the latter in Job 4:13; 33:15; Daniel 8:18; 10:9. In Isaiah 29:10 the prophet uses the paradox of including both ideas by proclaiming that a deep sleep will fall upon the prophets themselves so that they can no longer prophecy.

How then are we to understand the meaning of the term in the book of Jonah. Nowhere at this stage of the story does a revelation come to Jonah; in fact he appears to be rather slow in recognising his responsibility for what is happening. Therefore the "Tardemah" of Jonah, must be the deep sleep that approaches death as the prophet cuts himself off from the storm and the sailors' activities and prayers, just as he has cut himself off from God's mission. We have here, therefore, the first hint of Jonah's "death wish," a theme which is more and more explicitly demonstrated as the story progresses: the request to be thrown overboard, the requests for death in Chapter 4.

But since this "death wish" is so clearly developed, the specific, emphatic usage of r-d-m must contain an additional meaning. If we look to the situation in Chapter 4 that most resembles this withdrawal, when Jonah sits beneath his booth, we might expect another "Tardemah," or at least some hint to the explanation of the usage of this word. But since no explanation is forthcoming, and since the usage of this rare word by the author has already forced us to look outside our immediate context to find its meaning, it is valid to look beyond the book of Jonah to answer this question.

The next step depends upon the logic of association, and assumes both on the part of the author and his audience a mind fully conversant with other Biblical texts, and an ear finely attuned to detecting similarities and differences in phraseology. Another prophet in flight once lay down and slept at a significant point in the story: what was written about him? In I Kings 19:5 the prophet Elijah, fleeing from Jezebel to the desert near Beer Sheba, sits beneath a broom plant, asks his life from God.
"and he lay down and slept": וישכב ויישן
We thus have here a phrase containing one word in common with Jonah (1:5) and one different. The "sleep" of the prophet Elijah is "replaced" by the "deep sleep" of Jonah. וישכב וירדם   If we work on the assumption that the specific purpose of the author in drawing attention to the unusual word was to bring to his readers the above association (12), then we can say at the very least that two prophets, both fleeing, both faced by imminent death, lie down and sleep; but whereas one sleeps a normal sleep, the other sleeps the "deep sleep" which is already cut off from contact with the world about him, a sleep which is itself already close to death.

Could we have got to this chapter of I Kings in any other way? The picture of a prophet sitting under a plant (the gourd) might have led us to the former prophet who sat beneath a broom tree; partly because the unusual word "gourd" would have puzzled us, let alone the need for two sources of shade on Jonah's head (4:5,6). Even stronger might be the word association that comes to mind when Elijah beneath his broom tree asks for death, as does Jonah in almost identical words:
וישאל את נפשו למות ויאמר רב עתה ה' קח נפשי כי לא טוב אנכי מאבתי
"...and he requested for himself that he might die; and said: 'It is enough; now, O YHWH, take away my life; for I am not better than my fathers'" (I Kings 19:4):
וישאל את נפשו למות ויאמר טוב מותי מחיי
"...and he requested for himself that he might die, and said: 'It is better for me to die than to live.'" (Jonah 4:8)

ועתה ה' קח נא את נפשי ממני כי טוב מותי מחיי

"'Therefore now, O YHWH, take, I beseech Thee, my life from me; for
it is better for me to die than to live.'" (Jonah 4:3)

One should add to these verbal associations the similar repeated question/
answer dialogue between God and his prophet that follows both with Elijah
(I Kings 19:9-14) and with Jonah (Jonah 4:4-11). To this also the similarity
of numbers - Elijah walks one day into the desert, Jonah walks one day
into Nineveh; Elijah is sustained for forty days in the desert, Jonah pro-
claims Nineveh's destruction after a forty-day period.

In passing, a peculiar feature of these associations may be noted, namely
that material contained in one chapter of the book of Kings is distributed
between two separate chapters of the book of Jonah: the association with
sleeping which occurs when Elijah is under the broom tree, actually occurs
in the Jonah story when he is in the ship; whereas the request to God to
take his life, is in both cases associated with the plant. It will be seen
later that this "dividing up" of material from a prior source between two
different "episodes" in "Jonah" occurs in other occasions (13).

To sum up: the use of r-d-m has led us to look outside the Book of Jonah
for an explanation; the place we reached (I Kings 19) has been shown to
contain a remarkable number of parallel themes (the prophet sitting beneath a plant - who asks to die - and then has a dialogue with God) and
phrases (one identical in both וישאל את נפשו למות ויאמר ; one similar
קח נפשי / קח נא את נפשי ממני and one that is similar precisely in the
contrast that led us here in the first place: וישכב וירדם / וישכב ויישן).
Can such an overwhelming amount of common material be mere coincidence,
or can one not say with a large degree of certainty that the author of the
book of Jonah looked to this chapter on the life story of Elijah while he constructed his work?

Such an elaborate explanation to arrive at a commonly accepted conclusion
(14) is important for two reasons:

i. that the author provides a number of "clues" to direct us to a quite spe-
    cific chapter of an earlier book, and

ii. that the combination of quotation(s) and contextual relationship is the
    most convincing evidence in establishing the existence of quoted materi-
    al.

"Innocent Blood" - the Paradoxical Quotation

When the sailors pray to God not to destroy them because of the "life of
this man" (Jonah 1:14) nor to "lay upon us innocent blood," the reader is
brought up with a start. Is this not a phrase out of Israelite tradition somewhere that these heathen sailors are quoting?! But is it a quotation at all,
or merely an independent statement? The combination of the phrase "in-

nocent blood" with the verb n-t-n (in the sense of "to be held responsible
for by God") occurs in only two other places in the Bible: Deuteronomy 21:8
and Jeremiah 26:15 (15). But do we follow Kaiser (16) to the former: "und
bitten ihn mit deuteronomischen Worten darum, ihnen dieses Leben nicht
zuzurechnen (vgl. 1:14 mit Dtn 21:8)"; or Feuillet (17) to the latter: "L'expression 'ne pas nous charger d'un sang innocent' veut peut-être rappeler
Jer 26:15 et souligner cette volonté droite par contraste avec l'acharnement
des ennemis de Jérémie."?

Do we have a way of establishing in the first place that we are dealing here
with a quotation at all? We can answer this in the affirmative by referring
to a stylistic device of the author. We have already noted in our analysis
of the "psalm" (18) that it can only be understood in its place in the book
if it is recognised that the author puts into the mouth of Jonah certain phrases from his tradition, which become ironic when spoken by Jonah within
the particular context. We must now pay attention to precisely the opposite
device which the author employs: namely to put "traditional Israelite" quotations into the mouth of the "pagans" (or use them in the narrative with
regard the "pagans"), thus reversing the ironic effect - the words now sound
perfectly correct, but it is the fact that they come from the last place the
reader would expect, that produces the irony.

i. Jonah says: "who made the sea and the dry land," thereby bringing to
mind Psalm 95:5 - "the sea is His, and He made it; and His hands formed
the dry land."

The sailors pray to God:

כי אתה ה' כאשר חפצת עשית

"for Thou, O YHWH, hast done as it pleased Thee," thus calling to mind
the Hallel psalms: Psalm 115:3

ואלהינו בשמים כל אשר חפץ עשה

"But our God is in the heavens; whatsoever pleased Him He hath done."
or Psalm 135:6

כל אשר חפץ ה' עשה בשמים ובארץ בימים וכל תהמות

"Whatsoever YHWH pleased, that hath He done; in heaven and in earth, in
the seas and in all deeps."

ii. When we read that the sailors "feared YHWH exceedingly" (1:16) we are
not very surprised; when, however, we read that the people of Nineveh
suddenly "believed in God" (3:5), we are astonished. We are more astonished
when we recognise the probable source of both reactions (19) - Exodus 14:31:

וירא ישראל את היד הגדולה אשר עשה ה' במצרים וייראו העם את ה'
ויאמינו בה' ובמשה עבדו

"And Israel saw the great work which YHWH did upon the Egyptians, and
the people feared YHWH; and they believed in YHWH, and in His servant
Moses." (All other uses of the root אמן in relationship to God are restricted to Israel's belief (or more frequent lack of belief) in God and in the prophets He repeatedly sends) (20).

CHAPTER IV - ANALYSIS OF QUOTATIONS

iii. In 3:10 when God sees the repentance of the people of Nineveh:

וינחם האלהים על הרעה אשר דבר לעשות להם ולא עשה

"and God repented of the evil, which He said He would do unto them, and He did it not." That this is almost word for word the phrase used of God's forgiveness of the children of Israel after the Golden Calf episode, we have noted already elsewhere (21).

וינחם ה' על הרעה אשר דבר לעשות לעמו

"And YHWH repented of the evil which He said He would do unto His people." (Exodus 32:14)

The phrase recurs three times in Jeremiah 26 (verses 3, 13 and 19) expressed first by God as a hope - "perhaps they will turn from their evil ways, then I will repent"; then by Jeremiah as a promise - "amend your ways, and YHWH will repent"; and then as a historical recollection from the time of Hezekiah who feared God and entreated Him - "and YHWH repented Him of the evil." Thus all these usages refer specifically to Israel (22). However, in the theology of Jeremiah, the possibility exists already for the extension of this idea to another nation - Jeremiah 18:8:(23)

ושב הגוי ההוא מרעתו אשר דברתי עליו ונחמתי על הרעה אשר חשבתי לעשות לו

"but if that nation turn from their evil, because of which I have spoken against it, I repent of the evil that I thought to do unto it." Though this takes us a step further towards the situation in "Jonah," it is still the shock of the similarity of the "Jonah" verse to Exodus which predominates, and the contrast that it emplies. We can also see how the author has used the formulation from an earlier stage of his tradition, mediated through a later theological concept. We can also note in the Jeremiah formulations a dependence upon the Exodus passage.

iv. While still within this context in Exodus, we can note a second significant parallel. Moses in his plea to God says (Exodus 32:12):

שוב מחרון אפך והנחם על הרעה לעמך

"Turn from Thy fierce wrath and repent of this evil against Thy people."

The king of Nineveh says (Jonah 3:9):

מי יודע ישוב ונחם האלהים ושב מחרון אפו ולא נאבד

"Who knoweth whether God will not turn and repent, and turn away from His fierce wrath, that we perish not."

These are the only two passages which combine the elements of God "turning from His fierce wrath" and "repenting of evil." Yet again an idea that was formerly restricted to the relationship between God and Israel is expanded to embrace the "pagan" world.

v. The phrase used by the king of Nineveh (3:8):

וישבו איש מדרכו הרעה

"let them turn each man from his evil way" is a phrase which otherwise occurs only in Jeremiah (24), and once again applies only, in the Jeremiah context, to Israel.

"INNOCENT BLOOD"

71

With these five examples behind us, and the sixth example of "lay not upon us innocent blood" with which we began, we may assert that the author of "Jonah" has repeatedly put into the mouth of his pagan characters, or into the narrative parts concerning them, phrases which in a variety of other texts (Exodus, Deuteronomy, Jeremiah, Psalms) apply only to, or are only used by, Israel in relationship to God. Since this is a consistent stylistic device it is likely that all the examples we have found represent deliberate "paradoxical" quotations from earlier texts.

We may now return to our original question - in quoting the phrase "do not lay upon us innocent blood," is the author of "Jonah" referring to the version in Deuteronomy or that in Jeremiah?

If we examine the phrase in Deuteronomy 21, we find that the structure of the quotation is almost identical with that in "Jonah"; and that it, too, takes the form of a direct address to God. (Jonah 1:14)

ויקראו אל ה' ויאמרו אנה ה' אל נא נאבדה בנפש האיש הזה ואל תתן
עלינו דם נקיא כי אתה ה' כאשר חפצת עשית

"Wherefore they cried unto YHWH, and said: 'We beseech Thee, O YHWH, we beseech Thee, let us not perish for this man's life, and lay not upon us innocent blood...'!"

Deuteronomy 21:7-8:

וענו ואמרו ידינו לא שפכה את הדם הזה ועינינו לא ראו.
כפר לעמך ישראל אשר פדית ה' ואל תתן דם נקי בקרב עמך ישראל
ונכפר להם הדם

"And they shall speak and say: 'Our hands have not shed this blood, neither have our eyes seen it. Forgive, O YHWH, Thy people Israel, whom Thou hast redeemed, and suffer not innocent blood to remain in the midst of Thy people Israel....'"

Nevertheless the context is totally inappropriate for the "Jonah" story. In Deuteronomy the point at issue is that a corpse has been found whose murderer is unknown. The innocence or guilt of the victim is of no consequence here (his blood being "innocent" only insofar as he is the victim of an unknown assailant) The only significant fact is that his blood has been shed, and that atonement must be made for his death by the symbolic killing of the heifer and the rest of the ritual (25). Secondly, the elders of the nearest town are not literally responsible for the killing of the victim, but are in some sense ritually (and perhaps underlying this, morally) responsible, and hence must perform the rite of atonement. This obviously does not connect directly with the situation of the sailors who are concerned with the probable murder that they themselves are about to commit - on a man who is actually in some sense "guilty" (at least before his God). Where then is Kaiser's deuteronomical quotation?

On the other hand our passage in Jeremiah 26 has a somewhat different structure of quotation and is directed not to God but to the people of Jerusalem. (Jeremiah 26:14-15)

אך ידע תדעו כי אם ממתים אתם אתי כי דם נקי אתם נתנים עליכם

ואל העיר הזאת ואל ישביה כי באמת שלחני ה' עליכם לדבר באזניכם
את כל הדברים האלה

"Only know ye for certain that if you put me to death, ye will bring innocent blood upon yourselves, and upon this city, and upon the inhabitants
thereof; for of a truth YHWH hath sent me unto you to speak all these words
in your ears."

Here we have the confrontation between a prophet and a mob who wish to
kill him. The relationship between them, however, is paradoxically different, as we have come to expect from our studies in "Jonah's" use of quotations. In Jeremiah the people (the "bad" people against whom the "good"
prophet has preached) wish to kill him; and he pleads for his life, not for
his own sake, but because his death will bring the stain of "innocent blood"
upon Jerusalem. In contrast Jonah (the "bad" prophet faced by "good" sailors) himself asks to be thrown overboard to his death, and it is the sailors
who do everything in their power to prevent this act. Not only that, but they
themselves are aware of the significance of the shedding of innocent blood
and pray to God not to hold the act against them, a problem which seems
to have escaped Jonah's attention in his concern to be rid of his mission.
Certainly in terms of context, we have the more likely source of quotation
in this passage. But where is Feuillet's quotation when the structure and
object of address are quite different?

The answer seems to lie yet again (26) in a synthesis made by the author
of "Jonah" between the two texts, i.e., taking the context of Jeremiah, but
bringing to it the formula actually used in Deuteronomy (27).

Do we have further proof, however, that the author of "Jonah" could have
made such a synthesis from two passages? Once again we must rely upon
the circumstantial evidence that this would accord with a stylistic device
employed a number of times by the author; which leads us to our next
section.

The Dividing up of Quotations

From what we have seen of the usage of quotations so far, two "complementary" devices are used by the author, though curiously enough they seem to
have been overlooked in the literature. These are: i. That the author divides
up material from a single source into two separate chapters in "Jonah";
ii. That he gathers into a single place in "Jonah" material from two separate places in the Bible.

i. The Separation of Texts

a. We have already seen (28) how the author has led us to I King 19. But
whereas the phrase about the prophet lying down and sleeping/deep sleeping
(c.f. Jonah 1:5 and I Kings 19:5) occurs with regard Elijah when he is under
the broom tree, it refers to Jonah when he is in the ship. However, all the

other elements which occur in both texts: the plant beneath which the prophet sleeps, the request to die, occur in Jonah in the fourth chapter.

b. The two reactions of the children of Israel to their rescue at the Reed Sea, "fear" and "belief" (Exodus 14:31) are divided between the sailors (Chapter 1) and the Ninevites (Chapter 3) (29).

c. The "appropriate" context for the "trial scene" in Jerusalem between the prophet and people would be in Chapter 3, after Jonah has prophesied in Nineveh, yet the author has put it, together with the phrase about "innocent blood" into Chapter 1. However, the thrice repeated sentence about God changing His mind about the evil He thought to do (Jeremiah 26:3, 12, 19) comes significantly in "Jonah" in Chapter 3 after the king's command to repent.

We thus have three examples where the author has taken material from a common source and divided it between different chapters in "Jonah." We can now examine in detail the converse process - the synthesising of material from different places in the bible into one single place in "Jonah."

ii. The Fusion of Texts

a. We have already noted in our discussion on "paradoxical quotations" (30) the use of Exodus 32:14 - "and YHWH repented of the evil which He said He would do unto His people", and have noted that its usage here is mediated through the theological "extension" of the verse in Jeremiah 18:8, and by its usage in Jeremiah 26. The quotation in Jonah 3:10 is nevertheless dependent for its wording upon the exodus version.

b. We have also dealt at length with the problem of "innocent blood" as it appears in Deuteronomy and Jeremiah (31). We need only note again that the phrase itself is based upon the Deuteronomy version, whereas the new context, without which it would not be comprehensible from its original situation, is dependent upon Jeremiah 26.

c. The third example deals in part with new material. When Jonah confronts God in his rage, he tells Him (4:2):

אנה ה' הלא זה דברי עד היותי על אדמתי. על כן קדמתי לברח תרשישה
כי ידעתי כי אתה אל חנון ורחום ארך אפים ורב חסד ונחם על הרעה.
ועתה ה' קח נא את נפשי ממני כי טוב מותי מחיי.

"I pray Thee, O YHWH, was not this my saying when I was yet in mine own country? Therefore I fled beforehand unto Tarshish; for I knew that Thou art a gracious God, and compassionate, long-suffering, and abundant in mercy and repentest Thee of the evil. Therefore now O YHWH, take, I beseech Thee, my life from me; for it is better for me to die than to live."

But when did Jonah "say" something when he was back in his own country? This is not merely a pedantic question, for we have seen too often the precision with which words are used. If Jonah insists that he said something, there must be a purpose. And since nothing is recorded of what he said

"back in his own country" we are justified in seeking an explanation, yet
again, in the usage here of a quotation; and indeed we can readily find one
which takes us again back to the context of the Reed Sea.

When the children of Israel stand on the shore of the Reed Sea and see
Pharaoh's chariots approaching, they complain to Moses (Exodus 14:12):

הלא זה הדבר אשר דברנו אליך במצרים לאמר הדל ממנו ונעבדה את
מצרים כי טוב לנו עבד את מצרים ממתנו במדבר

"Is not this the word that we spoke unto thee in Egypt, saying: Let us alone,
that we may serve the Egyptians? For it were better for us to serve the
Egyptians, than that we should die in the wilderness."

That this is indeed a quotation is likely from the fact that we have another
passage quoted from this chapter (Exodus 14:31) and possibly from the use
of יבשה we have already noted (32). Furthermore the relationship of meaning is quite clear. Within the Jonah context alone, the phrase is redundant;
in connection with our passage in Exodus two ideas are emphasised. Both
reflect the unwillingness of Israel (Jonah or the children of Israel) to leave
a previous security ("Egypt"/"my land") at God's command to face a new,
dangerous situation. The second part shows an inverted relationship between the two expressions. The children of Israel prefer slavery to apparent death; Jonah prefers death to life. In this association, however, (as
in the problem with the "innocent blood" and Deuteronomy), we seem to
be missing an intermediate stage which links up these two thoughts. However, we have already encountered the solution in our analysis of the connection with Elijah (33).

In I Kings 19:4, Elijah, who has fled from Jezebel, sits beneath the broom
tree and asks God to take his life.

והוא הלך במדבר דרך יום ויבא וישב תחת רתם אחד וישאל את נפשו למות
ויאמר רב עתה ה' קח נפשי כי לא טוב אנכי מאבתי

"But he himself went a day's journey into the wilderness, and came and
sat down under a broom tree; and requested for himself that he might die;
and said: 'It is enough; now O YHWH, take away my life; for I am no better
than my fathers.'"

If we compare this verse with Jonah 4:2, we find the same "take away my
life" and the same construction "ki tov...mi..." (common to our Exodus
passage and Jonah) though here expressed in the negative form. Thus
"Jonah" once again links together the context of one passage (Elijah's
flight and request for death) and the terminology from another - the words
of the children of Israel before the Reed Sea. The effect is to set up a
series of very powerful "echoes" in which each text interacts with the
other, and both react within the "Jonah" context itself. It also has the
effect of giving an interpretation to Elijah's puzzling statement that "I
am no better than my fathers," linking it now with the unwillingness of
the children of Israel to leave behind their slavery, both of which situations
depend upon trusting in the word of God despite apparent danger. However,

THE DIVIDING UP OF QUOTATIONS

it is difficult to see how far the author of "Jonah" intended the ripples of his associations to spread (34).

Thus we have three passages where the author has made a synthesis of the words and contexts of two separate but related passages, in the construction of his story. We may now return to the examination of other passages from which the author seems to quote.

The Repentance of Kings

Before turning to more problematic passages, there is a further text which Feuillet (35) cites as relating "Jonah" to Jeremiah, namely the description of the events which take place in Nineveh and in Jeremiah 36 (36). He presents the outline of the comparison as follows:

"Le thème fondamental des deux passages est le même: la possibilité du non-accomplissement de l'oracle divin en cas de conversion...." "De plus, c'est la même marche générale des évenements: menace divine (Jonah 3:4, c.f. 1:2; Jeremiah 36:7b); - publication d'un jeune extraordinaire et général avec, de part et d'autre, une expression qu'on ne trouve que là: קרא צום (Jonah 3:5; Jeremiah 36:9); - la nouvelle arrive aux oreilles du roi entouré de ses ministres (Jonah 3:6; Jeremiah 36:12-20)."

It should be noted that the sequence of events is not quite the same; in Jeremiah 36 the fast has already been proclaimed before Baruch reads from the scroll; whereas in "Jonah" it is the reaction of the people consequent to the prophetic call. Nevertheless the author of "Jonah" could well have interpreted the events described in Jeremiah as the penitent actions of the people of Jerusalem:

a. The subject of the phrase "they called a fast" (Jeremiah 36:9) could as well be the "people" as the "anonymous authorities" (37);

b. Significantly no adverse reaction of the people is recorded to Baruch's words, in contradistinction to the angry response to the Temple sermon (38).

Feuillet continues (39): "Il est dit dans Jérémie 36:24: 'le roi et tous ses serviteurs qui entendirent toutes ces paroles ne furent point effrayés et ne déchirèrent pas leurs vêtements'; c'est l'attitude inverse que prennent le roi de Ninive et ses grands (Jonah 3:6-8); - l'impénitence de Joakim, qui fait brûler le rouleau de propheties de Jérémie, provoquera la réalisation de l'oracle de menaces: la destruction des hommes et des bêtes à Jerusalem (Jeremiah 36:29-31); la pénitence de Ninive lui vaudra d'être épargnée tout entière, hommes et animaux (3:10; c.f. 4:11)."

The above description brings out very clearly the paradoxical relationship we have so often noted in the work of our author - the "Ninevites" responding correctly when Israel does not.

Feuillet continues (40) by discussing the problem of the redundancy of the king's proclamation calling for a fast, after the people have already done so. He argues against Böhme (41) (the two document theory) and Schmidt (42) (that 3:6-9 was a later addition), by showing the dependence of the passage on the Jeremiah model: first the people responded, then the king. Though this accounts for the outline of events, it does not explain the double proclamation of fasting and the wearing of sackcloth (first by the people, then by the king). However, as we have seen (43) this can be understood in terms of "traditional" and "new" penitential responses.

Thus we can say with Feuillet, that the use of a common term קרא צום and similar contexts (in inverse relationship to each other), would support the thesis that "Jonah" is here dependent upon Jeremiah 36.

Problematic Quotations

With these illustrations and analyses behind us, we can now tackle two of the major problems concerning the use of "quotations" in "Jonah": the first being the relationship between Jonah 3:9a and 4:2c and Joel 2:13-14a; the second, between "Jonah" and Ezekiel 26-28 and Psalm 107.

i. Jonah and Joel

Jonah 3:9a reads:

מי יודע ישוב ונחם האלהים ושב מחרון אפו ולא נאבד

"Who knoweth whether God will not turn and repent, and turn away from us His fierce wrath, that we perish not."
Jonah 4:2c reads:

כי ידעתי כי אתה אל חנון ורחום ארך אפים ורב חסד ונחם על הרעה

"For I knew that Thou art a gracious God, and compassionate, long-suffering, and abundant in mercy, and repentest Thee of the evil."
Joel 2:13-14a reads:

וקרעו לבבכם ואל בגדיכם ושובו אל ה' אלהיכם כי חנון ורחום הוא
ארך אפים ורב חסד ונחם על הרעה.   מי יודע ישוב ונחם והשאיר אחריו
ברכה מנחה ונסך לה' אלהינו

"And rend your heart, and not your garments, and turn unto YHWH your God; for He is gracious and compassionate, long-suffering, and abundant in mercy, and repenteth of the evil. Who knoweth whether He will not turn and repent, and leave a blessing behind Him, even a meal-offering and a drink-offering unto YHWH your God?"

Though it is possible that both authors might utilize a common source for each phrase, the coincidence of two such phrases, so clearly inter-related in each case, in such similar contexts (a last opportunity for repentance before destruction comes), without some sort of mutual interrelationship is unlikely (44). We have noted already that within "Jonah" both phrases stand in their usual ironic relationship to the speaker: the king of Nineveh quoting Israel's tradition about God's attributes in hopeful anticipation of salvation; Jonah quoting Israel's tradition about God's attributes in condemnation of that very salvation. Joel conversely cites the attributes of God, and logically applies them to Israel's situation. If one author is responsible for the coining of both phrases, how can we demonstrate which is dependent upon the other? (45)

Ideally, in assessing the relationship between two books for the dependence of one upon the other, both should first be fixed in time independently, as far as possible (46). However, critical opinion gives such a wide range of dates to both books (from the 10th to the 2nd century for Joel; from the 9th to the 2nd century for "Jonah"), though on the whole bringing them both into the 4th century (47), that no clearcut historical relationship can be evoked. We are thus left with an examination of internal literary criteria for our analysis.

To the argument that "Jonah" is quoting Joel, we can bring the following pieces of evidence from our analysis.

a. That "Jonah" regularly uses quotations in the construction of his story. However, so also does Joel; and whereas "Jonah" quotes Jeremiah and perhaps Ezekiel (48), but none other of the post-exilic prophets, it is generally accepted that Joel (3:5) quotes Obadiah (17); and Joel 2:11; 3:4 are dependent upon Malachi 3:2, 23 (49). Though it cannot be argued from "Jonah's" failure to quote later sources that he must necessarily be earlier (as they may simply not have suited his purpose), nevertheless it is a factor which may be significant in the light of other evidence.

b. "Jonah's" use of paradoxical quotations suggests that, if he has not coined the actual formulation used by the king of Nineveh, it is likely that, as elsewhere, he is again here using his usual technique - and that the source of the paradoxical quotation is Joel. However, Joel himself seems to employ something of the same procedure, reversing the ideas found in other prophets by use of amended quotations (50). Likewise, prophetic warnings against Egypt (Ezekiel 30:2) and Babel (Isaiah 13:6) are "reversed" in Joel and directed against Jerusalem (Joel 1:15) (51). Whether it is more paradoxical for "Jonah" to put words from Israel's tradition into the mouth of the king of Nineveh; or for Joel to quote the king of Nineveh in encouraging Israel to repent, both possibilities remain open within the stylistic framework of both writers (52).

c. We have noted that "Jonah" sometimes divides up material from the same source into two separate chapters. In line with this, the Joel passages could have been divided into its two elements and placed in Chapter 3 and 4. However, Joel has a tendency to bring together passages from different prophetic books, and even from different places in the same prophet (53), so that yet again the customary devices of either writer could be at work here.

d. We are thus forced to examine the phrases within their context and see who is the most likely writer to have created them in their present form.

If we examine the words of the king of Nineveh, we can see that the whole sentence stands, within the context of the book, in parallel with the words of the captain of the crew (1:6):

אולי יתעשה לנו האלהים ולא נאבד

" ...perhaps God will think upon us, that we perish not."
Jonah 3:9:

מי יודע ישוב ונחם האלהים ושב מחרון אפו ולא נאבד

"Who knoweth whether God will not turn and repent; and turn away from His fierce wrath, that we perish not?"

Here "who knows" is in parallel with "perhaps," both standing within a context of imminent destruction, both expressing the hope that God will intervene and save their lives, "that we perish not." It is thus clear that this hopeful anticipation of God's merciful action by pagans is one of the motifs of the book, and it is therefore more likely that the author coined both of these parallel expressions, than that he was fortunate enough to find exactly the phrase he needed ready at hand in Joel. To support this, the theme of "knowing" is one that again forms a sub-motif throughout the book (54): it is as important that the pagans can only say "who knows?", about God's actions, whereas Jonah can say (4:2) "I knew!", also about God's actions. Thus two submotifs of Jonah that run consistently through the book come to a climax in this phrase - whereas in Joel, among the many eschatological themes, this only plays a periferal role. Thus the likelihood is that the author of Jonah coined the phrase.

Furthermore, we have noted already that "Jonah" utilises the full quotation from Exodus 32:12 in constructing the words (in line with the author's use of the other quotation from this chapter). That Joel could quote a foreshortened version of Jonah's text is therefore more likely than that "Jonah" found the Joel version (which may or may not have been based on the Exodus passage) and used it to reconstruct the connection with the full Exodus text (55).

Finally if we accept that it was "Jonah's" author who worked with the two passages in Exodus, it is consistent with this that he would have amended the version of the "attributes of God" to the form he quotes in 4:2, with its terminal phrase "and repentest Thee of the evil." Since this is the central issue of the final chapter it is again likely that "Jonah" composed it in this form for his purpose. Once again, whereas in Joel it stands as an isolated phrase, within "Jonah" it is part of a theme that pervades the whole book. It is therefore our contention that Joel, as in other places, extracted the two sentences from an earlier "prophetic" book and wove them into his own material.

ii. Jonah and Ezekiel and Psalm 107

In his analysis of the Biblical sources to "Jonah," Feuillet (56) asks the valid question: "D'où a pu venir à l'auteur l'idée étrange de faire s'embarquer son héros sur un vaisseau allant à Tharsis: pour le montrer voulant se dérober à sa mission, point n'était besoin de lui faire prendre la mer; Jérémie avait seulement souhaité d'aller se cacher au désert!" In seeking an answer, he turned to Psalm 107 (verses 23-32) and Ezekiel 27, as the only other two passages in the Bible which deal with a sea journey (57). In recognising linguistic affinities with the Psalm, he assumed that it was dependent upon Jonah, citing in evidence only the suggestion that it was possible on historical grounds, as the psalm seems also to quote from Job (58). However, he went no further in analysing the stylistic relationship of the two texts. He then turned to Ezekiel 27 as the source of the sea voyage in "Jonah," but had to admit certain difficulties:

a. Certain words are common to Ezekiel and "Jonah," but appear nowhere else: מלחים "sailors" in Jonah 1:5 and Ezekiel 27:9, 27, 29; חבל "pilot" in Jonah 1:6 and Ezekiel 27:8, 27, 28, 29; but as technical terms they are as likely to be used independently in either context.

b. Both texts are concerned with ships going to Tarshish or "ships of Tarshish" (Ezekiel 27:25-26) - but this latter terminology is not unique to Ezekiel (59).

c. In Ezekiel 27:26 come three elements common to "Jonah":
במים רבים הביאוך השטים אותך רוח הקדים שברך בלב ימים
"Thy rowers have brought thee into great waters; the east wind hath broken thee in the heart of the seas." - i.e., a destructive East Wind sent by God (which in "Jonah" occurs only in the fourth chapter (4:8), whereas the wind in Jonah 1:4 is only described as "great"); a ship that is "broken" (c.f. Jonah 1:4 "the ship was like to be broken"); and "the heart of the seas" (c.f. Jonah 2:4). However, the terminology of "Tarshish ships" being "broken" by an "East Wind" appears also in Psalm 48:8 and II Chronicles 20:37 (the ships of Jehoshaphat that were broken and unable to go to Tarshish - see also I Kings 22:49). Feuillet finds the most significant literary affinity in the phrase "heart of the seas" which recurs six times in Ezekiel 27:28 (60). He ties this to "Jonah" by pointing out that" "Ézéchiel avait prédit que Tyre-bateau, avec tout son équipage, irait s'abîmer 'au coeur des mers' (27:26-27); dans le livre de Jonah, le navire de Tharsis et tous ses marins paiens sont sauvés par Yahweh, mais c'est Jonas qui est jeté 'au coeur des mers' (2:4...) ...L'expression 'au coeur des mers' se retrouve Ezekiel 15:8; Psalm 46:3; Proverbs 23:34; 30:19; mais périr ou etre jeté au coeur des mers, c'est là une idée qu'on ne rencontre que Jonah 2:4 et Ezekiel 27:26-27" (61).

However, notwithstanding the fact that "the heart of the seas" occurs six times in Ezekiel, it does also occur in other places, notably Exodus 15:8 which also uses תהמת and במצולת (c.f. Jonah 2:4, 6) (62). Thus the only strong evidence so far for a connection is the alleged ironic relationship between Ezekiel predicting the sinking of the "Tarshish ship" into the heart of the sea, and Jonah's being thrown into the heart of the sea. Feuillet is thus forced to find a background of theological controversy to explain the relationship of the two texts, precisely in connection with this single point: "il semble ne faire appel au voyant de Tell-Abib que pour en prendre le contrepied. Ne dirait-on pas, en particulier, qu'il a voulu se donner le malin plaisir de faire subir passagèrement (63) à son héros le sort que le fils de Buzi avait prédit pour toujours à Tyr avec ses mariniers: elle devait être à jamais engloutie au coeur des mers?"(64) Hence the satirical character of the book of Jonah "a pour but d'expliquer le non-accomplissement des oracles contre les nations" (65).

This is indeed one of the themes of the book, however, equally one of the themes is the complementary problem of the inability of the prophet himself to go against the word of God. One can state the paradox as follows: God's word comes to the prophet; the prophet tries to avoid the task, but God's word must be fulfilled - and the prophet is forced through a series of extraordinary supernatural interventions to perform it. God's word comes to Nineveh stating that in 40 days it will be destroyed, and God's word must be fulfilled. The Ninevites repent, and such is the power of repentance that God's word is not fulfilled! Thus the non-fulfillment of oracles is the second complementary part to the story of Jonah's flight. However, the episode of Jonah's request to be thrown into the sea is still a stage in his attempted flight from God, i.e., that part of the book concerned with the inevitable fulfillment of God's word. Thus to relate it to the non-fulfillment of the prophecies against Tyre (or rather the paradoxical fulfillment of them in the casting of the prophet into the sea), does not accord with the context of Jonah at all (66).

Thus on linguistic grounds and on thematic grounds it cannot be proven that Chapter 1 in Jonah is dependent upon Ezekiel 26 (67).

Psalm 107:23-32 appears, at first glance, to be a more rewarding place to find a source for Jonah's storm. If one lists mechanically the words common to both texts, it seems quite impressive:

יורדי הים – אניות – מלאכה – במצולות – ויעמד
– רוח סערה – תהומות – ויצעקו אל ה׳. – ישחקו

However, as in previous examples, it too is the relationship of words or phrases to context that we must examine if we are to be certain of a connection between two texts. Whereas the storm description in Psalm 107 is a highly graphic account of the experience of a storm (the rising and falling of the ship, the reeling to and fro of those aboard, the uselessness of all their technical skill), "Jonah's" is almost academic in comparison, forming in reality only a background against which the dialogue with the sailors can take place (68). Only three repeated phrases are used to describe it:

a. 1:4 YHW <u>hurled</u> a great wind onto the sea - the key word "hurled" carrying through the entire episode (the sailors "hurling" the vessels, and eventually Jonah, overboard);

b. 1:4 "and there was a mighty tempest in the sea" developed in verses 11 and 14 "for the sea grew more and more tempestuous";

c. Verse 11 "that the sea may be calm unto us," which reappears in verse 12. None of which phrases (with the sole exception of the root שתק) appear in Psalm 107. Thus the Psalm does not provide the language of the storm.

Likewise if one turns to the context alone, a superficial glance suggests certain features in common: travellers on the ocean who see God's wonders; a storm sent by God; the inadequacy of the skills of the crew to save them; prayers to God in distress; God calms the storm with the subsequent joy of the travellers. However, many of the details do not correspond in the two texts, and the central problem of both passages is significantly different. In the Psalm it is precisely the prayers to God of the travellers which are effective - in "Jonah," although prayers are addressed by the sailors (pagan who "convert"!), they are ineffective; for whereas in the Psalm this prayer out of distress which is answered is the recurrent theme (verses 6, 13, 19, 28), it is only peripheral to this part of the Jonah narrative, being one of the several measures employed by the sailors. In "Jonah" everything hinges instead of the reaction of the prophet to the storm, and behind the storm, to his mission. (Even if the author's customary "paradoxical" quotation is evoked, it would not help us here, for the paradox of heathen sailors praying to YHWH would only be effective if their prayers <u>were</u> answered.) Thus on linguistic and contextual grounds the dependence of "Jonah" upon the Psalm is unlikely (69).

iii. Jonah and Psalm 139

We are thus forced to return to Feuillet's original question - where did the author get the idea of making his hero embark on a ship for Tarshish? Obviously such a question cannot be answered with any real certainty, however, it may be that one need look no further afield than Psalm 139: 7-10 (70):

אנה אלך מרוחך ואנה מפניך אברה
אם אסק שמים שם אתה ואציעה שאול הנך
אשא כנפי שחר אשכנה באחרית ים
גם שם ידך תנחני ותאחזני ימינך

"Whither shall I go from Thy spirit? Or whither shall I flee from Thy presence? If I ascend up into heaven, Thou art there; if I make my bed in the netherworld, behold, Thou art there. If I take the wings of the morning, and dwell in the uttermost parts of the sea; even there would Thy hand lead me, and Thy right hand would hold me" (71).

The first point to be noted is that the concern of the author of "Jonah" with the "sea voyage" is secondary to his concern with the attempted flight from the mission of God - thus we are justified in turning to a passage dealing with such a "flight," rather than looking just to passages concerning sea voyages.

Secondly, the point of the Psalm is the impossibility of such a flight - yet, as we have noted throughout this work, it is precisely Jonah's problem that he can always come up with the correct traditional formulation without ever seeing that it does also literally apply to himself; to attempt to flee from God when one already knows, at least on one level of consciousness (72), that such a flight is impossible is the first paradox presented by the book.

Can we set this suggestion into a more concrete textual basis? Certainly there are two suggestive linguistic usages. It would not be beyond the customary wit of the author to interpret verse 7a literally as "Whither can I go from Thy 'wind'," since it is precisely the "great wind" which pursues Jonah into the sea, and God's East Wind which causes him so much discomfort when the gourd is destroyed. Perhaps a more certain association can be seen in the difference between the two words מפני and מלפני , which already exercised Ibn Ezra (73). He noted that "when I searched the whole Bible, I never found a word about flight except in connection with the word פני (such as Psalm 139:7; Judges 11:3). And I did not find in regard to Jonah's prophecy that he fled מפני God, 'but only' מלפני God.'" Conversely he notes the usage of לפני in relationship to standing before the presence of God, standing, like Elijah, in God's service (I Kings 17:1), i.e., in acceptance of God's mission (74). Important for our immediate theme is the fact that Jonah's attempt "to flee from before the presence of YHWH" is repeatedly emphasised in the chapter (twice in verse 3); and that it is a coinage used only by the author of "Jonah." The implication is that he knew the phrase of the Psalm and deliberately substituted the unusual form מלפני to emphasise that Jonah's flight was not merely physical, but was also flight from the mission itself and its implications. Perhaps we can go even further and note that a clue to the meaning of מלפני is given by the author himself within verse 2, when God explains that "their evil has come up 'before me' (לפני)." The problem of Nineveh has come into the area of immediate "concern" of God - Jonah flees from this place of "concern" (75). In the closing sentence of the book God challenges Jonah with the opposite proposition: You had "concern" for the gourd... should I not have "concern" for Nineveh...?"

The phrase "if I dwell in the uttermost parts of the sea" (Psalm 139:9b) would thus have been the starting point for the "horizontal" direction of Jonah's flight to the uttermost part of the sea, to Tarshish. Of significance, however, in the light of our analysis of the structure of the "Psalm" in Chapter 2 and its relationship to Chapter 3 (76), is verse 8:

"If I ascend up into heaven, Thou art there; if I make my bed in "sheol,"
behold, Thou art there." This is precisely the implication of the "Mirror
image" structure we have found to these two chapters. At the bottommost
point of Jonah's descent he finds God waiting, who draws him up (2:7); at
the topmost point of the Ninevite's spiritual rise, at the peak of their
penitent acts (3:10), there is God waiting for them.

Summary

In this section we have analysed the technique of the author of quoting
material from other passages in the Bible, and noted various ways in
which he has drawn the attention of the reader to the existence of these
quotations. We have thus been led to Exodus 14 and 32; to Deuteronomy
21; to I Kings 19; to Jeremiah 26 and 36; to Psalm 139.

We have further demonstrated certain methodological tools for comparing
two passages containing similar material with a view to determining
whether one is indeed quoting the other, and which is being quoted and
which quotes. We have thus shown with regard certain problematic passages that Joel quotes "Jonah," and that there is no clear evidence of a
relationship between "Jonah" and Ezekiel 27 or Psalm 107.

We have noted a distinction between "quotations" and "reminiscences."
It remains now to draw together the material we have gathered about the
surface narrative of the book, the quotations and reminiscences, to try
to determine the underlying motifs and ideas that tie these together.

וַיָּקָם
יוֹנָה
וַיֵּלֶךְ אֶל
נִינְוֶה
כִּדְבַר

יְהֹוָה:

Chapter V

ANALYSIS OF THEMES

We have delayed discussing the "themes" of the Book of Jonah until now,
because, before doing so, some account of the various levels on which it
has been constructed was first required. An interpretation which ignores
the presence, for example, of quotations, or the various "key words" and
literary constructions, can only give a partial explanation of the ideas contained in the book.

In restricting ourselves to "inner Biblical criteria" (1), and avoiding the
more general symbolism of the book, we are attempting to accept the in-
vitation given by the author himself, to enter into a discussion with certain key ideas and experiences of his own Biblical tradition. This gives
us at least some objective controlling measure in terms of material, and,
albeit in a problematic way, some background knowledge of his religious
environment.

Ambiguities

As a preliminary to our analysis, however, we must tackle the problem
of whether the book has indeed a single "message," as is usually affirmed
by most commentators - though with a large measure of disagreement as
to what precisely the message is (2); or are there indeed several "messages," some primary, some secondary. In his study of the book of Ruth,
Rauber (3) lists a couple of such "single message" explanations of that
book, and warns: "But under these assertions is an hubristic assumption
that for a work of high literary art we can say with confidence, 'The purpose of X is....' and fill in the blank with 25 words or less. It is, I maintain, one of the main functions of the literary critic to oppose this view.
The task of the literary critic is to explore the complex world of the artist
and to suggest ways in which we can respond as fully as possible to its
multiplicity, its suggestiveness, its richness. But all this is denied us if,
lurking in the back our minds is the secret conviction that art is really
little more than the decorative embellishment of the prosaic, that the purpose of a great artist can be reduced to copybook maxims" (4). Rauber
sees his work as complementary to that of the scholar, who, for example,
tends to fix attention on matters like the legal discussions in Ruth 4, which
are, in Rauber's reading, only periferal in terms of the artistic significance of the book as a whole.

Perhaps even more challenging, and certainly it has evoked a dramatic
response, has been the analysis of the Biblical story of David and Bathsheba by two literary critics, M. Perry and M. Sternberg (5). Central
to their argument is that in this narrative: "the narrator evades an explicit

rendering or formulation of thoughts, but directs the reader to infer them from what is rendered explicitly (6)... The narrator exploits the fact that the reader must (if he wishes to make sense of the story) supplement what is not explicitly communicated, and uses the system of gaps as a central device for the creation of irony." In the David and Bathsheba narrative, one of the main gaps left open is whether Uriah is aware or not of his wife's adultery, and they proceed to show how the text provides no definite answer, and the reader can construct general arguments to support either thesis. Neither argument, however, can be proven to be exclusively correct, but both add to the ironic depiction of David.

The significance of this for "Jonah" becomes evident when we examine two problems (7):

a. Why does Jonah ask to be thrown overboard? Is his primary motivation to commit suicide? Or is it to save the lives of the sailors? Or is it a mixture of both? Reading the story in terms of the first interpretation, we can see a straight line between the "deep sleep," the casting into the sea, and the request for death in Chapter 4. However, in contrast to this we have Jonah's prayer of thanksgiving when he is recued - an apparent psychological paradox which has led some commentators to question the authenticity of the "Psalm" (8). On the other hand, if we interpret it as his wish to save the sailors, which fits in well with the fact of his confession of guilt in 1:12, and is the sort of magnanimous gesture that might convince God that he was, after all, worth saving, then we have to explain his indifference to the danger he was putting them in by making them guilty of shedding "innocent blood" (1:14) - and anyway, why did he not ask them to take him back to shore, since he knew that his flight from the mission had caused the storm in the first place? That is to say that both explanations of Jonah's behaviour (which can only be guessed at from the events described) are valid, but not completely so (9). Some sort of synthesis between them is possible, but only if we accept a more complex picture of the character of Jonah - one that contains both possibilities - altruistic self-sacrifice and stubborn rebelliousness, concern for others and a desire to see their destruction. Thus we are not dealing with a black and white depiction of one-dimensional character, but indeed a person who can be seen in as unfavourable light as in the list of opinions compiled by Keller (10), ranging from "ludicrous" to "bloodthirty" (11), to the corrective (though overly sentimental) reconstruction of Keller himself of the suffering, isolated prophet (12). From our own study (13) we recognise a tendency towards the more unfavourable depiction of his character, bearing in mind, nevertheless, that there are ambiguities and that despite all of Jonah's failings, God still chooses and uses him, and is prepared to reason with him to the end. Perhaps the best characterisation comes from Goitein (14): "The whole tenor of the story is much too earnest for a satire; Jonah is not painted with the brush of mockery or disdain, but drawn with the pencil of deep and sympathetic insight into human weakness."

CHAPTER V - ANALYSIS OF THEMES

The significance of this problem, however, lies in the fact that the reader himself is once again forced to participate in the events being described, if he is to understand them, and must himself choose at least a provisional explanation of Jonah's motivations, since these are not explicitly stated.

b. With the second problem, however, we face the other point in the book where a gap in the explanation forces one into highly significant speculations. From the very beginning we must deal with the question: Why does Jonah run away? The answer he himself gives (in 4:2), which is rightly recognised as one of the focal points of the book, leaves out one important step in Jonah's thought process, and it is this which has opened the doors in the various interpretations of the book. He says, in brief, "I ran away because I knew You are a compassionate God... who repents of evil." But to what specifically does Jonah object?

(i) Is he shocked at a miscarriage of justice - that evil Nineveh was let off so lightly? Jonah fighting for justice against God's mercy (15).

(ii) Is he concerned at the specific relationship of Nineveh to Israel, anticipating that destruction will come at the hands of the Assyrians (16)?

(iii) Is he worried that his reputation will suffer if his prophecy is not fulfilled (17), or generally reluctant to make a prophecy which he knows will not come true (18)?

(iv) Is he angry that this compassion of God, once exclusively Israel's, has now come to be applied to all nations, including enemies (19)? By which token the book reflects an inner Jewish struggle between a narrow nationalistic outlook and a broader universalistic one.

(v) Or has the author deliberately, or unconsciously left the question open, so that the problem here is less a specific issue than the nature of the psychological type that Jonah represents whom the reader is asked to study, laugh at, and learn from (20)?

If we may sum up these two points, there are certain problems built into the text itself which lend to ambiguity, precisely because insufficient information is given to the reader at key points. No one single explanation satisfies all the possibilities the text raises, nor can it do so. That is to say that by choosing a narrative form to convey his ideas, the author has found a medium which forces the reader to live with some degree of uncertainty, particularly with regards the motivation of one of the central characters. We find ourselves continually switching between identifying with, and then rejecting, the prophet, and then sympathising with him again, and so on. We are thus being taught the lesson of tolerance, of seeing the world through the eyes of others and accepting their right to exist, implicit in the message of the book, through the very form in which it is written. It repeatedly makes us change our standpoint, thus forcing us into insecurity, a state that can only be supported because of the ever-present humour, and the reassuring picture of God's continuing guidance and control at every stage. Thus form and content contribute simultaneously to the lesson being conveyed.

Anticipations

There is yet another level in which ambiguity works, arising once again out of device of the author to involve the reader. As well as asking what Jonah's answer in Chapter 4 means, we must also ask why has the author delayed his answer until this particular chapter (21)? Cohn (22) points out that the answer serves no purpose earlier, since Jonah is not being punished because he challenges God's pity, but because he flees. Only in the fourth chapter does the purpose of his flight become significant, and there it is mentioned. But a necessary complement to this explanation is the remark of Bacharach (23) that because of this we are forced to ask ourselves throughout the narrative the question, why does he run away; until finally we come to the fourth chapter That is to say that in all his experiences we are unconsciously seeking clues to the reason for the flight. We may add to this the observation of Wolff (24) that the presence of quest- ions in the book itself, e.g., of the sailors to Jonah, increases the for- ward movement of the book. If we tie these elements together, we can now see that the reader becomes involved on two levels: he is himself forced on by his own question about Jonah's motivations to move on to the answer in Chapter 4; he must identify himself even more closely with the sailors' questions in seeking clues to the explanation of Jonah's behaviour (25).

But this has further consequences, for the seeking of clues requires the making of provisional explanations for Jonah's acts (such as his motive for asking to be cast overboard discussed above), and thus the anticipating of future events. Yet precisely this anticipating of events is one of the them- atic and structural keys of the book itself. Jonah himself states that he fled from God's mission because he "anticipated" (4:2) (קדמתי) God's com- passionate response. Yet this prophet of YHWH who can anticipate what God will do is surprisingly slow to understand what is happening aboard the ship in the storm - in every event, the sailors are exactly one step ahead of Jonah. They recognise from the beginning the need of prayer in this situation, and have to remind the prophet to do so. They are aware that someone is responsible for the storm (1:7) and throw lots to find out whom. They ask Jonah "tell us" (הגידה-נא) you who are responsible for the storm, who you are, etc. After Jonah's response they know that he has fled from YHWH "for he had told them (הגיד). Does this phrase mean that some of the actual conversation has been omitted (26), or does it mean that in Jonah's words about fearing YHWH, he actually revealed to them that he was fleeing (27)? That this latter is the more likely is shown by the fact that Jonah only confesses to being responsible for the storm after the sailors have asked what should be done to calm it down. That is to say, the prophet only becomes aware, or is prepared to admit, his responsibility, after it has been thoroughly recognised by everyone else. By the repetition of הגיד - הגידה the irony of Jonah's unconscious revelation of more than he intended is emphasised. When the sailors try to row back to the dry land, they anticipate what should have been Jonah's correct reply - namely to take him back so that he could complete his mission.

In Chapter 2, the timing of the "psalm" becomes less of a problem when it is recognised that it is precisely the sort of prayer that is offered by a pious person who has been rescued from immediate danger (from the sea into the fish) in anticipation of future restoration to normal circumstances (28). The comic implications of Jonah's final words about God's salvation, followed by being vomited out of the fish, have been discussed above (29). In Chapter 3, the Ninevites anticipate the edict of the king, and are already wearing sackcloth and ashes before he hears of the matter. Most signific- ant of all is the king's statement, "who knows, perhaps God will repent," as a hopeful anticipation of God's response. That is to say that both the people and the king read into Jonah's words a concealed meaning, as have done the sailors before them. Finally Jonah himself, the one who theoretic- ally is most able to anticipate God's moves, is nevertheless the one who tried to flee; the one who "knows" God's ways in fact does not know - from the storm that drives him back, to the fish that saves his life from drown- ing, to the final irony - that God's compassion and patience are less strech- ed by the pagan Ninevites than by His own recalcitrant prophet.

Thus the reader, in order to understand even the timing of events, the sequence of which is often apparently inverted, is forced to think beyond the simple description of time relationships offered by the narrative to the much more paradoxical relationships between "before" and "after," between words and realities, between what people know and what they only think they know, with which the author is playing.

Polarities

In order to do justice to all these problems a different type of approach is required, one which recognises the ambiguities and tries to demonstrate the various arguments in the book through which certain ideas are conveyed. Recognition of the existence of a variety of themes, some major and some minor, has been made by a number of commentators (30), and recently Kaiser (31) has attempted to clarify them through analysing the Tendenz of each scene, thus recognising the major theme and minor themes that accompany it. He has also made valuable use in his study of the "quot- ations" as setting a further dimension of contrast behind a particular scene. The value of this technique lies in its recognition of the complexity of ideas contained in any given part, however it has the weakness that it is too tied to the individual scene and thus sometimes misses the overarching struc- tural elements that give further dimensions of meaning. Furthermore in seeing each historical association in isolation, the implications of this device of the author are lost.

We are dealing here with at least three levels of communication within the book:

1. The overt narrative text.
2. The "subliminal" level of word play and repetition.
3. The level of quotation and reminiscence.

All these must be brought into the discussion in trying to analyse the messages of the book.

We have found that the clearest way to present this material is by the isolation of four main sets of contrasting ideas. Under these four propositions the different layers of material can each be investigated separately. Though this is one selection of "polarities," it is not the only way of "reading" the material, nor are these propositions mutually exclusive, but must necessarily overlap (32).

The four polarities are:

i. Knowledge of God/Disobedience of God.
ii. Particularism/Universalism.
iii. Traditional Teaching/New Experience.
iv. The Power of God/The Freedom of Man.

We can now proceed to analyse each of these propositions in terms of the three levels of "communication."

i. Knowledge of God/Disobedience of God

Here we deal with a theme within which is usually considered the relationship of God to His prophet (33). Behind it, as we shall see, stands however the whole paradox of Israel's relationship to God, repeatedly examined by the prophets. How can Israel know God, and all God has done for her, yet still be disobedient? How can God, despite all Israel's failures and failings, continue to choose this people? This latter is one of the unspoken (and almost never discussed in the literature) problems of the book - why does God bother with Jonah, what does He see in the prophet that makes Him continue to use him (34)? What is sometimes discussed is how Jonah, knowing God, can still attempt to disobey. The problem is neatly expressed by Haller in relation to the sailors' response of fear on knowing that Jonah is fleeing from YHWH: "Das Erkennen wird zum Fürchten. Bei ihnen erfolgt die echte Wechselbeziehung zwischen Gott erkennen und Gott Fürchten (bei dem rechtgläubigen Jona ist dieser Wechselbezug unterbrochen)."(35)

a. Narrative

Jonah is ordered to go to Nineveh and he flees to Tarshish. He knows that excape to the sea is useless, for he affirms that he fears YHWH "who made the sea and dry land" (1:9). Nevertheless despite acknowledging this he still asks to be thrown into the sea, rather than be taken back to shore. On being rescued he offers thanks from the belly of the fish, and by implication suggests that in gratitude he will now return to Jerusalem to fulfil his vows (36). Yet again God has to order him to Nineveh. Resigned, Jonah goes on his way, partially enters the city, says his words once. Thus far, though Jonah knows that God's word must be fulfilled (his admission that he was responsible for the storm confirms this), he has attempted to disobey, then reluctantly obeys. When Nineveh repents, Jonah is angry, and spells out his anger by pointing out that he knew from the very beginning the nature of God's compassion, and precisely for that reason he fled. Thus we have here explicitly the paradox - and also the overlapping of two propositions, for some aspect of Jonah's own personal desires must be motivating him (37).

Jonah can also know, yet nevertheless refuse to accept - which seems to lie behind his problematic behaviour when he leaves the city. If he knows already that Nineveh has repented and that God has forgiven them (which the sequence of events clearly shows) (38), why does he sit outside the city "until he might see what would become of the city"? Once again the author has given us a riddle, one capable of at least three solutions.

1. He suspects that the Ninevites' repentance might be short-lived and that during or after the forty days they will revert to their old ways. In support of this we have one interpretation of the phrase in the "Psalm" (2:9) "Those who (continue to) regard lying vanities will forsake their own mercy" (39).

2. Knowing that this is not so, he nevertheless is pitting his will against God, as if trying to force God to destroy them after all (40). Such defiance, against all logic, is quite in line with his attempt to flee from God's word in the first place and his readiness to die (41).

3. He may just be recording his protest.

All three explanations, however, have in common that what Jonah knows, and what he is prepared to accept, are two quite different things. Knowing God's decision he still hopes to "flee" from it, to force his own reality upon it (42). The further implications of this argument will be picked up in the final section (43).

In the final question to Jonah, God spells out even more fully what His compassion implies, and Jonah is left with the question as to whether he is prepared yet to accept this knowledge for himself.

On a more subtle level, however, the extent and quality of Jonah's knowledge is also questioned, as we have seen from the discussion on "anticipations" (44). He knows his tradition, and recites it at three significant points (in answering the sailors, in his prayer from the belly of the fish, and in his self-justification before God in Chapter 4). Yet, as we

have already noted (45), the irony lies here in the fact that what he quotes
has a paradoxical relationship to what he actually does, his very disobedience illustrating the distance between his formal knowledge of tradition
and his experienced knowledge. Conversely he applies his knowledge that
God "repents of the evil" grudgingly to God's treatment of Nineveh; without recognising that without that patience of God he himself would not have
survived.

b. Word Usage

The key word which underlines this proposition is "to know." As we have
seen above (46) it appears in Chapters 1, 3 and 4, and its meaning develops
from the desire of the sailors to know what is going on, who is responsible
for the storm (1:7), to an awareness that somehow the relationship of Jonah to his God lies behind the storm (1:10). (Just as their fear grows to a
fear of God (47), so does their knowledge.) Jonah's acknowledgement of
his responsibility (1:12), brings us into the category of "knowledge of God"
and His ways that is to characterise the meaning of the word in the rest
of the book. The king of Nineveh (3:9) speculates on God's repentance -
"Who knows, perhaps He will turn and repent" (3:9). Jonah asserts that
he knew God's nature (and hence His reaction to the Ninevites) before he
left for Tarshish (4:1). However, the final usage of the word in the book
introduces another element, which we have already noted underlines the
use of words in the last chapter. For the knowledge of God implies choice -
to obey God or not. Thus the categories which echo throughout the fourth
chapter in the repeated words טוב and רעה, חיים and מות (good and evil,
life and death) are those which typify the choice demanded of Israel by God
(Deuteronomy 30:15). Thus the Ninevites are characterised as those who
do not know to distinguish between right and left, for whom God feels particular compassion. Nevertheless by implication, they can come to know
God as well as Israel (for the king's speculation, and its accompaniment
by repentance, has pointed the way forward). Thus the choice of Jonah of
death rather than life (4:3, 8), of "evil" (48) rather than "good," echoes
on a deeper level the problem of knowledge of God, yet disobedience, with
all the consequences it implies.

The nature of "coming to know" is also conveyed in the book by a remarkable technique which we have discussed in the section on the "Growing
Phrase" (49). The repetition of whole phrases, both "growing" ones and
those that remain the same, enables us to see the same events but after
some intervening experience has considerably altered their meaning. Jonah hears the same order in Chapter 3 as in Chapter 1, but his response
is now different because of all that has happened in between. The sailors
have a quite different understanding of the storm and their fear of it after
it has calmed down. Even when the same characters are not involved, we
can feel the change in significance between the similarly phrased statements of the captain of the crew (perhaps God will think of us 1:6) and the
king of Nineveh (who knows if God will not repent 3:9) both culminating in

the same "that we perish not." But the same technique also points up Jonah's stubbornness, for despite the experience of the gourd, Jonah repeats
his identically phrased request to die.

We have already noted a further element that also comes under this category of "knowing, yet disobeying," namely Jonah's "partial confessions"(50).

1. Twice the sailors ask "through whom" this evil is upon them (1:7,8);
Jonah finally acknowledges that "through him" "this great storm" is upon
them (1:13).

2. Three times his flight is characterised as being "from before the presence of YHWH" (1:3,10); but when Jonah speaks of it to God, he only acknowledges "fleeing to Tarshish" (4:2).

3. The "Psalm" with its pious confession and thanksgiving, nevertheless
makes no mention of his running away or wishing to fulfil his mission.

Finally Jonah is brought to know the extent of his responsibility through
the repeated usage of אבד - first that he almost causes the destruction
of innocent sailors (1:6,14), then that he is responsible for giving the Ninevites the chance to repent, without which they will "perish" (3:9), and
perhaps ultimately that he has some responsibility towards the gourd that
perishes as part of his lesson (4:10) (51).

c. Quotation

Two sets of quotations belong to this theme, which at the same time take
us beyond Jonah as an individual, and fill in a background from his tradition which allows us to see him as the representative of Israel. The first
does so indirectly, namely in the comparison between the repentance of
the people of Nineveh and its king, and that of King Jehoiakim as recorded
in Jeremiah 36 (52). In the latter the king, in flagrant disregard of the
word of YHWH (unlike his predecessor Josiah), knowing the consequences,
chooses to disobey. To the reader this is just one of a number of elements
which at first contrast the behaviour of the pagan world with that of Israel
and thus forces him to identify a message aimed at Israel itself; Nineveh
is the extreme opposite to, and thus paradoxically a model for, Jerusalem. That later Rabbinic Midrash (53) recognised in Jonah's flight his
knowledge that the pagan world was near to repentance and thus would put
Israel into guilty contrast, is no more than a development of a theme latent within the book itself.

The "complementary" quotation from Exodus 14:31 (54) reinforces this
effect. The Ninevites "believed in" God and did repentance; Israel after
the crossing of the Reed Sea also "believed in" God, but their history
showed a constant unwillingness to behave in accordance with this belief
(55).

To summarise our findings in this section, the problem of knowing the will
of God, yet disobeying Him, has been presented to the reader on various

levels: to have the word of God, yet not to accept it; to have only an intimation of what God requires, yet to act fully, and successfully, upon it; to know, yet not to know, - the gap between inherited knowledge and experience; all of which problems are compounded by the repeated intrusion of the wider perspective of Israel's history, its knowledge of God and what it did with that knowledge. Thus one is forced to re-examine each of these positions, in turn identifying with Jonah the prophet who can act in the full knowledge of what God requires in a given situation, yet is prevented by his own private desires from doing so; and with the far more uncertain (but "realistic") position of the sailors and Ninevites faced with these sudden intrusions into their world who surrender their own desires to what little they can perceive of as God's desires. Thus whether one attempts to draw concrete lessons from these problems, or leave them to echo in one's mind, the story has forced the reader to know more of his situation and recognise that he knows less; and to question both historically and in the contemporary situation of the author and his readers, why Israel did not do what it knew so clearly that it had to do, and what it knew of the role now demanded of it by God.

ii. Particularism/Universalism

Unlikely Israel, just as the unlikely prophet Jonah, was nevertheless chosen, and repeatedly called to new tasks. The danger of chosenness is the sense of exclusiveness, or particularism, it may engender, the chosen one seeing himself as the centre around which the universe must revolve. Whereas the chosenness demanded by God, is that God be seen as the centre, and that he see himself as chosen to serve God's wider purposes. Such particularism can apply to an individual or a people as a whole, and in "Jonah," though we deal overtly with the individual prophet, the people is always alluded to beneath the surface. These themes are explored in "Jonah" under the second set of propositions.

a. Narrative

On the level of the narrative, the most obvious characteristic which conforms with this proposition is that the pagans are "good," and Jonah is, if not thoroughly "bad," at least highly problematical! That is to say that by reversing the usual roles of Biblical situations (the good prophet against the evil people) the author forces the reader to re-examine both positions which he has come to take for granted. One can note that he develops equally well the "character" of the pagans as a collectivity, as that of Jonah.

First the sailors in their series of reactions to the storm. Their first response is the pious one of crying to their gods (1:5), before turning to their technical methods (throwing the vessels overboard). Then the captain becomes aware that someone has not prayed, and tells Jonah to do so. His reason is that perhaps God will think of them "that we perish not," a religious hope that is to be extended by the king of Nineveh. Recognising, somehow, that this storm is caused by someone aboard, they cast lots - yet when the lot reveals Jonah as the culprit, instead of throwing him overboard at once, they open formal court proceedings in the middle of the storm (56), to ascertain the truth of the matter. Hearing Jonah's confession they are shocked that he has run away from his God, and ask him what to do. When he tells them to throw him overboard, they do everythin in their power to return to shore rather than commit murder. When this fails, they pray for forgiveness, acknowledging that they are utterly in God's hands. Their mounting fear, is converted into fear of YHWH when the sea miraculously calms, and immediately they make vows and sacrifices, perhaps even fully converting to the religion of YHWH.

No less astonishing is the behaviour of the people of Nineveh and its king in their instant repentance on hearing the warning of the prophet.

That is to say that the author has painted in spectacular colours the qualities of the pagan world - it is pious; it has an intuitive grasp of God's wishes; it tries desperately to preserve the life of a fellow man, even a stranger, however guilty he may be and into whatsoever danger it may lead them; it is close to repentance and given the chance does so in a most spectacular fashion; it is ultimately innocent, not knowing left from right.

By contrast we have the selfishness of Jonah which we have repeatedly noted (57). If we may summarise, bearing in mind that we are here concentrating on the aspects that reflect badly on the character of Jonah for the sake of the contrast, he is unwilling to obey his God; he would rather see Nineveh destroyed than give it the chance to do repentance; his flight puts the lives of others into danger, nevertheless he sleeps through the storm and only admits responsibility when forced to; though he should have asked to be returned to shore, he asked to be thrown overboard, thus jeopardising further the lives of the sailors by making them shed "innocent blood"; he is of doubtful piety, quoting his tradition in a way which shows that he has no real relationship to it.

Thus by forcing the reader to sympathise with the "other," the pagans, against his "own" Jonah, the author opens the door to a wider and more tolerant viewpoint. The fullest "expression" of this viewpoint is put into the character of God as described in the story. A compassion and benign tolerance is attributed to Him - but the picture is saved from sentimentality by the strong measures He is prepared to take to teach His prophet. The dimensions of His concern, however, open up the picture even further, for it extends beyond the human characters in the story, pagan and hebrew alike, to the animal world as well. In fact it is a sign of the wider "universalism" of the book that the entire world of nature (animals, fish, worm, plants, winds, sea) (58) respond to His word and are dependent upon Him; thus the context of the story comprehends far more than it need do if it were only (59) dealing with the particularism/universalism problem of Israel, however important an element this latter may be.

b. Word Usage

As we move into the second level, we have a good opportunity to see how the three sets of "characters" in the book, (God, Jonah and the pagans) interact with each other (60).

1. By using the device of parallel literary structures and verbal forms with different subjects, the author suggests various levels of contrast. More attention is paid to the details of these structures elsewhere (61), so it will only be necessary to sum up the results here.

I. Jonah and the Pagans

The contrast between Jonah and the king of Nineveh is shown by the use of the verbs ויקם and וישב (62). Jonah's response to God's call to "rise up" (1:2) was indeed to "rise up" - but to flee to Tarshish. In 3:3 he "rose up" and went to Nineveh. The same verb form is used to describe the immediate response of the king upon hearing of Jonah's prophecy, (3:6) and he "rose up" from his throne to do penitence at once. Part of his penitence included "and he sat" in ashes (3:6). Jonah, in response to the deliverance of Nineveh, also "sat" - under the shade of the succah. (The verb is repeated before and after the building of the succah so that the emphasis on the verb is clear, as also is Jonah's concern with his comfort.) While the king "sat" in discomfort inside Nineveh hoping for the city's deliverance, Jonah "sat" in comfort outside Nineveh hoping for its destruction!

Both the sailors and Jonah pray, and both use the same "introductory formula" and structure of prayer. However, whereas the sailors continue immediately with genuine prayer to God, Jonah's anger breaks through. Furthermore, as Cohn has noted (63), whereas the sailors want to rescue the "soul" of Jonah, Jonah wants the destruction of his "soul" (4:3).

II. Jonah and God

Jonah and God are set up "in opposition" to each other (64) by the use of the same verbs (ראה, חרה, חוס) for both, and the device of changing the word order so as to put emphasis on the subject, thus setting Jonah and God against each other. These will be further examined below (65).

III. God and the Pagans

The "better" behaviour of the pagans in their relationship to God, the mutuality of their interaction, is made evident by the play on the verb שוב in 3:8-10 and the use of עשה and רעה in the same context. Both these are analysed below (66).

All three "characters" are played off against each other on this level of presentation. The net effect is to reinforce the quality of the pagans over against Jonah, both in their mutual interaction and in their relationship to God.

2. The self-centredness of Jonah is developed particularly in Chapter 4, when he is free to complain to God. Wolff (67) has noted how the "I" of Jonah is emphasised: "Im Urtext kommt allein in Vers 2 fünfmal ein Ausdruck der 1. Person vor ("Das ist's ja, was ich dachte, als ich noch in meinem Lande war, weshalb ich auch eilends fliehen wollte; denn ich wusste...") und in dem kurzen Vers 3 viermal ("Nimm, Herr, meine Seele von mir; denn mein Sterben ist besser als mein Leben."). Wolff notes that Jonah's concern has been with himself right the way through, and we would add that our analysis of the Psalm (68) (with the development particularly between 2:5,8 and 10, where the "I" briefly disappears) confirms this reading of his character.

3. On the other hand the words used to designate the sailors and Ninevites give them a different quality. For though the sailors are designated by the term מלחים when they are introduced (1:5), it is immediately stated that each "man" איש (1:5) cried to his god (69); and they are subsequently designated as איש (1:7); רעהו "his neighbour" (1:7); and אנשים (1:10, 12, 13, 16). They even refer to Jonah himself not as "an Hebrew," but as "this man" (1:14). That is, they are all "fellowmen" tied together in the same fate. The people of Nineveh are also called "men of Nineveh" (3:5) - who "believe in God"; and in the one act they are required to do which demands individual responsibility ("and let each man turn from his evil way" 3:8), they are designated איש . For the rest they are bound together with the animals as, perhaps, "common humanity" (70) (אדם) (3:7, 8; 4:11) who cannot distinguish their right hand from their left. By this reading which recognises all the uses of אדם , the last sentence of the book seems to refer to all the inhabitants of Nineveh, and not just the children (71) - that is all humanity who have not yet had Israel's revelation of God.

Within the context of the different designations of characters within the book, we must obviously refer back also to our section on the "names of God" (72), where we distinguish between the "gods" of the sailors; the "one God" recognised by the captain of the crew and the king of Nineveh, who is identified by the sailors as YHWH (73). Though this scheme applies to Chapters 1-3, we have already noted that in Chapter 4, Jonah's private dialogue with God, a different system is involved, which explores the "inner" aspects of God's compassion - private knowledge for Israel alone. Thus here too the distinction is made between the special relationship to God of one people, and the general awareness of God current in the pagan world (74) - an awareness that can nevertheless become fully realised, as in the case of the sailors.

4. We have noted already in the section on the "Growing Phrase" the significance of the designation of Nineveh as a great city "to God" (75).

c. Quotations

Perhaps the most dramatic example of the "universalising" of a principle which had previously only applied to Israel is the hope of the king of Nineveh that God may "turn and repent," and the fulfilling of his hope in 3:10, which is almost word for word a quotation from Exodus 32:14, when God forgives the children of Israel after the Golden Calf (76). Nor should one overlook the importance of Jonah's quotation of the "Thirteen Attributes" (77) in 4:2, because the contrast, and Jonah's anger, spell out the application of these attributes to God's dealings with all humanity, and not merely Israel (78).

Within the context of "paradoxical quotations," we should also add the two other cases where the pagans cite Jonah's own tradition, in their prayer (1:14) (79), and the occasion when the king of Nineveh breaks through to a new level of repentance, citing Jeremiah (80).

On a quite different level are a set of "reminiscences" that have significance here (though they could equally be tackled under the proposition Traditional Teaching/New Experience). We have noted already that the words used to designate Nineveh, and the destruction threatening it, echo the words used to describe the generation of the flood, and the desctruction of Sodom and Gomorrah (81). The effect of this is to give a "pre-history" to Nineveh, and spell out the degree of evil it represents; but on the other hand it is a sign of the wider dimensions of God's compassion being exhibited here, that destruction is no longer inevitable (82).

Equally significant is the alteration to the phrase in Psalm 31:7 when it is quoted in Jonah's "Psalm" (83) - the "I hate" of "I hate them that regard lying vanities" has been dropped, as a further sign of a new relationship to the pagan world.

If we try to summarise the material that has been gathered in this section, it becomes clear that the author has used a method equivalent to the shifting focus mechanism of a camera. He presents us in "close-up" Jonah as an individual, depicting certain of his characteristics as a person, whereby the greatest "particularism" of them all, the individual ego, is displayed. It is as a character in response to the call of God with its wide, "selfless" implications, in response to his meeting with the sailors, Ninevites, other parts of God's creation, that Jonah is described with all his selfishness, and the few hints at a better side to his nature, and a capacity to grow. As the focus shifts, however, Jonah becomes fitted into the background of the history and traditions of his people as a whole - never explicitly stated (except in the ambiguous "I am an Hebrew") (84), but always hinted at in the symbolism of names (Tarshish, Nineveh, Jaffa), in his quotations from his tradition, in the analogies to earlier prophets

CHAPTER V - ANALYSIS OF THEMES

and experiences in the history of Israel (85). Thus Jonah's "particularism" at least as the wider perspective unfolds, is Israel's particularism; and the characters and situations he encounters as an individual, become the challenges presented to Israel at a certain stage in its history (86).

Conversely the pagan world is depicted in glowing colours, in its piety, in its humanity and its readiness to come to Israel's God. That such a picture is as much a caricature of reality as the portrayal of Jonah, need hardly be said (though surprisingly enough it rarely is), particularly in view of the contrast between the real Nineveh and the city depicted here. Thus the message conveyed here cannot simply be "look how nice the pagans are," for presented on so simplistic a level, it becomes an insult to the bitter experience of Israel following the destruction and exile. Rather it would seem that the very extremes being depicted here "wicked Nineveh/holy Nineveh," and the balancing more neutral figure of the sailors, represent an attempt yet again to tease the reader out of a conventional attitude into a re-thinking of relationships. Such a reappraisal can be in reaction to a strong contemporary particularistic tendency, a part of an assimilationist movement, a prelude to a missionising programme, or even the private humanitarian vision of an exceptional person, all of which have been suggested. Yet precisely because all of these are possible, great caution must be used in attempting to localise the book into too particular a historical context based upon some such an interpretation alone (87). As Ackroyd puts it: "...we should endeavour to see what the book is concerned to do, and to understand its place in the life of a community which could be both narrow and open, and in which the problem of what the community was to be and how it was to be preserved was not one which admitted a simple answer" (88). Or even more concisely in the words of Von Rad: "...it is wrong to suggest that the Book's universalism wished to see covenant and election finally severed from their restriction to Israel; it addresses those who know covenant and community; and it is those men whom it warns against the temptation of using their peculiar position in God's sight to raise claims which compromise Jahweh's freedom in his plans for other nations" (89).

iii. Traditional Teaching/New Experience

With this category we enter one of the most significant, yet least recognised or explored aspects of the book. Yet Jonah's conflict with his God is intimately connected with the whole burden of tradition he carries, a tradition with the consequences of which he must try to reconcile himself. Though it has been noted that the quoted material within the book serves more than an archaising purpose (90), and the contrast between Jonah and Elijah, Jeremiah and Moses has been frequently discussed in their individual significance, nevertheless the full implications of this abundant material have not been explored (91).

Under this heading, therefore, we are concerned with the religious tradition out of which Jonah and (to some extent) the pagans come, and the tension between this traditional way of viewing God and His demands, and the new challenge that He brings. This tradition can be used for evasive purposes, a screen behind which to hide (92), a justification of the status quo; or it can be seen in its full implications and streched to incorporate the new situation (93). Jonah is told to go to Nineveh which will require the revising, among other things, of the responses and expectations of his tradition. How does he fare?

a. Narrative

On the level of the narrative, perhaps the most signifcant feature is that at crucial moments in the story, when asked to explain himself to the sailors, and in attempting to justify himself to God, Jonah offers a theological formulation from his tradition. That there is a gap between the implications of the statements and Jonah's usage of them we have noted in several places, nevertheless it is to his tradition that Jonah turns in crisis moments. The only statements that he makes which are independent of this past are the request to be thrown overboard (even the request to die echoes the words of Elijah).

But the pagan world, too, has its religious tradition, as exemplified by the initial response of the sailors in praying to their various gods; and in the response of the people of Nineveh in donning sackcloth and ashes. That more is expected of them than these traditional forms, we have already suggested in our discussion of the structure of the book and the specific new idea expressed in the king's decree (94).

The significance of the past is also conveyed by a further detail of Jonah's reply to the sailors. Much ingenuity has been expended in trying to solve the riddle of his answer - how to the four questions of the sailors, he gives an answer which might answer at most two of them, but hardly all four. "An Hebrew" might answer the question of his land and people, but hardly his "occupation" (unless we understand מלאכה as "mission"). Likewise the appended theological confession about "fearing YHWH" seems to have no bearing upon the questions at all, unless their burden is in the preliminary phrase about "through whom this evil is upon us," the questions trying to define the nature of the god who is pursuing Jonah (95). Nevertheless, whatever the problem the answer of Jonah raises, this dislocation between question and answer forces us to pay particular attention to the first word of his response - Ibri, an Hebrew (96). We are immediately struck by its peculiar archaic quality within the context (97). It is the term used by the Israelites for themselves when speaking to foreigners (e.g., Genesis 39 and Exodus 1-10 to Egyptians; I Samuel 4:6 to Philistines), but not so in any post-exilic text. But is its effect, as Keller suggests (98), to hint indirectly at all YHWH has done for His people; or does the significance lie, as for Jepsen (99), in the second part of the formula, so that Jonah's

CHAPTER V - ANALYSIS OF THEMES

LIBRARY
LA SAINTE UNION
COLLEGE OF HIGHER EDUCATION
SOUTHAMPTON

emphasis lies not on the particular people to which he belongs, but to the class of all those people who "fear" YHWH? It seems to us that both interpretations are possible, using the familiar observation that what Jonah says with one intention (to express his highly particularistic identify as "an Hebrew," with all its traditional overtones) can be seen by the reader in view of the overall situation (Sailors who also come under the category of those who "fear" YHWH), as a highly universalistic concept. What is, however, of importance in our present discussion, is that the use of such an archaic term, with its reminiscences of Abraham (Genesis 14:13) and the slavery in Egypt, once again evokes the historic roots of the people, the tradition out of which Jonah comes.

b. Word Usage

The only features which are particularly relevant to our discussion are the repetition of the phrase "to Your holy Temple" in the Psalm, and the formal promises to "offer sacrifices" and "fulfil vows" made by Jonah and the sailors, since both of these allude to quite specific religious traditions. However, we should also note again the way the "fear" of the sailors develops to become a "fear of YHWH," i.e., it enters into, and thus expands and reinterprets, the formulation that Jonah himself has used (1:9) (100).

c. Quotations

In this section we have the bulk of the problem which confronts us. For with the use of quotations throughout the book, the author has put us firmly within the traditions of Israel, has evoked several scenes from the past, has set up Jonah in comparison with certain great prophetic figures, and thus put into awesome perspective his attitudes and behaviour.

As a starting point let us briefly note the structural problem we have previously examined (101). We have seen the Jonah's "Psalm" is built up on quotations and reminiscences from several Psalms, and that the author quarrels with at least one concept in them in his removing of the word "I hate" from the quoted version of Psalm 31:7. Further, at the crucial moment in Jonah's "descent," when he reaches the deepest point, the farthest distance from the God who has cast him out, the words of his tradition are left behind, and he himself describes his desperate situation in his own words - and precisely at this point God is waiting to meet him. When he breaks out beyond the formulations of the experience of his tradition to his own direct experience, God is there. Conversely, the proclamation of the king of Nineveh in going beyond the "traditional" measures of his people to an ethical form of repentance, meets the approval of God. Thus tradition, and the transcendence of tradition, are both evoked.

What are the situations out of Jonah's tradition which are recalled by the use of quotations throughout the rest of the book?

Firstly the burden of the prophetic tradition itself. Jonah's flight is no more than the logical end of a spectrum of prophetic attempts to avoid the call. Moses, Elijah, Isaiah and Jeremiah at the outset of, or after a crisis in, their career, tried to avoid the burden of their mission. It may be that the starting point of the author was to take precisely the next logical step - what would happen if a prophet actually did try to run away? However, if we try to remain within the particular passages to which our examination of the quotations has led us, two prophets are directly evoked: Elijah in Horeb, asking for death; Jeremiah in Jerusalem facing death at the hands of the angry citizens (102). The irony of the former situation lies in the fact that Elijah's wish to die comes after the apparent failure of all his prophetic activity, whereas that of Jonah comes after his resounding success in Nineveh (103). Furthermore all the special care with which God looked after Elijah (ravens to feed him, angels to accompany him, a plant to shade him) find their echo in Jonah, in even more miraculous form (the great fish, the gourd). The tragic question to the defeated Elijah (I Kings 19:9): "What are you doing here, Elijah?" is almost parodied by the captain of the crew's anxious cry (Jonah 1:6): "What are you doing sleeping?"; for Jonah's "deep sleep" goes far beyond the exhausted "sleep" of Elijah (104). All these elements magnify the difference between the two prophets, and diminish the stature of Jonah even further in the comparison. Yet is that all that the author wished to convey with so detailed a comparison? Two further elements must surely be discussed since the Elijah tradition has been evoked: what was the mission with which he was concerned as a prophet; what was the conclusion of the scene our author has evoked? In terms of the situation of flight from Jezebel, the background is his battle against the prophets of Baal, and the tendency towards syncretism in Israelite religion, that is to say a crisis in Israel's relationship to YHWH and the surrounding people. What was the conclusion of this episode? Despite the revelation of God to Elijah in the wind, earthquake, fire and "still, small voice" (I Kings 19:11-12), he did not pick up his prophetic burden, and had to appoint a successor in his stead (105); despite being "jealous for the Lord God of hosts" (I Kings 19:10, 14), he was "no better than my fathers" (I Kings 19:4). Furthermore precisely the qualities which were important for Elijah in his time, zeal, jealousy for God, intolerance, readiness to kill the prophets of Baal, are very far away from the tolerance towards even the evil city of Nineveh that characterise "Jonah." That is to say that the effect of the quotations works two ways. Just as the destruction of Sodom and Gomorrah must be re-examined in the light of the fate of Nineveh, so the story of Elijah must be re-examined in the light of Jonah. Though Jonah is diminished further by the comparison with Elijah, the attitudes of the latter are questioned by the caricature of them that Jonah presents. On several levels, "Jonah" forces us to re-read the tradition.

Whereas the allusions to Elijah work by means of direct comparison, the quotations from Jeremiah 26 and 36 work by means of inversion. Whereas

Jeremiah in chapter 26 pleads for his life on the grounds that with his death "innocent blood" will be on the heads of the people of Jerusalem, it is not Jonah who tells this to the sailors, but the sailors themselves who must pray to God, and thus remind Jonah, of this danger. The two-way effect to this is to diminish Jonah in comparison with Jeremiah (106), and elevate the quality of the sailors. It also brings the fourth party, the citizens of Jerusalem, into the picture, their reaction to Jeremiah now being contrasted to that of the sailors to Jonah. In the same way the allusions to Jeremiah 36, which contrast the actions of king Johoiakim with those of the king of Nineveh, bring out further the contrast between the pagans, and the citizens and leadership of Jerusalem. Thus on one level Jeremiah's theology of repentance is being directly applied to the pagan world, with wondrous effect - the universalising tendency again; and on the other side the attitudes and behaviour of Jerusalem in the last moments before the Babylonian invasion, destruction and exile are being evoked and criticised (107). Thus in this series of quotations Jonah is identified only in an inverted way with Jeremiah, and directly with the citizens of Jerusalem - his character corresponds more to theirs than to that of the prophet. This is important as we shall see from the third "model" with which Jonah's character is compared - it is also an argument against the attempt of Feuillet (108) (and Keller) (109) to see Jeremiah as the direct model for the prophet, which requires an oversentimentalising of the character of Jonah as depicted in the book.

With the third traditional evocation the picture becomes much clearer. We have noted (110) that Jonah's complaint to God in Chapter 4: "Was this not my saying, when I was yet in mine own country...?" is a quotation from Exodus 14:12. From the same context of the crossing of the Reed Sea comes the quote from Exodus 14:31, and the repeated allusion to יבשה (111). Here the identification with the children of Israel is quite direct, and their fear of leaving the security of slavery to take a chance upon the freedom offered by God, finds its echo in Jonah's preference of death to living with the implications of the new dimension of God's revelation. Again, as we have noted (112), the figure of Elijah forms an intermediate stage in the development of ideas from the Reed Sea episode to Jonah.

We have delayed till now dealing with one of the most difficult problems of the book, namely the relationship between the Jonah of this book and the Jonah ben Amittai of II Kings 14:25. Yet this has been used to justify opinions varying from Jonah's "supreme nationalism" (113) to his tragic awareness of the imminence of destruction (114). It has been argued that no connection was originally intended between the two figures at all (115), that the meaning of the name Jonah, "dove," was significant (116), and that the very obscurity of the prophet in II Kings left the author free to write anything about him that he wished (117).

That Jonah is a supreme nationalist is suggested by his prophesying during the time of Jeroboam ben Joash "who did that which was evil in the sight of YHWH," but nevertheless "restored the border of Israel from the entrance of Hamat to the sea of the Arabah"; thus he was a prophet of a period of national expansion. However, the reference continues with an explanation of God's purposes - "For YHWH saw the affliction of Israel that it was very bitter; for there was none shut up nor left at large, neither was there any help for Israel. But YHWH did not say to blot out the name of Israel from under heaven; but he saved them by the hand of Jeroboam ben Joash." (II Kings 14:27.) That is to say that Jeroboam's expansionism is belatedly given YHWH's blessing as a way of saving Israel despite the sins of Jeroboam. Thus Jonah's role is not that of a "nationalist" but of a prophet speaking the authentic word of YHWH (II Kings 14:25b) at a particular moment of history, which must presumably include a realisation of the sins of Jeroboam and perhaps, too, the imminence of being "blotted out" which is also YHWH's word (II Kings 14:27a); i.e., in a context which displays two sides of God's reasoning, Jonah is accredited as being a true spokesman. The ambiguity of his role in II Kings is thus similar to the ambiguity of his position in the Book of Jonah itself (118).

Out of this background, when the last reprieve of the Northern Kingdom before destruction is recorded, comes the figure of Jonah ben Amittai. The author knowing this text could well have projected it into his story and hence the suggestion that a temporary reprieve was likewise granted to Nineveh (119).

We have already noted in our discussion of "Universalism" that the phrase used for God's forgiving of the Ninevites is that used when he forgives the children of Israel after the episode of the Golden Calf (Exodus 32:14).

With one final evocation, our material will be complete for an explanation of the total picture. When Jonah in Chapter 4 quotes back at God in anger and frustration His qualities of compassion and mercy, we are forced to recall the source of this statement in God's self-revelation to Moses (Exodus 34:6), and more specifically, Moses' usage of them in his desperate flight to save the people after the "evil report" of the spies, and the people's rebellious wish to return to Egypt (Numbers 14:18). Once again the comparison between irritated Jonah, and the desperate Moses, diminishes the former. Furthermore the awesome implications of this formulation are seen afresh through the absurdity of Jonah's argument, let alone the spelling out of the universalistic dimension. But beyond even this, the crisis against which Moses is acting, must also come into the minds of the reader, which enables us now to develop the pattern that lies behind all these reminiscences:

1. The children of Israel at the Reed Sea are forced to choose between the security of slavery and taking a chance on the freedom offered by God - with their subsequent avowal of belief in God and His prophet Moses.

2. The children of Israel during the very period of the revelation to Moses on Mount Sinai build for themselves a Golden Calf to worship - yet never-

CHAPTER V - ANALYSIS OF THEMES

theless they are forgiven by God after Moses' intercession.

3. The children of Israel wish to turn back in fear from the dangers of entering the Promised Land, despite all their experience of God's providence. The role of the prophet is developed as spokesman of God, as mediator between God and the people, and defender of the people before God.

4. In Elijah's time comes the struggle within the land to establish the proper worship of YHWH against the syncretistic tendency of the people and leadership - with the despairing surrender of Elijah of his mission.

5. The time of the historic Jonah, when the ultimate doom of the Northern Kingdom was spelled out.

6. The last days of the kingdom of Judah and the final struggle of Jeremiah in Jerusalem to avert disaster by the call to repentance - rejected first by the people and finally by the king (120).

7. Jonah, summoned out of "my land" to bring the threat of destruction, and hence the implicit message of repentance and turning to the God of Israel, to the pagan world.

This latter is thus put into its historic perspective as the latest challenge, the new crisis, for Israel. After evoking the memories of past stages in the challenges, failures, yet continued survival and progress of the people, the question now arises of their relationship to the pagan world around them. Furthermore memories of the clash between prophet and people are evoked, the two being blended in the character of Jonah - the messenger of God with the attitudes of the people (121). Thus by the evocation of tradition and the continual need to break out beyond traditional positions and limitations in the light of a new demand by God, the author faces Israel with the challenge of the outside world, and also the new role the people themselves must play, being identified (both positively and negatively) with the prophet.

It is tempting to stop at this point and let this interpretation stand by itself, however, since it seems to be almost too "tidy" a construction, some possible objections must be examined.

Is one reading too much into the quotations that appear in the book? We have attempted to limit outselves to the actual quoted material itself, only going beyond it to the immediate context out of which it comes. Since we have already demonstrated (122) that the precise identification of the context is important in justifying the assumption of quoted material at all, it is reasonable to assume that the author intended the whole context to speak. The scenes at the Reed Sea, Elijah in Horeb and Jeremiah in Jerusalem are quite explicit; the argument of Moses with God when he first quotes the "thirteen attributes" in defence of Israel could well be intended here in view of the author's repeated use of paradoxical quotations. However, once the presence of this quoted material is accepted, it is right to seek the organising principle behind it; not merely for the sake of our own desire for a logically satisfying construction, but because of the remarkable precision that has characterised every other aspect of the author's work - from the formal construction of the book as a whole, to the balance of old and new materials, to the precision of word usage (123). If he had a formal framework for every other level of construction, then it is conceivable that he had one for the historical memories he evoked.

Furthermore this reading of one level of construction of the book sheds some light on the problem of the inclusion in the canon among the twelve minor prophets rather than among the Writings. For in its evocation and criticism of these key events in the history of the people and the development of prophecy itself it is precisely in line with the re-interpretative methods of the prophets themselves, critically assessing Israel's traditions in the light of new challenges (124).

With regards Elijah, we have suggested that there is both some level of critique of him as a prophet (125) alongside of the recognition of his place at a crucial stage in the development of Israel's relationship to God. We would take this first argument a stage further by re-examining part of the materials that identify the two prophets - namely the supernatural interventions by God. Elijah stands on one side of the borderline between legend and history, where legendary material is shaped to fit a theological intention; whereas Jeremiah stands on the other side, where accurate witnessing of events and the precision of historical records (e.g., the names of the princes and other characters in Jeremiah 26, 36) mean that the identification of the hand of God in history works on a more mundane level (126) - it is not in the supernatural intrusions, but in the correct interpretation of contemporary events. Thus the presence of all the wonders and marvels in Jonah appears at first glance to be naive returning to the Elijah tradition. We would argue, however, to the contrary - that precisely the absurdity of these supernatural interventions, coupled with the technical devices like the repetition of the same root m-n-h to accompany them (127), and the hyperbolic description of everything (the 14 uses of the root g-d-l) shows that we have here an ironic imitation of that tradition (128). That is to say that Jonah's "miracles" are literary miracles, designed as much to amuse and enchant his readers, as to illustrate their ultimate absurdity in the world in which they lived (129). This common thread throughout the book which magnifies events to absurd proportions (the "goodness" of Nineveh; the wondrous miracles; the prophet with the character of the people), again and again teases the reader out of his preconceptions and forces him back upon himself. There is thus a "democratising" process here, as much of the prophetic vocation (130) as of the tradition itself. All these associations from Israel's past, the struggles of the great prophets with and against the people, the challenge of bearing God's word in the world, culminate in Jonah, and through him lead the reader to an awareness of his own responsibility.

CHAPTER V - ANALYSIS OF THEMES

iv. The Power of God/The Freedom of Man

Two statements, both by "pagans," summarise the problem. The sailors
in praying to YHWH (1:14) point out "for You, O YHWH, have done as it
pleased You." The king of Nineveh, in leading his people in repentance,
proposes the question: "Who knows whether God will not turn and repent
...?" God creates and rules the world according to His own plan, He is
free to act as He wishes, is ultimately responsible for all that happens,
and can force mankind to do His will - and yet in certain circumstances,
man can himself successfully oppose God's decree. But in what circumstances, under what conditions, and with what consequences? (131)

a. Narrative

The first few sentences establish the problem: God's word comes to Jonah, Jonah flees so as to avoid performing it. God, master of all creation,
sends one of His "messengers," a great wind to force Jonah back; even
in the casting of lots God's hand can be felt in indicating Jonah as the guilty
party. When Jonah attempts the flight into death, surely the last refuge
from the will of God, there is the fish waiting for him, to rescue him and
ultimately to bring him back to dry land. As an ironic aside Jonah has even
been incidently responsible for the full-scale conversion of the sailors to
the fear of YHWH - Jonah's very rebelliousness can be turned to serve
God's purpose! (132)

Again the call, which Jonah must now obey (133), though meeting only the
minimum requirements of his mission - one third of the way into the city,
five words of unconditional warning. Yet the miracle of Nineveh's repentance takes place and God revokes the decree of destruction. Not because
of their "belief" in God (3:5), nor because of their sackcloth and fasting,
but because of turning away from the evil in their hands, the impossible
occurs and God changes His mind - the thing that Jonah could not achieve,
to force God to accept his wishes, the pagan Ninevites have done with repentance. Thus in the first three chapters, the paradox is firmly placed
before the reader, reinforced, as we shall see in the next section, but the
underlying use of language. God's word must be fulfilled, by the repentance of man can overcome the evil decree - or as formulated by Jepsen:
"dieses Gottes Barmherzigkeit überwindet das Gericht und will das Leben" (134).

The fourth chapter shows that God is not satisfied with the effect of His
words on Nineveh (and the sailors) alone, but that they also should have
consequences for the messenger (135). Though Jonah, apparently feeling
himself free of his burden at last, institutes the "discussion" with God in
Chapter 4 ("and the word of Jonah came to YHWH," so to speak), God's
questioning replies and the episode with the gourd show that He is still in
control of the situation. What exactly the nature of this new development
is, will become clearer after we have examined the word usage in the
next section. Suffice it to say for now that the essential problem is the

"repentance" of Jonah himself (136), in part from his own "evil," but also towards a higher understanding of God, as befits his role as God's messenger.

b. Word Usage

At this point it is only necessary to recall briefly the materials we have gathered during this study.

1. Throughout the book the use of infinitives in reference to the acts of God have accompanied acts that reached fruition; when accompanying the acts of man (Jonah's attempt to flee, the sailors' attempts to return to dry land, etc.) the act has failed (137). The single exception is precisely at the significant point in the story when God Himself changes His mind about a course of action (3:10): "and God repented of the evil which He said to do to them; and He did it not." Jonah's relative freedom after completing his mission is thus shown by his intention to sit outside Nineveh (4:5):

עד אשר יראה מה יהיה בעיר

"till he might see what would become of the city." - no longer infinitive but a conjunction with a finite verb (138).

2. We have noted that the three words of Jonah's call: "Rise, go, call" - remain echoing in the air (e.g., two of them repeated by the captain of the crew) until Jonah actually completes his mission (139). Furthermore the act of flight by Jonah causes God to "hurl" a great wind - and this "hurling" repeats itself until Jonah is "hurled" into the sea. Finally the four-fold repetition of וימן (2:1, 4:6, 7, 8) points to a consistent pattern of behaviour by God in dealing with Jonah.

3. From the point of view of "man" in the story, there is also a hint towards such consistency of action. Jonah's "descent" is emphasised by the three-fold repetition of the root y-r-d in Chapter 1 and its recurrence in Chapter 2 in the "Psalm." Conversely the exact balance between the acts of God and of man with regard the key problem of "repentance" is revealed by the four-fold usage of the verb שוב in Chapter 3:

וישבו איש מדרכו הרעה ומן החמס אשר בכפיהם.   מי יודע ישוב
ונחם האלהים ושב מחרון אפו ולא נאבד
וירא האלהים את מעשיהם כי שבו מדרכם הרעה .....

3:8b "'... let them turn every man from his evil way, and from the violence that is in their hands. Who knoweth whether God will not turn and repent, and turn away from His fierce anger, that we perish not? And God saw their works, that they turned from their evil way....'"
The initiative of "turning" is taken by the people of Nineveh, and in response God "turns." Significantly when the initiative to turn does not come directly from man, it is to no avail - in 1:13 the sailors try to "turn" back to the shore (there is no object to the verb which could either refer to the boat or Jonah), but because the initiative is theirs, and not Jonah's, they have no success.

CHAPTER V - ANALYSIS OF THEMES

In the same context of the repentance of the Ninevites, the reciprocity is further shown by the use of עשה and רעה .

וירא האלהים את מעשיהם כי שבו מדרכם הרעה וינחם האלהים על הרעה
אשר דבר לעשות להם ולא עשה

God sees their "doings" that they turn from their "evil"; God repents of the "evil" He said He would "do" - and did it not." (The further significance of the use here of עשה lies in the fact that it has been otherwise used twice of God in sentences which emphasise His total power and freedom: 1:9 - who made the sea and dry land; 1:14 - for You, YHWH, have done as it pleased You.)

4. An interesting possibility of demonstrating that God's word is fulfilled, in a certain sense, no matter what happens, is the interpretation of נהפכת given by Rashi and Abarbanel, and among recent scholars, Good: "But the verb (haphak) can also mean 'to be changed' in a positive sense, from something bad to something good. The latter is certainly not in the prophet's mind, but given the response of the populace, may we not say that it is in the author's mind? 'Forty days hence, Nineveh will be a different place.'" (140)

5. The above examples are necessary preliminaries to an examination of two other sets of key words. Jonah, in attempting to flee from God's word, has set up his own will in opposition to that of God. He himself recognises this, if not completely, in the inner meaning of the "psalm," as discussed above (141). That man can influence God in a certain way has been shown by the success of the Ninevites. But now a further level of understanding is to be accorded Jonah, through examining those qualities of man that approach those of God. That Jonah cannot escape from the lesson is clear from the events in Chapter 4; that he is still free to accept or refuse it is clear from the question mark at the end of the book; that the issue is the significance of certain qualities as contained in God and in man, is revealed in the emphatic comparison of "You" (Jonah) in 4:10, with "I" (God) in 4:11 (142). The nature of the discussion depends upon the recognition of two key words - חרה and חוס .

Jonah is in a state of רעה after learning that Nineveh will be saved (4:1). To deliver him from his רעה God brings in the gourd (4:6). But the thrust of the argument seems to lie in God's repeated challenging question:

ההיטב חרה לך

"Are you right to be angry?" To understand the question we must return to the statement of the king of Nineveh (3:9) that perhaps God will turn from חרון אפו "His fierce anger," the righteous anger he feels because of the wickedness of the city. When they repent, God indeed forgives them - and Jonah becomes in turn angry ויחר לו (4:1), with a self-righteous anger (143). Jonah, in not accepting God's judgment, puts himself in God's place in judging Nineveh, and in God's place he can still hope for the failure of their repentance and hence the destruction (144). In answer to God's first question, he stalks out of the city and sits there to await events. His anger at the non-destruction of Nineveh is only matched by his anger at the destruction of the gourd, when, because of his own personal physical suffering, he finally speaks. Then God is ready to explain the meaning of the lesson - if man is to try to imitate the "feelings" of God, let it not be the "anger" of God, which is God's prerogative alone, but rather His pity חוס . "You had pity on the gourd...should not I have pity on Nineveh?" Beyond the message of destruction and repentance that Jonah must bring to the pagan world, he must himself come to understand the inner quality of that very pity in God that can forgive, overcoming his own wilfullness in the process (145). Then the freedom of man will come to accord with the will of God.

c. Quotations

The theme of the inevitable destruction of an evil city conjures up Sodom and, at least on the level of "reminiscence," we cannot overlook the distant evocation of Abraham. With Sodom appears the argument between the first "prophet" and God about its fate. "Shall I hide from Abraham that which I am doing; seeing that Abraham shall surely become a great and mighty nation, and all the nations of the earth shall be blessed by him? For I have known him to the end that he may command his children and his household after him, that they may keep the way of YHWH, to do righteousness and justice..." (Genesis 18:17-18). The parallels are striking. God reveals the coming destruction to a prophet. God "knows" Abraham will teach his children to do "righteousness and justice" - Jonah "knows" God is compassionate and merciful. Abraham (the "Hebrew" - Genesis 14:13) argues against God - how can He destroy the righteous with the wicked, for the sake of the righteous can they not all be spared? - Jonah (the "Hebrew" 1:9) is rebuked - "should not My pity extend to such a large city whose people do not know right from left and so many animals?" In the Abraham story God wants Abraham to come to understand the concepts of righteousness and justice - and God's right to conform to them, yet remain free to transcend them. In our book God wants Jonah, who understands about justice, to come to appreciate something of this pity of God which transcends justice. Through Abraham all the nations shall be blessed; through, or rather despite, Jonah, the pagans come to be blessed. All of which associations are too loosely tied to the text to be "proved" to be intentional. Yet given the key of Sodom," 'Ibri," and perhaps the "knowing" (of God Genesis 18:18, of Jonah 4:2), they argue very persuasively that such was also the purpose of the author.

But with the dimension of repentance offered to the threatened city we come to the quotations from Jeremiah, and immediately the challenge before Israel enters into the picture before us. We would only add here a problem raised by Eerdmans, though in the context of the dating of the book. "It seems improbable that an author would intend to demonstrate the mercy of Jahu by pointing to a famous town, long ago destroyed by Him. If the story shall have any sense Ninive must exist" (146).

CHAPTER V - ANALYSIS OF THEMES

There is a further problem to add to that of Eerdmans, within which, however, lies the resolution. The reader not only knows that Nineveh was indeed long since destroyed, but also that Nineveh/Assyria was responsible for the destruction of the Northern Kingdom. Thus to the whole story there is an added pathos. At a certain time Nineveh might have been destroyed but because of their repentance they were saved - and thus ultimately became weapons in the hand of God to destroy the Northern Kingdom. If subsequently their evil was too great (147), then it was inevitable that they, in turn, would be destroyed. Yet if Nineveh could repent, why could not Israel, and then Judah (Jerusalem) have repented, for they too could have survived. To the ironies of the book itself is added the irony of history. "At one instant I may speak concerning a nation and concerning a kingdom to pluck up and to break down and to destroy it; but if that nation turn from their evil, because of which I have spoken against it, I repent of the evil that I thought to do unto it. And at one instant I may speak concerning a nation, and concerning a kingdom, to build and to plant it; but if it do evil in My sight, that it hearken not to My voice, then I repent of the good, wherewith I said I would benefit it. Now therefore speak to the men of Judah, and to the inhabitants of Jerusalem...." (Jeremiah 18:7-11a).

This section is best summarised by examining a further problem posed by the book - namely the two explanations given for God's sparing of Nineveh. The first is that God repents of the evil He said He would do on seeing their repentance. However, at the end of the book, in challenging Jonah to understand His pity, God says, in effect, "should I not have pity on Nineveh with its so many people and animals." Did God forgive them because of their repentance, or because of His pity? In not making a clear distinction between these two stages, a great confusion of motives is possible. In accepting the repentance of Nineveh, expressed in terms of the ethical category of turning away from the violence in their hands, we have the working of the familiar viewpoint presented by the quotation from Jeremiah: turning from evil can make God Himself "turn." The matter is not guaranteed, as the cautious "who knows" of the king of Nineveh clearly shows, but it is a well-established theological position in Israel. In the tension between strict justice and mercy, tešubah can lead God's mercy to prevail over His justice.

With the second explanation, the limits of the system are extended to all peoples, who are to be seen in the light of God's compassion, of His disinterested love, something which man can only partly grasp by arguing from the limited experience of his own compassion "You had pity on the gourd... should not I have pity on Nineveh?". But this quality of God extends as well in the dimension of time, for just as the "toil" attributed to Jonah in 3:10 (in tending the plant) has no counterpart in the sentence about God (148), so also the time factor (that grew in one night and perished in one night) has no counterpart - God's pity is open-ended, both in space and in time. Thus the borders which man erects in defining who may or may not come under God's compassion, themselves disappear into the timelessness of God. Nineveh was yesterday's enemy, but today exists no more. Israel and Judah, as they once existed, are no more. The only eternal things are the protagonists of the book: God, and the man who is sent with His message, the very nature of which forces him to grow beyond his own limitations to a perception of the divine.

Summary

We have tried to display the complex relationship in the Book of Jonah between form and meaning; to separate out those elements which have led to the multiple interpretations of the book, and trace the various directions in which they lead. Different emphasis on any single element or group of elements can result in quite different readings. That such ambiguity exists and that no single reading is the "true" one, is no more, and no less, a problem than the attempt to recognise and understand the word of God itself at any given time. In trying to contain and describe his experience within the form of a narrative, the author has added to the problem of revelation itself, that of the conveying of revelation. To do so he has used a splendid paradox - a remarkable, almost mathematical, technical precision in his narrative style, so as to convey imprecision and ambiguity. The whole is summed up in a phrase which has been applied both to drama and to ritual - strategic mystification.

If nevertheless we may extract a theme which seems to have become clarified through our analysis, it is precisely the freedom of God to be beyond any definition by which man would limit Him. God is not contained in Jonah's categories (149). He is free to deal with Nineveh as He wants, and not as Jonah wants. It may be that with regards Nineveh, Jonah wants "justice" - the destruction of the wicked; but God is ready to accept their repentance. Jonah wants his own relationship to God (a controlling one!) to be maintained (whether this is Jonah's egoism or Israel's particularism) - but God is free both to maintain this privileged relationship (though on His terms) yet extend His concern at the same time to all mankind, and all creation. Jonah would contain God within his tradition - yet it is only at the point where his tradition proves inadequate, where he must break through to his own experience (whether in the depths of Sheol, or in the heights of repentance) that he can encounter God, waiting to meet him. For Jonah thinks he knows God and can disobey - but he does not know God, and ultimately cannot disobey.

112

טוֹב
מוֹתִי
מֵ"

ABBREVIATIONS

ABR	Australian Biblical Review
AJA	American Journal of Archaeology
AncB	Anchor Bible
ATD	Das Alte Testament Deutsch
AThANT	Abhandlungen zur Theologie des Alten und Neuen Testaments
BiKi	Bibel und Kirche
BiLe	Bibel und Leben
BiTod	The Bible Today
BK.AT	Biblischer Kommentar, Altes Testament
BS	Bibliotheca Sacra
BZ	Biblische Zeitschrift
CBQ	Catholic Biblical Quarterly
CTh	Cahiers Théologiques
CTJ	Calvin Theological Journal
EstB	Estudios Biblicos
EuA	Erbe und Auftrag
EvTh	Evangelische Theologie
FRLANT	Forschungen zur Religion und Literatur des Alten und Neuen Testament
GuL	Geist und Leben
HAT	Handbuch zum Alten Testament
HK	Handkommentar zum Alten Testament
HSAT	Die Heilige Schrift des Alten Testaments
HUCA	Hebrew Union College Annual
ICC	International Critical Commentary
IDB	Interpreter's Dictionary of the Bible
IntB	The Interpreter's Bible
JBL	Journal of Biblical Literature
JPOS	Journal of the Palestine Oriental Society
JSSt	Journal of Semitic Studies
JThS	Journal of Theological Studies
KAT	Kommentar zum Alten Testament
KHC	Kurzer Hand-Commentar zum Alten Testament
KK	Kurzgefaßter Kommentar zu den Heiligen Schriften
MG	Miqra'ot G'dolot
MGWJ	Monatschrift für Geschichte und Wissenschaft des Judentums
NThT	Nieuw Theologisch Tijdschrift
NTT	Norsk Teologisk Tidskrift
OTL	Old Testament Library
PastB	Pastor Bonus
PR	Psychoanalytic Review
PTR	Princeton Theological Review

RB	Revue Biblique
RGG	Die Religion in Geschichte und Gegenwart
RSEHA	Revue Sémitique d'épegraphie et d'histoire ancienne
SJT	Scottish Journal of Theology
TEH	Theologische Existenz Heute
ThR	Theologische Rundschau
ThStKr	Theologische Studien und Kritiken
ThZ	Theologische Zeitschrift
VT	Vetus Testamentum
VT.S	Supplement to Vetus Testamentum
ZAW	Zeitschrift für die Alttestamentliche Wissenschaft
ZKTh	Zeitschrift für Katholische Theologie

NOTES

Introduction

1) Though this technical detail is an essential basis, it may be pre-
   ferred in the first instance to move on directly to the argument
   itself, beginning page 31.

2) A. Feuillet, "Les Sources du Livre de Jonas," RB, 54 (1947),
   pp. 161-186. A. Feuillet, "Le Sens du Livre de Jonas," RB, 54
   (1947), pp. 340-361.

3) Throughout the study the term "Jonah" will be used to mean the
   book itself; the name Jonah, without inverted commas, refers to
   the prophet himself. Wherever biblical quotations do not follow
   the translation in The Holy Scriptures of the Jewish Publication
   Society of America, Philadelphia, 1917, they are our own translation.

Chapter I

1) Just to give a few examples: H. W. Wolff, Studien zum Jonabuch,
   Köln, 1965; Phyllis L. Trible, Studies in the Book of Jonah (Un-
   published Doctoral Dissertation), Columbia University, 1963. G.
   Cohn, Das Buch Jona Im Lichte Der Biblischen Erzählkunst (Studia
   Semitica Neerlandica 12), Assen, 1969. O. Kaiser, "Wirklichkeit,
   Möglichkeit und Vorurteil. Ein Beitrag zum Verständnis des Buches
   Jona," EvTh 33 (1973), pp. 91-103. Further literature will be cited
   at relevant places.

2) Since two quite different meanings are present in the use of טעם ,
   it forms a border-line case.

3) See Analysis of Structure, page 55ff.
4) See below page 16ff.

5) The appearance of the root עבר in עברי (1:9) is again a borderline
   case for consideration, since the relationship between the two is
   problematic.

6) See below, page 20, 26.
7) See below, page 118 n 49.
8) See Analysis of Structure
9) e.g., ישב page 19f ; חרה , ראה page 20.

10) c.f. Wolff, Studien, p. 39; Cohn, Erzählkunst, p. 66f, 98. A. Jepsen,
    "Anmerkungen zum Buch Jona," Wort-Gebot-Glaube (W. Eichrodt
    Festschrift), Zurich, 1970, pp. 297-305, p. 298.

11)   One can already note a device of the author here, namely that rather than use diverse synonyms he repeats a key word within a total phrase which itself "grows" with each repetition - from סער in verse 4 to וסער הולך in verse 11. See below, page 31ff.

12)   See page 31ff.

13)   c.f. Wolff, Studien, p. 95. E. Haller, "Die Erzählung von dem Propheten Jona," Theologische Existenz Heute, N.F. 65, München, 1958, p. 17. W. Rudolph, Joel-Amos-Obadia-Jona (KAT Band XIII 2), Gütersloh, 1971, p. 341 (hereafter referred to as "Commentary").

14)   Against E. M. Good, Irony in the Old Testament, Philadelphia, 1965, p. 45, who sees the use of the verb with regards the sailors as an act of "sympathetic magic" on their part.

15)   Thus we can understand the phrase in the "Psalm" (verse 4) "For Thou didst cast me..." as being a true account of what happened - the sailors were the agents - but it was the initial "hurling" by God of the wind that led to the "hurling" overboard of Jonah. Against Trible, Studies, p. 78.

16)   Verse 2.
17)   c.f. Cohn, Erzählkunst, p. 74. Good, Irony, p. 44.
18)   See further discussion, page 29.
19)   Verse 3 (twice), 5.

20)   ויונה ירד Most commentators understand the use of the verb here in a pluperfect sense - "and Jonah had already gone down" (prior to the appearance of the storm); e.g., J.A. Bewer, A Critical and Exegetical Commentary on Jonah (ICC), Edinburgh, 1912, p. 32, 34. M. Delcor, Les Petits Prophètes. Jonas (La Saite Bible), Paris, 1961, p. 278. Haller, Erzählung, p. 17f. Cohn, Erzählkunst, p. 56. C.A. Keller, Jonas (Commentaire de l'ancien testament X1a), Neuchatel, 1965, p. 272 (hereafter referred to as "Commentary"). T. H. Robinson, Die zwölf kleinen Propheten (HAT), Tübingen, 1938, p. 120. A. Van Hoonacker, Les Douze Petits Prophètes (Etudes Bibliques), Paris, 1908, p. 327. Others see Jonah's action as his response to the storm: e.g., O. Loretz, Gotteswort und menschliche Erfahrung, Freiburg, 1963, pp. 20, 23. J. Halévy, "Recherches Bibliques. Le Livre de Jonas," RSEHA 14 (1906), pp. 1-49; 7, 9. N. H. Snaith, Notes on the Hebrew Text of the Book of Jonah (Study Notes on Bible Books), London, 1945, p. 13. S. D. Goitein, "Some Observations on Jonah," JPOS 17 (1937), pp. 63-77; 67, n9. Goitein, in defending this view, points out that וה' הטיל two verses before is likewise adversative, and ויונה ירד sounds like the response to those words. No one translates וה' הטיל in the pluperfect, and it appears that the grammar can support both meanings, the translation depending upon the interpretation put upon the events.

21) c.f. Cohn, Erzählkunst, p. 64. G.M.Landes, "The Kerygma of the Book of Jonah," Interpretation 21 (1967), pp. 3-31; 25. A. Neher, L'essence du prophétisme (2nd Ed.), Paris, 1972, p. 293. E. Simon, "Flight from God - and Return," Commentary 16 (1953), pp. 214-218; 214f. It is interesting to speculate whether the use of נשא (to take up), which might otherwise be superfluous, is used here (1:12, 15) to suggest a movement back "upwards" - Jonah's descent being to some extent "corrected" by his offer to be thrown overboard, thus saving the sailors.

22) See Analysis of the "Psalm," page 39ff.

23) c.f. Landes, Kerygma, p. 25.

24) יבש in the other chapters where it appears is in the form יבשה where it has the "positive" meaning of the safety of dry land.

25) It is perhaps no more than a coincidence of this selection, but the total number of "bad" words and "good" words is in each case 15.

26) c.f. J. More, "The Prophet Jonah: The Story of an Intrapsychic Process," American Imago, Spring 1970, pp. 3-11, p. 8. Though one may quarrel with the psychological model presented here, it gives a useful insight into the turmoil and anger of Jonah.

27) H. Gunkel, "Jonabuch," RGG (2nd Ed.), Tübingen, 1929, Vol. 3, Col. 638-643; 641. Haller, Erzählung, pp. 44.

28) e.g., I Kings 17:9; Deut. 10:11; Joshua 7:10; Numbers 22:20; Jeremiah 13:4,6. Kaiser, Wirklichkeit, p. 93.

29) e.g., I Kings 17:10; Jeremiah 13:5,7; Numbers 22:21.

30) c.f. A Lods, Histoire de la Littérature Hebraique et Juive, Paris, 1950, p. 595. D. F. Rauber, "Jonah - the Prophet as Shlemiel," BiTod 49 (1970), pp. 29-38; p. 32.

31) The highly formal usage of קום can now be clearly seen. God says "rise up," Jonah "rises" to flee, and the captain tells him again "rise up." The second time God says "rise up," Jonah "rises up" to do his task, and now the king must "rise up." Chapter 1: קום .... Chapter 2: ויקם ..... ויקם ..... קום ..... ויקם קום

32) See Analysis of Themes, page 96.

33) Jonah also "prays" (4:2) as do the sailors (1:14), using similar forms of lament. (For a full comparison the these prayers, c.f. Trible, Studies, p. 216, p. 229.)Significantly, Jonah having begun like the sailors with the correctly submissive אנה ה' cannot contain his anger which breaks through with his words of complaint, "Was not this my saying when I was yet in mine own country!" Only at the end does he return to the "correct" formula of petition in asking for death.

34) See below, page 25f.

35) Ibid.

36) In noting that in such antithetical statements both elements should have the same content, Leah Fränkel, "Ha'antitezah k'yesod siphruti b'miqra'," Hammiqra' v'toldot yisra'el, Jerusalem, 1972, pp. 129-146, p. 142f, points out that the reference to Jonah's "toiling" over the gourd is not matched by a similar remark about God "toiling" over Nineveh. She concludes: "More than the Lord has pity on Nineveh for His own sake (because it was the fruit of His work), He has pity on it for its own sake...." (The article is hereafter referred to as "Antitezah.")

37) 4:1, 4, 9 (two times). c.f. Wolff, Studien, p. 37. It suits the author's ironic intention, though it is probably not meant deliberately, that Jonah is quite literally "four times" as angry as God.

38) c.f. Lohfink, N. "Und Jona ging zur Stadt hinaus (Jona 4:5)," BZ 5 (1961), pp. 185-203, p. 190

39) See further discussion, page 153 n 133.

40) e.g., I Kings 17:9; Isaiah 38:4, Jeremiah 1:4, 11; 2:1; 13:3; etc.

41) Once again the change in "meaning" of דבר coincides with its appearance in the fourth chapter, thus further marking off the units 1-3, 4.

42) See page 116 n 20.

43) c.f. Trible, Studies, p. 210, 235, who notes the emphasis on Jonah, but assumes it is to show the contrast to the sailors' behaviour.

44) See Analysis of Structure, page 55.

45) See page 90ff.

46) The following discussion deals only with the Ninevites, but it is worth noting again in this context that הטיל is used both of God and the sailors.

47) c.f. Wolff, Studien, p. 37f.

48) For an overall glance at this complexity see Diagram 1.

49) We have noted above (page 16) the curious fact that the verb שוב appears first in Chapter 1 (1:13), when the sailors try unsuccessfully to "turn back" to shore. Since שוב is only otherwise used in a "penitential" context, it is tempting to see a symbolic meaning here - the sailors trying to "turn" Jonah back to his mission, to "repent" for him. Since the initiative is theirs and not Jonah's they cannot succeed. c.f. L. Fränkl, "W'rahamaw 'Al Kol Ma'asaw", Ma'ayanot, Jerusalem, 1967, pp. 193-207; p. 195 n. 7

50) See Diagram 1a, page 23. See also a further example of this device, page 30.

51) See Diagram 1c, page 23.

52) The frequent repetition of רעה , in various grammatical forms, as one of the "Leitworte" has been analysed by Cohn, Erzählkunst, pp. 54, 65-7. See also Wolff, Studien, p. 38f.

53) So Goitein, Observations, p. 72. But see against his view, Rudolph, Commentary, p. 334, note c, to 1:2. There is also the further problem as to whether "their evil is come up before me" is part of God's explanation to Jonah as to why he must preach "because their evil..." or the content of his preaching "that their evil..." See below, page 153 n 133.

54) We see no valid reason to omit the second appearance of this phrase (despite variant readings in some MSS) once its point in building this contrast is recognised. Against Trible, Studies, p. 22. See below, page 133 n 14 for further confirmation of this view.

55) c.f. J. Bacharach, Jonah Ben Amittai W'Eliyahu, Jerusalem, 1959, p. 21.

56) A second example also depends upon variations of a similar phrase:

ויקם יונה לברח תרשישה מלפני ה' .....
לבוא עמהם תרשישה מלפני ה'
כי ידעו האנשים כי מלפני ה' הוא ברח .....
על כן קדמתי לברח תרשישה

(1:3) "But Jonah rose up to flee unto Tarshish from before the presence of YHWH...to go with them unto Tarshish, from before the presence of YHWH. (1:10) For the men knew that he fled from before the presence of YHWH. (4:2) Therefore I fled beforehand unto Tarshish..." Of the two elements of his flight: that it was to Tarshish; that it was from before the presence of YHWH, the sailors rightly recognised that the flight from God was significant. In confessing to God, Jonah only dwells on the geography! For a third example of a "partial confession," see page 52 below.

57) c.f. Wolff, Studien, p. 38f; Cohn, Erzählkunst, p. 74.

58) It thus serves the same purpose as 2:1-2, which carries us from the closing act of the sailors to the "response" of Jonah - introduced (just as Chapters 1 and 3 are introduced) with almost identical words:

(2:3)   ויתפלל יונה אל ה' אלהיו ממעי הדגה ויאמר .....
(4:2)   ויתפלל אל ה' ויאמר .....

For further discussion on the transitions, see below, page 55.

59) Furthermore it adds yet one more element to the complex inter-relationships of 3:8b-10 we have noted above, through the addition of חרה . A new chiastic relationship is established between the חרון אפו of God (3:9) and the רעה that God does not do (3:10),

with the רעה that comes upon Jonah and his חרה in 4:1. (Following Rudolph, Commentary, p. 363).

60) For further discussion of the "attributes," see page 27 f.

61) For discussion on the relationship between these passages, see Analysis of Quotations, page 77.

62) So also does the double form of the name of God. See section on the "changing Names of God," page 36.

63) c.f. Cohn, Erzählkunst, p. 64.

64) For a discussion on the "Multidimensionalität" of language with particular reference to רעה , see Cohn, Erzählkunst, p. 63ff.

65) See page 85 ff.
66) See above, page 17.
67) See above, page 15.
68) c.f. Simon, Flight, p. 215.
69) What he "knew" when first he fled is told in 4:2.
70) See above, page 24.
71) See section on the "growing phrase."
72) Exodus 34:6-7; Numbers 14:18.

73) e.g., Psalm 86:15; 102:8; Neh 9:17. For further study, see J. Scharbert, "Formgeschichte und Exegese von Ex 34:6f und seiner Parallelen" Biblica 38 (1957) pp. 130-150; R. C. Dentan, "The Literary Affinities of Exodus 34:6f" VT 12, (1963), pp. 24-51, and the discussion of both these by Trible, Studies, pp. 231f, 257-259. See also Wolff, Studien, p. 68f; J. Schildenberger, "Der Sinn des Buches Jonas," EuA N.F. 38 (1962), pp. 93-102, p. 94f; O. Loretz, "Herkunft und Sinn der Jona-Erzählung," BZ 5, (1961), pp. 18-29, p. 26f.

74) This problem in meaning has led to the usual suggestion that children are meant by this image. But see the discussion on this in the Analysis of Themes, page 147 n 71.

75) Indeed this interpretation is reinforced by the other uses of ידע where it means to "distinguish between." Three times in Genesis (2:9,17; 3:22) in connection with the "tree of the knowledge of good and evil"; twice with regards being too old (II Samuel 19:36) or too young (Deut 1:39) to distinguish "good" from "evil"; the only other usages, outside "Jonah," being Ezekiel 22:36, where it is used to distinguish between "ritually unclean and clean" in parallel with distinguishing between holy and profane, c.f., Ezekiel 44:23.

76) See further discussion in the Analysis of Themes, page 92 f.
77) See section on the "Growing Phrase," page 32.

78) See for example Bewer, Commentary pp. 50-52; A. Parrot, Nineveh and the Old Testament, London, 1955, p. 85.

79) c.f. Rudolph, Commentary, pp. 355ff, who gives an account of the various attempts to explain Jonah's behaviour. See also Kaiser, Wirklichkeit, p. 98, and further discussion below, page 121 n 91.

80) c.f. Wolff, Studien, p. 38.

81) See above, page 16.

82) Page 25 f.

83) Page 117 n 31.

84) Thus all three roots have the function of "key words." See F. Rosenzweig, "Das Formgeheimnis der biblischen Erzählung," Kleinere Schriften, Berlin, 1937, pp. 167-181. M. Buber, "Leitwortstil in der Erzählung des Pentateuchs," Die Schrift und ihre Verdeutschung (M. Buber und F. Rosenzweig), Berlin, 1936, pp. 211-238. c.f. Wolff, Studien, p. 40.

85) This construction of the "bracketing" of two uses of עשׂה with regards the acts of man, by two uses with regards the acts of God, is the "obverse" of the bracketing we have examined above (page 22) with the root שׁוב . There the acts of man provided the context, and hence some measure of control, over the acts of God. Here it is God who controls the situation in which man must try to respond. The subject of the bracketing verb "acts," the subject within the brackets "reacts."

86) See above, page 22.

87) The beginning of this countermovement is probably implied in the submission of the sailors to God's will, through which they are saved.

88) See above, page 21.

89) While accepting with Wolff, Studien, p. 34 and Cohn, Erzählkunst, p. 58 that the effect of the infinitives is to hurry the action on, the meaning conveyed by this form should not be overlooked.

90) Good, Irony, p. 47. c.f. Trible, Studies, p. 205, who notes that by changes in both vocabulary and form continuity is broken between the call and the response.

91) The usual assumption here is that this points to Jonah's reluctance to fulfil his mission. It is however possible to argue that the emphasis is rather on the fantastic suddenness with which Nineveh repented, i.e., it would have taken Jonah three days to cover the whole city, however, he had only just begun to enter and said his words just once, when his hearers all believed and spread the word! This would be in line with the midrash (Yalkut Shimoni 3:25) that Jonah's voice carried throughout the whole city.

92) See page 107 f.

93) The technique of repeating sentences or even larger passages is a feature of Biblical narrative - the significance usually lying in some minor change in the repeated version, reflecting the different stand-point, or interpretation of events, of the first and second speaker. Compare, for example, Genesis 24:1-22 with verses 34-49 (especially verse 4 with verse 41); c.f. also three versions of the events between Potiphar's wife and Joseph in Genesis 39 - compare verses 12-13, and 17-18. Significant also is the repetition of a sentence without a change in language despite an intervening event, such as in the dialogue between God and Elijah (I Kings 19:9-14), where Elijah's failure to change his response leads to his rejection by God for a further mission. See further to this the Analysis of Themes, page 102 ff. Nehama Leibovitz, ʿIyunim Hadašim B'sepher Š'mot, Jerusalem, 1970, p. 120 n 4, credits Nahmanides as the first Jewish exegete to draw attention to this feature, citing his commentary to Genesis 42:34.

94) e.g. W. Baudissin, Einleitung in die Bücher des Alten Testaments, Leipzig, 1901, p. 595f; Bewer, Commentary, p. 4.

95) In particular the development of the fear of the sailors has been studied. e.g. Haller, Erzählung, p. 27. H.W.Wolff, Die Bibel - Gotteswort oder Menschenwort?, Neukirchen, 1959, p. 28f. Wolff, Studien, p. 37. R. Pesch, "Zur konzentrischen Struktur von Jona 1" Biblica, 47, (1966), pp 577-581, p. 578. Landes, Kerygma, p.14n 44. Keller, Commentary, p. 273. C.A.Keller, "Jonas, Le Portrait d'un Prophète," ThZ 21 (1965), pp. 329-340, p. 333. Good, Irony, p. 46.

96) Fränkel, Rahamaw, p. 195.

97) Cohn, Erzählkunst, p. 54. It is interesting that the whole storm description is actually built upon very few repeated elements. See further the Analysis of Quotations, page 81 f.

98) See discussion by D. Winton Thomas, "A Consideration of Some Unusual Ways of Expressing the Superlative in Hebrew," VT, 3 (1953), pp. 209-224. It is possible that Jonah's author intended to give to an idiomatic expression a fresh nuance. Certainly the other example given by Thomas (p. 226) from Jonah 4:9 עד מות , cannot just mean "very much" in the context which focuses so much upon Jonah's wish to die.

99) The great size of Nineveh is shown "subliminally" by the threefold appearance of forms of the root רבב in this sentence: רבו , הרבה and רבה .

100) Each time a different name of God is used. See section on "The Changing Names of God," page 33 ff.

101) c.f. H.C.O. Lanchester, Obadiah and Jonah (Cambridge Bible), Cambridge, 1918, p. 69. On the sentence: "So Jonah was exceedingly glad because of the gourd," he remarks: "The selfishness of Jonah's character is vividly brought out. Everything is judged in relation to his own peace of mind or body."

102) c.f. B. S. Jacobson, Ḥazon Hammiqra', Vol. 2, Tel Aviv, 1959, p. 386f.

103) Cohn, Erzählkunst, p. 54.

104) c.f. Fränkel, Antitezah, p. 145.

105) For a general review, see M. Weiss, "Einiges über die Bauformen des Erzählens in der Bibel," VT 13 (1963), pp. 456-475, p. 466ff. For examples in Jonah, see Cohn, Erzählkunst, p. 69ff. See also Analysis of Themes, page 97.

106) e.g. W. Böhme, "Die Komposition des Buches Jona," ZAW 7 (1887), pp. 224-284. See discussion in Bewer, Commentary, p. 13ff.

107) K. Marti, Das Dodekapropheton (KHC XIII), Tübingen, 1904, pp. 242-243. A. Bentzen, Introduction to the Old Testament, Copenhagen, 1951, p. 145. J.D. Smart, The Book of Jonah (Int B), New York, 1956, p. 874. A. Weiser, Einleitung in das Alte Testament, 5th Ed., Göttingen, 1963, p. 222. O. Eissfeldt, The Old Testament: An Introduction, Trans. P.R. Ackroyd, Oxford, 1965, p. 406. Delcor, Jonas, p. 267. Cohn, Erzählkunst, p. 70. For further literature, see J. Möllerfeld, "Du bist ein gnädiger und barmherziger Gott (Jonas 4:2)," GuL 33 (1960), pp. 324-333, p. 325n4.

108) c.f. Halévy, Recherches, p. 2. Lohfink, Jona, p. 186. M. Burrows, "The Literary Character of the Book of Jonah," Translating and Understanding the Old Testament (Essays in Honour of H.G. May), Eds. H.T. Frank and W.L. Reed, New York, 1970, pp. 80-107, p. 87. J. Schreiner, "Eigenart, Aufbau, Inhalt und Botschaft des Buches Jonas," BiKi 1962, pp. 8-14, p. 10. Trible, Studies, pp. 67-104.

109) c.f. Marti, Dodekapropheton, p. 242. Bewer, Commentary, p. 64.

110) Rudolph, Commentary, p. 367; c.f. Bewer, Commentary, p. 64. "The real difficulty is in Chapter 4, for here YHWH and Elohim or HaElohim are used promiscuously, without any reason for the variation." c.f. Lohfink, Jona, p. 198. Trible, Studies, p. 83. N.K. Gottwald, A Light to the Nations, New York, 1959, p. 522, makes the general statement that "it is best, however, to lay the discrepancies for the most part to the redundancies and illogicalities of an Oriental storyteller, with the possibility of a gloss here

and there." In view of the precision that marks the choice of virtually every word, phrase, sequence of sentences and chapters of
the book, this seems a little strong, and sheds little light.

111) Rudolph, Commentary, ibid. See also his critique of various similar interpretations in n 13. Möllerfeld, Du bist, p. 325.

112) Th. Boman, "Jahve og Elohim i Jonaboken," NTT, 1936,
pp. 159-168.

113) c.f. Bacharach, Jonah, pp. 60-65. H. Rosin, The Lord of God,
La Haye, 1955, pp. 6-33. Cohn, Erzählkunst, p. 71 - basing himself on U. Cassuto (Torat Hat'udot, Jerusalem, 1953, p. 31ff).
Wolff, Studien, p. 81f, 120 (63f). Wolff suggests (p. 81f) "'Der
Gott' ist offenbar in der Sprache unseres Erzählers Jahwe, wie er
von den Heiden angerufen wird, wie er aber auch an den Heiden
handelt. An den Gott der Heiden will der Erzähler wohl erinnern,
wenn er von der harten Schule spricht, in die der zornige Jonah ge-
nommen wird...Die Heiden finden zum Gott Israels, während Israel noch in die besondere Schule Jahwes als des Gottes der Heiden
hineingenommen werden muss." It is ingenious, but fails to take
into account the fact that it is YHWH who hurled the storm into the
sea which might have cost the sailors, as well as Jonah, their
lives - which is as tough a "schooling" as anything that "Elohim"
handed out. J. Schildenberger, Sinn, p. 100, suggests that the
double name YHWH-Elohim in Chapter 4 is to show that YHWH,
the convenantal God of Israel is at the same time the God of nature
and all mankind - hence all the names of God previously used are
introduced into this chapter. But this does not explain the systematic changes of the name in this chapter.

114) c.f. the scheme given by Möllerfeld, Du bist, p. 325f, which, however, makes no distinction between Elohim and HaElohim as he
himself points out, p. 327 n6.

115) See below, page 35. Nor it is the "previously mentioned Elohim"
(Robinson, Commentary, p. 120; Good, Irony, p. 44), as this does
not accord with the usages in 3:10.

116) See discussion on "paradoxical quotations," page 69 ff.

117) Significantly the king is here quoting Jonah's tradition - a phrase
from Exodus 32:14, quoted also in Jeremiah 26:19, which has until now only referred to Israel, and has only been expressed with
the name YHWH. See further discussion, page 71 f.

118) c.f. Möllerfeld, Du bist, p. 327.

119) c.f. D.K.Andrews, "Yahweh the God of the Heavens," Essays in
Honour of T.J.Meek, Toronto, 1964, pp. 45-57, p. 53-54. J.H.

Hertz, Pentateuch and Haftorahs, 2nd Ed., London, 1962, p. 965
to verse 6.

120) The identification of Elohim as YHWH by the sailors is discussed
by Pesch, Struktur, p. 580, who makes, however, no distinction
between Elohim and HaElohim, and confines his remarks to Chapter 1.

121) c.f. Haller, Erzählung, p. 36. Bewer, Commentary, p. 54.

122) One can also express this same idea by pointing out that the first
three chapters are "defined" by God's word to Jonah. It is the
prophet's mission to the non-"Hebrew" world with which God is
here concerned, and until God's word is fulfilled (or, since Nineveh repents, His purpose is satisfied), it is how God is recognised
in the world at large which is important. By this reading, also,
Chapter 4 begins a new problem, God's "internal" dialogue with
His prophet, for whom a further refinement of the understanding
of God's actions is needed.

123) One can argue that the name YHWH here fits rather into the usage
of Chapter 1-3. It certainly does not contradict this usage, however the association with ויְמַן ties it strongly with the three other
"appointings" in Chapter 4 (unlike the "great wind" that YHWH
"hurls" in 1:4).

124) See above, page 25.

125) This explanation of the conjoined name removes the need to make
the association with Genesis 2, which has occasionally been suggested (e.g., Robinson, Commentary, p. 125, Bentzen, Introduction, p. 145), without being satisfactorily justified within the
context of the book.

126) A weakness of this argument is the change in the chapter as well
between Elohim and HaElohim which cannot have the same significance as in Chapter 1-3. The answer may simply be that for Chapter 4 a general distinction between YHWH and Elohim/HaElohim
is all that the author intended, but all the variants were introduced
to show the underlying unity of God despite all the names - c.f.
below, page 37.

127) It has been well pointed out (e.g., L. Gautier, Introduction à
l'Ancien Testament II, 1914, pp. 494-495) that the very compassion
Jonah gratefully accepts for himself (e.g., in the Psalm) he is not
prepared to allow God to grant to others!

128) See above, page 33.

129) Although it is beyond the scope of this thesis, it is worth speculating whether we can see here the roots of the later Rabbinic

doctrine of the interpretation of the names of God. This idea is
expressed most succinctly in Genesis Rabbah 33:3

בכל מקום שנאמר ה' – מדת הרחמים

בכל מקום שנאמר אלהים – מדת הדין

In every place where the name YHWH is used, it refers to God's
attribute of mercy. Wherever the name Elohim is used it refers
to His attribute of justice. Further material on this theme in Rabbinic thought can be found in A. Marmorstein, The Old Rabbinic
Doctrine of God, London, 1927, pp. 43-53, 181-208. For further
literature, see E.E. Urbach, Hazal, 2nd Ed., Jerusalem, 1971,
pp. 29-52. Whether this separation of names was the invention of
the author of Jonah, or already represents the formalisation of
a known usage of the divine names in earlier Biblical tradition
(or interpretation of this usage), takes us beyond our immediate
concerns, however such a study might throw light on other texts
where the interchange of divine names can be shown to have a
significance in the narrative itself. Along these lines see W. Rudolph, "Jona," Archäologie und Altes Testament. (Festschrift für
Kurt Galling), Tübingen, 1970, pp. 233-239. p. 238f. Also, Rudolph, Commentary, p. 367.

130)   See above, page 15.
131)   c.f. the discussion on דבר pages 21, 30.
132)   c.f. Smart, Jonah, p. 885; Delcor, Jonas, p. 282.
133)   c.f. Haller, Erzählung, p. 28n36; see Analysis of Themes, page 106.
134)   See Analysis of the Psalm, page 43.

135)   It is possible that the author intended that "YHWH, my Elohim"
in the mouth of Jonah at this point might imply that Jonah too saw
God as his own private god whom he could manipulate. But this
may be taking the ironic intention of the author a little too far.

Chapter II

1)   For reviews of the general grounds for excluding the "psalm", see
A.R. Johnson, "Jonah II:3-10: A Study in Cultic Phantasy," Studies
in Old Testament Prophecy, Ed. H.H. Rowley, Edinburgh, 1946,
pp. 82-102, p. 82f; and more recently Rudolph, Commentary,
p. 347f; Landes, Kerygma, p. 10; Trible, Studies, p. 75ff.

2)   Lohfink, Jona, p. 196, n35, 37, suggests that the chiastic structure
of verses 1a, b, 2 and 11 is interrupted by the "Psalm." However
there is no a priori reason why such structures should not be sepa-
rated in a book constructed in so complex a way as Jonah - c.f.,
for example, the various "interrupted" chiastic structures in Diagram 1. See also the chiastic relationship between 1:5,6 and 3:5,6
described by Trible, Studies, p. 297.

3) e.g. R. Pfeiffer, Introduction to the Old Testament, 3rd Ed., New York, 1948, p. 589: "The psalmist cried out 'of the belly of hell'... not that of a fish." But he goes on to point out that the imagery of drowning led to the selection of this particular "psalm." c.f. Landes, Kerygma, p. 13, especially n43; p. 30.

4) e.g. Rudolph, Jona, p. 236, who suggests also the omission of verse 2 (c.f. Eissfeldt, Introduction, p. 406). (See further remarks on this in Analysis of Themes, p.142 n 12.) c.f. Rudolph, Commentary, p. 348f. G. Von Rad, Der Prophet Jona, Nurnberg, 1950, p. 13, makes the cautious observation that the very inappropriateness of the "psalm" makes one wonder whether it was really inserted so carelessly.

5) e.g., Ibn Ezra to Jonah 2:2 argues already against the suggestion that the "psalm" ought to appear in the text after Jonah has been vomited onto the dry land. He explains the timing of the "psalm," and the use of the Perfect, as a form of "prophetic perfect." Similarly Radak to 2:3: "Since he was still alive, he knew he would emerge from the fish in peace." (c.f. his commentary to 2:5,7.) c.f. P.A.H. De Boer, "Jona," Zoals er gezegd is over Jeremia, (Phoenix Bijbel Pockets) Antwerp, 1964, pp. 93-102, p. 99. For the argument that the fish could be understood as having already saved Jonah, see discussion in Rudolph, Commentary, p. 348.

6) e.g., Abrabanel who refers to the midrash that Jonah was the son of the widow of Sarephath whom Elijah restored to life, so that the "past" deliverance mentioned in the "psalm" is this episode.

7) c.f. Simon, Flight, p. 216ff, on the midrash.

8) e.g. Ch. Aalders, The Problem of the Book of Jonah, London, 1948, p. 23f; R.K.Harrison, Introduction to the Old Testament, London, 1970, p. 915. See also the forthright statement of J. Ellul, Le Livre de Jonas (Cahiers Bibliques de "Foi et Vie"), Paris, 1952, p. 43. "Comme d'habitude, l'historien qui a imaginé cette solution a considéré que les commentateurs qui ont modifié ce texte étaient des imbéciles. Pourquoi auraient-ils choisi un text qui convenait aussi mal?...D'alleurs, si nous en supposons le compilateur capable, pourquoi pas l'auteur du livre de Jonas lui-même; l'un n'est pas plus vraisemblable que l'autre...Il faut partir à priori avec l'idée que le texte est authentique et chercher à trouver son sens profonds, et seulement si l'on n'y arrive pas, l'on peut se lancer dans les hasardeuses hypothèses de remaniements de textes."

9) c.f. Cohn, Erzählkunst, p. 93f, and the article of Landes, using arguments based on the symmetrical construction of the book. Most recently Kaiser, Wirklichkeit, p. 97f, argues for the originality of the "psalm" on a number of grounds: it contains a mixture of

taken-over quotations and new elements in the same way as the narrative part of the book; it is exactly adapted to Jonah's situation; it could be intended to show the contrast in Jonah's character between his wish to die and wish to live; or else express the irony of the grudging giving of thanks where none is intended at all.

10) An interesting alternative was suggested by Sir Philip Magnus, "The Book of Jonah," The Hibbert Journal, 16 (1917-18), pp. 429-442, 439, namely to preserve the "psalm" as original to the book and re-move, instead, the fish. The suggestion does not appear to have been taken up by other scholars.

11) c.f. Johnson, Phantasy, p. 83; R.B.Y.Scott, "The Sign of Jonah," Interpretation 19 (1965), pp. 16-25, p. 22. The argument sometimes raised that Jonah's words of praise do not constitute a "prayer," (namely a lament or supplication) has been criticised by Landes who rightly warns against defining the concept of prayer in the Old Testa-ment too narrowly. We would add to this that precisely the fact that "thanksgiving psalms" could be inserted as "prayers" of Hannah and Hezekiah, implies that such a broader concept was indeed in existence at some stage, otherwise such intrusions would hardly have been tol-erated. If the insertions pre-date the composition of Jonah, they could have furnished the author with a model. If they were inserted later in some or all cases, the argument that such a concept of prayer must have been current, still holds good.

12) H. Gunkel, Ausgewählte Psalmen, 3rd Ed., Göttingen, 1911, p.289.

13) S. Mowinckel, The Psalms in Israel's Worship (2 Vols), Oxford, 1962, II, p. 33. c.f. H. Gunkel, Einleitung in die Psalmen, Ed. J. Begrich, Göttingen, 1933, p. 269. But see the classification of C. Westermann, Das Loben Gottes in den Psalmen, Göttingen, 4th Ed., 1968, p. 76ff.

14) See page 31 ff.

15) For this meaning of נהר c.f. Johnson, Phantasy, p. 84, n 10, and Landes, Kerygma, p. 6 n14.

16) On the anachronism of a Northern prophet praying towards the Jeru-salem temple, see the discussion of Kaiser, Wirklichkeit, p. 97f. As to whether the earthly or heavenly temple is meant does not affect the issue here - c.f. Rudolph, Commentary, p. 354.

17) See discussion, page 32, c.f. Cohn, Erzählkunst, p. 93.

18) e.g., Psalm 111:10, 11; 24:7-8, 9-10; 103:20, 21, 22; 107:5, 15, 20, 31, etc. c.f. J. Muilenburg, "A Study in Hebrew Rhetoric: Re-petition and Style," VT.S 1 (1953), p. 97-111, p.100 f; N.H.Ridder-bos, "The Psalms: Style-Figures and Structure," Studies on Psalms (Oudtestamentische Studien 13), Ed. P.A.H. De Boer, Leiden, 1963, p.43-76, p. 46, 51. N.H.Ridderbos, Die Psalmen (BZAW 117) 1972.

19) e.g., Psalm 69:3, 16-- מצולה ; 22:13, 17-- סבבוני ; 31:7b, 15a-- בטחתי

20) e.g., Psalm 18:5; 30:4; 40:2; 69:1-3, 15-16; 88:3-8; 115:17; 124:3-5; Lam. 3:54-56.

21) For a study of this language, see C. Barth, Die Errettung vom Tode in den individuellen Klage- und Dankliedern des Alten Testaments, Zollikon, 1947.

22) We have examined this theme of continuing descent in connection with the use of the word ירד - see page 17.

23) See, for example, the discussion of the root טול , page 16.

24) We adhere to the Masoretic Text here and do not follow Theodotion. This is in line with Johnson, Phantasy, p. 84 n11, but for precisely opposite reasons; namely that the note of assurance expressed by the reading of the M.T. does indeed come too early in the "psalm," and therein lies its purpose, as the further discussion will show. c.f. Landes, Kerygma, p. 6n15; N. Snaith, "The Meaning of the Hebrew 'ak," VT 14, 1964, pp. 221-225; J. Pedersen, Israel, Its Life and Culture I-II, Oxford, 1926, p. 467f.

25) For words common to the psalm and the other chapters of the book, see above page 15.

26) Cohn, Erzählkunst, p. 93.

27) c.f. Cohn, Erzählkunst, p. 93. It is worth speculating whether the use of the root עלה does not also hint forward to Chapter 4, when God prepared a gourd "and made it to come up over Jonah."
ויעל מעל ליונה   The effect of the paronomasia here is to emphasise the root עלה , and the role of the gourd is indeed analogous in this episode to that of the sudden saving intervention by God spoken of in the "psalm." In the "psalm" the speaker "goes down" and God makes his soul "rise" to deliver him; in Chapter 1, the fleeing prophet "goes down," and in Chapter 4 God makes the gourd "rise" to "deliver him from his evil." The use of חסר in verse 9 also brings us into connection with Chapter 4. See below page 46. For further hints toward Chapter 4, see below page 145 n 28.

28) Most commentaries provide a list of parallel verses: e.g. Delcor, Jonas, p. 282; Robinson, Commentary, p. 123. See also the standard editions of the King James and Luther Bibles. For a recent list, see Kaiser, Wirklichkeit, p. 97n22.

29) c.f. Rudolph, Commentary, p. 352.
30) See below page 65 ff.

31) It is beyond the scope of this study to deal with the controversial problem of the metrics of the "psalm." We would note, however, in passing, that the division by sense units shown in Diagram 2 also separates the staccato rhythm of the middle column describing Jonah's physical descent from the more leisured "inner reflections" of Jonah in the lefthand column. It also shows the effect of the sequence in the central column, the five lines which describe his descent, building a crescendo, until "the bars of the earth are about him forever," to be interrupted dramatically by the break, both in sense and rhythm, by the phrase: ותעל משחת חיי ה' אלהי
This reading at least does not require the artificial sense division in verse 7 which is generally assumed (e.g. Johnson, Phantasy, p. 84, v. 13; Robinson, Commentary, p. 122) and retained in the new Biblia Hebraica Stuttgartensis. For recent studies in Hebrew poetry, and further literature, see F. Horst, "Die Kennzeichen der hebräischen Poesie," ThR, 21 (1953), pp. 97-121. J. Muilenburg, "Biblical Poetry," Encyclopaedia Judaica, Vol. 13, Col. 671-693, Jerusalem, 1971. S. Segert, "Problems of Hebrew Prosody," VT.S 7, 1959, pp. 283-291. R. Gordis, "The Structure of Biblical Poetry," Poets, Prophets, and Sages, Indiana, 1971, pp. 61-94. The remarks on varying metre (p. 68ff) are of particular interest.

32) See discussion, page 41.

33) c.f. Delcor, Jonas, page 283, arguing against Böhme.

34) Against Kaiser, Wirklichkeit, p. 97, who suggests the author quoted from memory and thus made a mistake. Apart from the general problem as to whether the author would have been so careless (in view of the correctness of other apparent quotes) it is unlikely he would have come to so unusual a form as this and not checked up on it.

35) c.f. Westermann, Psalmen, p. 88.

36) c.f. Deut. 32:12.

37) חסד is a word linking us with the divine attributes in Chapter 4 - and is anyway a synonym for God (c.f. Psalm 144:2). c.f. Johnson, Phantasy, p. 85n16.

38) See discussion, page 49.

39) c.f. Psalm 18:7, 116:1; etc.

40) c.f. Psalm 31:23b; 116:1; 145:19.

41) Psalm 102:11 - but see also Psalm 51:13; 71:9.

42) e.g., Psalm 69.3, 16; 107:24.

43) The former בלב ימים occurs six times in Ezekiel 27-28. See further discussion in Analysis of Quotations, page 80 f.

44) See discussion, page 40.

45) II Samuel 22:5; Psalm 18:5; 116:3.

46) Such a "scissors and paste" way of composing a prayer seems a little strange until one recalls that many of the classic prayers and poems of later Jewish liturgy were composed in such a way, thus allowing traditional words and phrases, with all their familiar echoes, nevertheless to say something new.

47) See discussion, page 129 n 27.

48) Eight times only in the Bible.

49) Around the word נפש is built the ambivalence of Jonah about continuing to live. The two appearances in the "psalm" refer to the imminence of death which he wishes to avoid; the two appearances in Chapter 4 to his two requests to die. We shall note again later the irony of the fact that the sailors pray (1:14) to save Jonah's נפש , and he prays in Chapter 4 to lose it.

50) But see also Psalm 50:14.

51) See discussion, page 41 f.

52) Likewise the contrast between קולי in verse 3 which cries out of distress and the קול תודה of verse 10. c.f. Gunkel, Einleitung, p. 275: "einst in tiefstem Herzeleid, jetzt in jauchzendem Frohlocken!"

53) We shall return to the further implications of this in the Analysis of Structure, page 62 f.

54) See section on "paradoxical quotations," page 69 ff.

55) The question as to how Jonah could have composed the "psalm" in such distressing circumstances is no more valid than asking how he could have survived three days and three nights. The author informs us that he did.

56) Especially Jeremiah 48:26; Isaiah 19:14; 28:8; Lev 18:25, 28; 20:22; Job 20:15.

57) c.f. Goitein, Observations, pp. 69-70, citing Abarbanel.

58) c.f., page 117 n 33.

59) In line with all the other "anticipations" in the book. See Analysis of Themes, page 88 ff.

60) c.f. Bacharach, Jonah, pp. 27-31. Rudolph, Commentary, p. 348, not recognising the irony, assumes the "psalm" to be inappropriate precisely because it contains no admission of remorse or vow of obedience. Recognition of irony in the placing of the "psalm" in its present position is made by Good, Irony, p. 54, though (ironically) he does not see this as being intended by the "glossator" who inserted it. c.f. Kaiser, Wirklichkeit, p. 98; Landes, Kerygma, p. 30n66.

61) The need to repeat to Jonah his duty to go to Nineveh, which he already knows (through the repeating of his "call words" through Chapter 1), suggests that Jonah's reference to "Fulfilling his vows" is not merely a stereotyped part of a Thanksgiving Psalm rendered superfluous by the present context, but is meant to be understood quite literally. On being released, Jonah intended to go piously to Jerusalem and offer a sacrifice at the Temple. God had to remind him that his first task was still to go to Nineveh! (Against Loretz, Gotteswort, p. 26, who seems to miss the irony, and assumes that had Jonah indeed gone to Jerusalem he would no longer be able to believe he could behave as he does in the following chapters.)

62) For Jonah's other "partial confessions," see page 24.

63) It is beyond the scope of this study to enter the controversy as to whether the book is to be described as a "midrash." As Burrows points out (Character, p. 85), "There is no reason a priori to suppose it is not a mixture of different kinds of composition. Certainly it must not be forced into any form defined in terms of classical or modern literature, or derived from the traditions of other peoples, ancient or modern, eastern or western, civilised or preliterary." For a study of midrash, particularly in relationship to evidence of the midrashic process within the Bible itself, see A. G. Wright, "The Literary Genre Midrash," CBQ, 28, 1966, pp. 105-138, 417-457. Wright excludes Jonah from the category midrash, though admits it is a borderline case (p. 531f). Insofar as we detect a homiletic purpose in the author's work, and recognise, the way he has woven certain traditional phrases into his text, both to teach them in a new context and, occasionally, to argue against them, e. g., Psalm 31:7, we call him a "midrashist."

64) But see further structural considerations in the Analysis of Structure.
65) See "Analysis of Quotations."

Chapter III

1) See above, page 53f. Cohn, Erzählkunst, p. 60, notes that in Chapter 1 and 3 Jonah enters society; in 2 and 4 he leaves it and is alone.

2) See also below, page 153 n 133.
3) See above, page 43.
4) See above, page 24.
5) Lohfink, Jona, p. 195.

6) See notes on the distribution of key words page 15f. and discussion on the names of God, page 35 ff.

7) Lohfink, Jona.

8) Keller, Portrait.

9) Pesch, Struktur.

10) Landes, Kerygma.

11) Trible, Studies, p. 206ff.

12) Cohn, Erzählkunst.

13) Based on Cohn, Erzählkunst, p. 51, following Pesch, Struktur, p. 578.

14) Cohn, Erzählkunst, p. 52, notes the interrelationship of these statements. בשלמי הרעה הזאת לנו – באשר למי הרעה הזאת לנו
מה זאת עשית – מה נעשה לך
This suggests additional structural evidence that both phrases about "through whom this evil is come upon us" are part of the author's original text. c.f. p. 119 n 54.

15) Rudolph, Commentary, p. 340n1.

16) In this connection the remarks of Trible, Studies, p. 199 on "symmetrophobia" are of value.

17) Lohfink, Jona, p. 202, deals with 3:1 - 4:4, a rather artificial division. c.f. Cohn, Erzählkunst, p. 52n1. Landes, Kerygma, p. 16f, compares the structure of 1:17 - 2:10 with 4:1-11, and (p. 26f) compares Chapters 1 and 2, and chapters 3 and 4, but the categories he constructs for comparison are again too artificial. For an analysis of the structure of individual sentences, see the very full study of Trible, Studies, pp. 206-234.

18) Keller, Portrait, p. 334, 335. See also the partial analysis of repeated phrases in Chapter 4 by Cohn, Erzählkunst, p. 53.

19) See next paragraph.

20) For further discussion on the possible interpretation of 4:5, see Analysis of Themes, page 91 . For a full account of the various attempts to resolve the problem, see Trible, Studies, pp. 92-102.

21) Trible, Studies, p. 101.

22) See above, page 19 f.

23) c.f. Ellul, Livre, p. 80.

24) It is perhaps significant that the text reads "in" the city, and not "to" the city, implying Jonah anticipates a change within (for example, a reversion to their evil ways), rather than some destruction that will fall upon them from without. Certainly the three-fold repetition of the word "city" in this sentence draws attention to Jonah's obsessional interest in it.

25) See Analysis of Themes, page 91.

26) See above, page 20.

27) One might bring to the phrase "till he might see what would become of the city" the remarks about "Interior Monologue." See below, Analysis of Themes, page 144 n 27.

28) In addition to their similarity of structure, they also contain numerous repetitions of the same words, unlike Chapters 2-3. See above, page 15.

29) For the final clue which brought into perspective the related structure of the "psalm" and Chapter 3, we are indebted to the observation of E. Simon, Flight, p. 217: "A rigorous architectonic movement organises the Book of Jonah, and its Midrashic interpretation, in the polar opposites of Fall and Ascent, Flight and Return. The same organising movement presides over the repentance of Nineveh, which starts with an initial popular swell and rises from below to engulf the king himself."

30) c.f. the form-critical analysis of Chapter 3 by Trible, Studies, pp. 226-229, which is an interesting example of how one can "describe" very accurately a structure, yet come no closer to understanding the function it fulfils. Since she has already ruled the "psalm" out of consideration, the structural relationship between Chapters 2 and 3 is not considered, but is it enough to record, for example, that the stress on the act of putting on sackcloth points up the importance of penitence in the story, without attempting to explain why the king makes explicit mention of this act in his decree when it is already redundant. Nor is it enough to put together as "Positive Instructions" the command "to put on sackcloth" and the command "to turn away from evil," without noting the significance of the qualitative difference between these two commands.

31) See Analysis of Psalm, page 41 ff.

32) It is worth recalling here that Jonah is also brought into comparison with the king through the use of the verbs קום and ישב . See page 19 f.

33) A possible objection to this analysis is that it does not take into account the whole structure of the "psalm." However, if one removes the formal elements (the introductory summary verse 3; and closing "moral" (verse 9) and vow (verse 10)), we are left with a complete unit beginning with "For Thou didst cast me into the depth" and ending with "Yet hast Thou brought up my life from the pit, YHWH my God." (See Diagram 2, which shows the concentric nature of this unit.) The "psalm" itself, as a whole, goes on to record the speaker's new humility and remembering of YHWH, which comes after YHWH has saved him. Thus YHWH is seen as taking the initiative when the speaker is at his lowest point - which is parallel to YHWH's rescuing of Jonah, despite his attempt to drown.

34) See Analysis of "Psalm", page 49.

Chapter IV

1) See works previously cited, especially Sources, p. 167ff; also
A. Feuillet, Le Livre de Jonas (La Sainte Bible), Paris 1966,
pp. 18-21.

2) Among earlier commentators, for example: J. Wellhausen, Die
Kleinen Propheten übersetzt und erklärt, 3rd Ed., 1898 (4th Ed.,
1963) p. 222, notes 4:3 and 4:6. S.R.Driver, Einleitung in die Literatur des alten Testaments, Berlin 1896, p. 345n1. Bewer,
Commentary, pp. 12-13. More recently Keller, Portrait, pp. 331,
338ff. J.C.McGowan, Jonah (Jerome Bible Commentary), London,
1968, pp. 633-637, p. 634. H.W.Wolff, "Jonabuch," RGG, Vol III,
Tübingen, 1959, 3rd Ed., Col. 853-856, Col. 854. Rudolph, Commentary, p. 328. Kaiser, Wirklichkeit, p. 92n7; 100. c.f. the
article of Schildenberger.

3) For a dissenting voice, see Aalders, Problem, p. 19ff, who incidently gives a good example of where quotation can be proved
by comparing Jer 49:14 with Obadiah 1.

4) The term "Reminiscenzen" is used by Baudissin, Einleitung, p. 596,
with reference to the phrases from the Elijah narrative which appear in "Jonah" and also the similarity between God's question to
Jonah in 4:4 and to Cain (Genesis 4:6). We use "quotation" for the
former because the exact wording is reproduced; "reminiscence"
for the latter since no complete phrase is reproduced.

5) c.f. E. Kaufmann, The Religion of Israel (Translated and abridged
by M. Greenberg), Chicago, 1960, pp. 283, 285; E. Bickermann,
Four Strange Books of the Bible, New York, 1967, p. 32, quoting
David Kimchi; Kaiser, Wirklichkeit, p. 99; Von Rad, Jona, p.7;
Cohn, Erzählkunst, p. 75; Haller, Erzählung, p. 14; Rudolph,
Commentary, p. 328.

6) Genesis 19:21, 25, 29; Deut 29:22; Isaiah 13:19; 34:9; Jeremiah
20:16; 49:18; 50:40; Amos 4:11; Lam 4:6.

7) c.f. Ellul, Livre, p. 79. See further discussion below, page 110.

8) H.M.Orlinsky, "Nationalism-Universalism and Internationalism
in Ancient Israel," Translating and Understanding the Old Testament; Essays in Honour of H.G.May, New York, 1970, pp. 206-236,
p. 228.

9) Of the 16 uses of יבשה , 7 relate directly to the crossing of the
Reed Sea (and Jordan) - Ex 14:16, 22, 29; 15:19; Joshua 4:22;
Psalm 66:6; Neh 9:11; two uses (Ex 4:9) concerning the turning of
water into blood, being in a sense a pre-figuration of the later
events, come into the same category; three times it concerns
creation - Gen 1:9, 10; Psalm 95:5; and once the "new creation"
in Isaiah 44:3; and the three times in Jonah.

135

10) See discussion on this problem with regard to Jeremiah: William L. Holladay, "The Background of Jeremiah's Self-Understanding. Moses, Samuel and Psalm 22," JBL 83 (1964), pp. 153-164, especially page 158. The problem of later editorial insertions hardly arises in "Jonah," as most critical opinion now recognises, due to the obvious unity of authorship (except for the problematic "Psalm").

11) Gen 2:21; 15:12; Jud 4:21; I Sam 26:12; Isaiah 29:10; Prov 10:5; 19:15; Job 4:13; 33:15; Daniel 8:18; 10:9.

12) Interesting in the light of this assumption is Robinson's remark on r-d-m, Commentary, p. 120: "In classical Hebrew another word, like יָשֵׁן , would have been chosen."

13) See section on "the Dividing up of Quotations," below, page 73 ff.

14) See for example, Wellhausen, Propheten, p. 222, note 4:3 and 4:6; Keller, Commentary, p. 331; McGowan, Jonah, p. 634; Bewer, Commentary, pp. 12-13; Kaiser, Wirklichkeit, p. 100.

15) From its context in Deut 21:8-9, it is clear that the usage of n-t-n is a technical term for legal responsibility for blood that is shed. c.f. Keller, Commentary, p. 275 to v. 14; K. Koch, "Der Spruch 'Sein Blut bleibe auf seinem Haupt' und die Israelitische Auffassung vom vergossenen Blut," VT 12 (1962), pp. 396-416, p. 406ff, especially p. 408. For more generalised usage the term used is שָׁפַך

16) Kaiser, Wirklichkeit, p. 95.
17) Feuillet, Livre, p. 33, note a.
18) See discussion on Analysis of the "Psalm," page 52 f.

19) For confirmatory evidence of this see discussion on the "dividing up of quotations," page 73 f.

20) c.f. Num 14:12; 20:12; Deut 1:32; II Kings 17:14; Psalm 78:22; II Chron 20:20. See also Isaiah 7:9.

21) See discussion on the "psalm," page 51. c.f. U. Cassuto. A Commentary on the Book of Exodus, (Translated by I. Abrahams), Jerusalem, 1967, p. 147.

22) The only other passages where God "repents of evil" which He intended to do refer to Israel: II Sam 24:16; I Chron 21:15; (But the same idea underlies Amos 7:3, 6; Judges 2:18).

23) The significance of Jeremiah's ideas standing at an intermediate point between a traditional concept and Jonah's usage will become apparent when we deal with the specific problem of "innocent blood."

24) Jer 18:11; 25:5; 26:3; 35:15; 36:3-7; 23:14,22. See to this W.L. Holladay, "Prototype and Copies," JBL 79 pp. 351-367, especially page 355.

25) See G. von Rad, Deuteronomy (OTL), London, 1966, p. 134ff;
S. E. Loewenstamm, "Law," The World History of the Jewish People,
Vol III, Judges, Tel Aviv, 1971, pp. 231-267, p. 259.

26) See the discussion on Exodus 32:14, page 71 above.

27) One is tempted to see already in Jeremiah's usage of the phrase
"you will bring innocent blood on yourselves and upon this city and
upon its inhabitants" the beginning of a re-working of the Deuteronomy passage. Jeremiah has elsewhere re-worked such legal passages for his own "homiletic" purposes (e. g., compare Jer 3:1 with
Deut 24:1-4; Jer 3:8 with Deut 24:1; Jer 2:34 with Ex 22:1-2). The
passage in Deuteronomy 21 is the only one which deals with the col-
lective responsibility of a city for murder committed within its vi-
cinity. The reference to "innocent blood" comes at a significant
point in Jeremiah's preaching where the emphasis clearly changes
from the Temple to the city itself. (Until now Jeremiah has preached
against the Temple first and then the city (verses 6, 9, 12), despite
the priests' and prophets' attempt to shift attention to the city alone
(in their formal accusation in verse 11 before the princes.)). But
the whole problem of what lies behind the construction of the chapter
would take us too far from our thesis.

28) See above, page 68 f.
29) See above, page 70.
30) See above, page 70.
31) See above, page 72 f.
32) See above, page 65 f.
33) See discussion in the section "Tardemah" and Elijah, page 67.
34) For further discussion, see Analysis of Themes, page 102 f.
35) Feuillet, Sources, p. 171.

36) c.f. Wolff, Jonabuch, p. 17f. For an analysis of Jeremiah 36 see
M. Kessler, "Form-Critical Suggestions on Jeremiah 36," CBQ 28
(1966), pp. 389-401; M. Kessler, "The Significance of Jeremiah 36,"
ZAW 81 (1969), pp. 381-383; G. Wanke, Untersuchungen zur sog.
Baruchschrift (BZAW 122) 1971, p. 59ff.

37) See J. Bright, Jeremiah, (AncB) New York 1965, p. 180.

38) The argument from "what is not there" is always dangerous, nevertheless it is significant that the princes who were formerly "neutral"
(Chapter 26), or anti-Jeremiah (c.f. Jer 26:22 and 36:25 re the
changing role of Elnatan ben Achbor) are now advocates of Jeremiah,
whether due to a spiritual change, or in the face of new political
dangers. (See Bright, Jeremiah, p. 181f.)

39) Feuillet, Sources, p. 171; c.f. Kaiser, Wirklichkeit, p. 100.
40) Feuillet, Sources, p. 172.

NOTES to Chapter IV

41) Böhme, Komposition, p. 224.

42) H. Schmidt, "Die Komposition des Buches Jona," ZAW 25 (1905), pp. 285-310.

43) See section on "The Analysis of Structure," page 62 f.

44) c.f. H.W.Wolff, Der Prophet Joel, (BK.AT Dodekapropheton 2), Neukirchen-Vluyn, 1969, p. 58.

45) The suggestion (without any supporting evidence) that "Jonah" quotes Joel is made by Lods, Histoire, p. 587; Pfeiffer, Introduction, p.588f; Bewer, Commentary, pp. 12-13; Rudolph, Commentary, pp. 328, 360, 363; B.D.Napier, Song of the Vineyard, New York, 1962, p. 366; Bickerman, Strange, pp. 41, 44; M.H Segal, Mavo' Hammiqra', Jerusalem, 1967, p. 475. The contrary suggestion, that Joel quotes "Jonah" (without any supporting evidence) is made by M. Delcor, Les Petits Prophètes. Joel (La Sainte Bible VIII (1)), Paris, 1961, p. 136, 159. Van Hoonacker, Commentary, p. 314, suggests that Joel is more dependent than "Jonah" on earlier Biblical sources and thus suggests that "Jonah" served as a model for Joel. He is followed by Feuillet, Sens, p. 355. Those who note the similarity without attempting to explain the relationship include J.A. Thompson, Joel (Interpreter's Bible), New York, Vol. 6, 1956, p. 731.

46) H.H.Rowley, "The Prophet Jeremiah and the Book of Deuteronomy," Studies in Old Testament Prophecy, Edinburgh, 1946, pp. 157-174, p. 158.

47) For a general survey of critical opinion on dating see, for example, Thompson, Joel, p. 732f; W. Neil, "Joel," IDB, Vol 2, 1962, p. 928; more recently H.W. Wolff, Joel, pp. 2-4, who places it in the first part of the 4th century; W. Rudolph, Joel (KAT XIII 2), Gütersloh, 1971, pp. 24-29, who favours a pre-exilic dating. With regards Jonah, we subscribe to a post-exilic date, since at least the Jeremiah texts, and also some degree of canonisation, are presupposed. The problem is somewhat periferal to our study, and since we have nothing new to contribute, we prefer to leave the question of a more precise dating open.

48) See discussion on Ezekiel, page 80 f.

49) c.f. Thompson, Joel, p. 732; G.F.Wood, Joel, Obadiah (Jerome Bible Commentary), London, 1968, pp. 439-445, p. 439f; Wolff, Joel, p. 4; Rudolph, Joel, p. 27, following his pre-exilic line, sees all these as a common background of terminology shared by all cultic prophets. However, if Joel is quoting "Jonah", it argues for a more formal textual relationship in all cases of apparent quotation.

50) c.f. Joel 2:3 with Isaiah 51:3; Ezekiel 36:35; Joel 3:10 with Isaiah 2:4; Mic 4:3.

51) c.f. Wolff, Joel, p. 11.

52) Schildenberger, Sinn, p. 96, also tries to assess the relationship of the two books in terms of their characteristic literary techniques. While noting that both use quotations, and that it agrees with "Jonah's" ironic technique to put a quotation from Israel's tradition in the mouth of the king of Nineveh, he has not noted that the same device is used by Joel. His assumption, therefore, that "Jonah" quotes Joel cannot be justified on these grounds.

53) c.f. Joel 2:10 with Isaiah 13:13; 10; Joel 4:17 with Ezekiel 36:11; Isaiah 52:1.

54) See discussion on "Knowing," page 26 f.

55) Though we have noted above in the section on the fusion of texts (page 74 ff.) the tendency of the author of "Jonah" to use a quotation in its original form, but mediated by a context in a second place, it has always been the context that was modified, not the form of the quote itself. If "Jonah" is quoting Joel here in modifying the form of the quotation, he is going against his usual technique. Though this is still only "circumstantial evidence," it is consistent with the other material we have assembled.

56) Feuillet, Sources, p. 176.
57) So also Wolff, Jonabuch, Col. 854.
58) Feuillet, Sources, p. 177.

59) c.f. Isaiah 60:9; I Kings 10:22 in connection with II Chron 9:21; I Kings 22:49 in connection with II Chron 20:36.

60) Beuillet, Sources, p. 178. (Eze 27:4, 25, 26, 27; 28:2, 8).
61) Feuillet, Sources, p. 178.

62) We have, furthermore, been directed by the author already to Exodus 14 and the crossing of the Reed Sea.

63) Author's italics.
64) Feuillet, Sources, p. 178f.
65) Feuillet, ibid., p. 179.

66) Likewise Feuillet's attempt (Sources, p. 179) to relate the actions of the "repenting" king of Nineveh (Jonah 3:6) to those of the "mourning" of the princes of the sea (Eze 26:16) or of the sailors (Eze 27:30-31) is too remote: "Ainsi donc quelque chose de l'oracle contre Tyre se réalise à Ninive, mais au lieu d'être l'expression du désespoir, c'est une manifestation de repentir! Il faut en dire autant de Jonah 3:5, 6, 8 qui ressemble beaucoup à Eze 27:30-31, mais dans un cas

il s'agit de rites de deuil consécutifs à la chute de Tyr, dans l'autre de rites de pénitence destinés à empêcher la destruction de Ninive!" Unfortunately even exclamation marks do not change mourning into repentance.

67) c.f. Rudolph, Commentary, p. 328. c.f. Aalders, Problem, p. 22f.

68) c.f. S. Abramski, "Jonah ben Amittai," Gazit 17, 1959, pp. 5-10, p. 9.

69) For another argument against Feuillet, See Loretz, Herkunft, p. 24. The possibility of the Psalm being dependent on "Jonah" is equally unlikely, except in the most general terms - the idea of a storm at sea. The much greater detail of the effects of the storm suggest rather a first-hand experience which is being described; in addition it must be seen within its context in relationship to God's care of lost travellers, captives and the sick.

70) The association with this passage is already suggested in the earliest Midrashic texts - Mechilta Bo (Introduction): "And Jonah rose up to flee to Tarshish from before the presence of YHWH." And could he really flee from before the presence of YHWH?! And is it not already written: 'Whither shall I go from Thy spirit?...?'" The same association occurs frequently in more recent literature: c.f. Haller, Erzählung, p. 16; Schreiner, Eigenart, p. 12. The earliest to suggest that the idea for the first chapter came from Ps 139 seems to have been A. Thoma, "Entstehung des Büchleins Jona," ThStKr 84 (1911), pp. 479-502, p. 490f. It was refuted by L. C. Stollberg, Jona (Doctoral Dissertation), Halle, 1927, p. 15, but only on the grounds of vocabulary, not the idea in the Psalm. Interesting is the remark of Gottwald, Light, p. 523, "Jonah's experience reads like an illustration of Psalm 139.

71) A clue to the possible relationship in time of the two texts would be of help here, but most commentators today refrain from dating the Psalm, e.g. H. J. Kraus, Psalmen, II (BK. AT Band XV/2), Neukirchen, 1960, p. 917; A. Weiser, Psalmen (ATD 14-15) (6th Ed.) Göttingen, 1963, p. 554; W. S. McCullough, The Book of Psalms (Int B Vol 4), New York, 1955, p. 713. An earlier tendency to date it in the Persian period or later (e.g. C. A. Briggs, A Critical and Exegetical Commentary on the Book of Psalms (ICC), Edinburgh, 1907, Vol II, P. 493; Gunkel, Ausgewählte Psalmen, p. 269) has been replaced more recently by a move towards a 7th century date (e.g. M. Dahood, Psalms III (AncB), New York, 1970, p. 285).

72) c.f. Weiss, Einiges, p. 464f.

73) Ibn Ezra to Jonah 1:1.

74) See among modern commentaries: Cohn, Erzählkunst, p. 63n3; Delcor, Jonas, p. 278; Goitein, Observations, p. 67; A. B. Ehrlich, Randglossen zur hebräischen Bibel (Vol 5), Leipzig, 1912, p. 263; Feuillet, Sources, p. 175.

75) c.f. Trible, Studies, p. 206f, "Evil comes into the presence of Yahweh, but Jonah flees from his presence."

76) See chapter on the "Analysis of Structure", page 62 f.

Chapter V

1) We have limited ourselves to factors like word usage and inner Biblical associations and left open the problem of the more general symbolism implicit in the book itself. Various studies have explored the mythological parallels behind episodes like the rescue by the "great fish," but in the end one is left with the result that although such themes might have been available to the author (itself almost impossible to prove), the significance lies rather in how he turned them to his own purpose. Analyses of the symbolic meaning of the fish, ranging from allegorical interpretations to poetic or psycho-analytic studies, have given fascinating insights, but are so sub-jective, or so tied to preconceived systems, that they bear increas-ingly little relationship to the text itself, which remains our primary concern.

2) c.f. the remark of H. Schmidt about the interpretations of the "Ten-denz" of the book among his contemporary scholars. "Absicht und Entstehungszeit des Buches Jona," ThStKr 79 (1906), pp. 180-199, p. 182. c.f. Driver, Einleitung, p. 345f. For a list of earlier opin-ions see J. Lippl, Die zwölf kleinen Propheten I (HSAT VIII, 3), Bonn, 1937, p. 160, and also B. Wolf, Die Geschichte des Prophe-ten Jona, Berlin, 1897, p. 8f.

3) D. F. Rauber, "Literary Values in the Bible: The Book of Ruth," JBL 89 (1970), pp. 27-37.

4) Ibid., p. 36; c.f. Von Rad, Jona, p. 11f.

5) M. Perry and M. Sternberg, "The King Through Ironic Eyes, The Narrator's Devices in the Biblical Story of David and Bathsheba and Two Excurses on the Theory of the Narrative Text," Hasifrut 1, Tel Aviv, 1968, pp. 263-292 (Hebrew) (English Summary, pp. 449-452). See also the discussion on this in Hasifrut 2, 1970, by B. Arpali and U. Simon, with Perry and Sternberg's reply. (For details see Biblio-graphy.)

6) The same point has, of course, long since been made about other Biblical narratives. With regards Jonah in particular, the formula-tion of Gunkel is helpful. In discussing Jonah's anger in Chapter 4, he asks (Jonabuch, col. 640) "Woher dieser Zorn? Es ist für hebrä-ische Erzählungskunst bezeichnend, dass sie nicht imstande ist, der-gleichen innere Zustände völlig deutlich zu machen und sich höchstens

mit einigen Andeutungen darüber begnügt." The problem, however,
particularly with so late a book as "Jonah," is whether this limitation
is due to inability, or deliberate unwillingness, to reveal inner states
directly - which is a central feature in the discussion aroused by
Perry and Sternberg, and c.f. Goitein, Observations, p. 66. In line
with Gunkel here is Feuillet's remark (Sens, p. 340): "Faut-il s'éton-
ner qu'il y ait tant d'interprétations divergentes du livre de Jonas" -
c.f. Burrows, Character, p. 88. Nevertheless, something of Jonah's
character is quite definitely conveyed, and Haller is closer than Gunkel to the mark (Haller, Erzählung, p. 7): "Im Fortgang der Erzählung wird Jonas Charakter psychologisch entschlüsselt, auf eine aller-
dings unpsychologische Weise, durch das reine Medium der Erzählung.
Welch eine hohe, reife Kunst, die den Glauben in einer seiner seltsa-
men Strukturen so darzustellen vermag!" c.f. Lods, Histoire, p.594f.
Though whether Haller's "almost pathological form of Orthodoxy"
(p. 6) is more correct than Lods (p. 595) "Jonas, c'est l'opiniâtreté
d'un coeur étroit et égoiste," reminds us that beyond the ambiguity
of the writer there will always be the subjectivity of the reader.

7) A third problem, why he sits outside the city, will be discussed in
the section "Knowledge of God/Disobedience of God," page 90ff. and
again at the end, page 109 f.

8) See Von Rad, Jona, p. 13f, and the discussion by Landes, Kerygma,
especially pages 4, 22ff, 25n64. More recently Rudolph, Jona, p. 236.

9) Good, Irony, p. 45, gives both explanations, but does not deal with
why both are possible.

10) Portrait, p. 329f.

11) The observation by A.D.Cohen, "The Tragedy of Jonah," Judaism 21
(1972), pp. 164-175, p. 169, that some interpretations of Jonah's
character are "strongly suggestive of some projection of personal
attitudes" could be well substantiated.

12) See Commentary, p. 275, especially in defence of Jonah's request to
be thrown into the sea. His position is criticised by Rudolph, Jona,
p. 233, and M.E.Andrew, "Gattung and Intention of the Book of Jonah,"
Orita (Ibadan, Nigeria) 1, (1967), pp. 13-18, 78-85, especially p.79ff.
Rudolph, Jona, p. 235f, in "writing off" Jonah ("Einen bekehrten Jona gibt es nicht." p.237), gives precisely the black and white interpretation which the book itself fights against. That Jonah is never
given the benefit of the doubt is perhaps acceptable, though to call
the words of his prophecy in Nineveh an attempt to "sabotage" God's
plan, has rightly evoked an objection from Kaiser, Wirklichkeit, p. 99.
More seriously, in order to prove his point, Rudolph has to cut out
not only the "Psalm" itself, but also the suggestion in 2:2 that Jonah
prayed, (Commentary, p. 349), on the grounds that it is inconsistent

with the picture of Jonah given before and after. Other objections
to the Psalm (e.g., its apparent inappropriateness - thanksgiving
when not yet delivered) he himself successfully answers. Thus the
reasoning is circular - it is inappropriate psychologically so must
be removed to prove how psychologically inappropriate it is -
which, to quote his own words, is "textwidrig und eine Verkennung
der Absicht des Verfassers."

13) See for example, the "partial confessions," p. 119 n 56, p. 52; his
selfishness, p. 33, p. 95.

14) Goitein, Observations, p. 74.

15) So Y. Kaufmann, Religion, p. 285. But see the critique of Cohen,
Tragedy, p. 164. c.f. Good, Irony, p. 51; Landes, Kerygma, p.29;
P.R Ackroyd, Israel under Babylon and Persia (New Clarendon
Bible), London, 1970, p. 340. "The excuse for his flight was his
knowledge of this will of God to forgive. There is here a profound
recognition of the fact that the idea of a God who is a strict adherent
of a rigid system of justice, reward and punishment, is an easier
concept than that of a God of love and mercy."

16) So Abarbanel, Commentary to 1:2,3 (See Goitein, Observations,
p. 65), F. Delitzsch, "Etwas über das Buch Jona" Zeitschrift für
die Gesammte Lutherische Theologie und Kirche 1,1840, pp.112-126,
p. 114; most recently Cohen, Tragedy, p. 174f.

17) So the midrash, Pirke R. Eliezer 10 (rejected by Ibn Ezra - Commentary to 1:2). See the review of early Jewish and Christian material along these lines in Wolf, Jona, p. 12. c.f. Burrows, Character, p. 97; Good, Irony, p. 51; Gottwald, Light, p. 523; Halévy,
Recherches, p. 21: "le démenti éprouvé par sa prédiction déplut
fortement à Jonas, qui se fâcha tout rouge à la pensée que tout le
monde le prendrait pour un faux prophète." Against this argument
see Bewer, Commentary, p. 57. Goitein, Observations, p. 73, sees
Jonah's tragedy in the very success he knows will attend the prophecy for "the successful propagation of an idea makes his own activities, nay, his very existence, superfluous."

18) c.f. Bickerman, Strange, pp. 40f, 43f; Driver, Einleitung, p.344;
Gunkel, Jonabuch, Col 640; F. Nötscher, Zwölfprophetenbuch (Echter Bibel IV) Würzburg, 1948, p. 83; Keller, Portrait, p. 337,
neatly, if unconvincingly, reverses the usual interpretation of Jonah's reluctance - Jonah does not wish to preach the destruction
of Nineveh because he cannot believe that a compassionate God could
really wish him to deliver so horrible a message. c.f. Magnus, Jonah, p. 430. For a highly sensitive reading of Jonah's reaction, see
Rauber, Jonah, p. 34.

NOTES to Chapter V

19) By far the commonest interpretation. e.g. Bewer, Commentary, p. 57; Delcor, Jonas, p. 275; E. König, "Jonah" Dictionary of the Bible, New York, 1911, pp. 744-753, p. 752; Landes, Kerygma, p. 19; Lippl, Commentary, p. 174; Rudolph, Commentary, p. 325.

20) c.f. Andrew, Gattung, pp. 15, 82f; Gottwald, Light, p. 521; Smart, Jonah, p. 872; B.S. Childs "Jonah, A Study in Old Testament Hermeneutics," SJTh 11, 1958, pp. 53-61, p. 61; Scott, Sign, p. 19; Schildenberger, Sinn, p. 96; Möllerfeld, Du bist, p. 328f, who makes a strong point about the purposelessness of Jonah's flight. Fränkel, Rahamaw, p. 200f comes to the opposite conclusion: that this gap exists because the book is not primarily concerned with Jonah's motives, but with the compassion of God - and hence with the degree to which man can imitate this, whatever his motives might be.

21) This is to make the same point as Lohfink, Jona, p. 187, about the placing of verse 4:5: "Es wurde stets gefragt: Wo ist die in 4:5 beschriebene Handlung in den objektiven Gang der Ereignisse einzusetzen? Nun ist zu fragen: Entspricht es der im Jonabuch entwickelten Darstellungstechnik, wenn der Erzähler die Handlung von 4:5 gerade an dieser Stelle und in dieser Form einführt?" Lohfink, ibid., credits Wolff with making this step, but that probably belongs to Stollberg, Jona, p. 13. See further M. Weiss, "Weiteres über die Bauformen des Erzählens in der Bibel," Biblica 46 (1965), pp. 181-206, p. 182ff.

22) Cohn, Erzählkunst, p. 55.

23) Bacharach, Jonah, p. 9. c.f. Haller, Erzählung, p. 5; Landes, Kerygma, p. 14.

24) Wolff, Studien, p. 36; Gotteswort, pp. 20, 30.

25) See also to this Jepsen, Anmerkungen, p. 299, who suggests other questions which the author leads us to ask through the dramatic tension he generates.

26) Either the text merely records the fact of further conversation, c.f. Van Hoonacker, Commentary, p. 328f; Landes, Kerygma, p. 14, or shows evidence of the history of the text itself, e.g. G.W. Wade, Micah, Obadiah, Joel and Jonah (Westminster Commentaries) London, 1925, p. 126, who assumes that in compiling the book from two sources some actual communication was omitted - against Wellhausen, Propheten, who sees it as a gloss.

27) So Lanchester, Jonah, p. 59, who adds "The last part of the sentence...reads like an unintelligent addition" - unless its purpose is precisely to show they had worked it out for themselves. See

also Lohfink, Jona, p. 193 (esp n 31), whose problem with the timing of events disappears when the "anticipatory" aspect is seen. Confirmation of this view comes from Weiss, Einiges, p. 464f, whose reading of the repetitions of מלפני ה' as a form of "Erlebte Rede" (Interior Monologue) suggests strongly that Jonah did <u>not</u> tell the sailors he was fleeing from YHWH.

28) c.f. Psalm Section, page 52. In the Psalm itself two phrases are suggestive of "anticipatory" thinking. It is possible that the statement in 2:9 is an expression of Jonah's hope that the Ninevites, though repenting at first, will revert to idolatry (c.f. Psalm Section, p. 45 f., 52). A further possibility is an ironic anticipation by the author himself in the word play between בהתעטף (2:8) and ויתעלף (4:8). The full context shows the effect:

בהתעטף עלי נפשי את ה' זכרתי ותבוא אליך תפלתי .....
ויתעלף וישאל את נפשו למות.

The drowning Jonah, when his <u>soul is fainting within him</u>, prays to God for life. The angry Jonah under the withered gourd faints and asks that his soul be taken from him!

29) Psalm Section, page 53.

30) e.g., Baudissin, Einleitung, p. 597f: Minor: That heathen, through God's leadership can find His grace; that man cannot go against divine destiny. Major: That God's warnings of destruction are dependent upon the response of man. U. Cassuto "Jona" <u>Encyclopaedia Judaica</u> IX, Berlin, 1932, Col. 268-272, Col. 269f, lists four: a. God's will is achieved despite all human opposition. b. Repentance lies not in external fasting and sackcloth, but turning from sinful conduct. c. True repentance averts the evil decree. d. For the sake of innocent children and animals all are spared. Gottwald, Light, p. 522f: The inescapability of God, the purity of the prophetic motives, and the universal love of God with the attendant universal obligation of Israel. c.f. Van Hoonacker, Commentary, p. 317, König, Jonah, p. 752, Lods, Histoire, p. 586.

31) Kaiser, Wirklichkeit, p. 93ff.

32) Thus sets (i) and (iv) (see overleaf) overlap, but in running them together a significant aspect of the book would be lost.

33) e.g., Goitein, Observations, p. 64. c.f. E. Jacob, "Sagen und Legenden im A. T.," RGG (3rd Ed.), Vol. 5, Göttingen, 1959, Col 1302-1308. Col 1306 on Jonah: "Das Gehorsam noch wichtiger ist als das missionarische Interesse." In this sense must be understood Keller's assertion that the book of Jonah is "l'histoire d'un prophète," with the emphasis on "prophète" (Portrait, p. 331). Along the same line, and even more directly describing our theme

is the remark of A. Neher to Jonah's request to be hurled into the sea (Essence p. 293): "A la vie enchaînée par Dieu, il préfère la mort dans les éléments déchaînés de la nature libre."

34) See, e.g. Haller, Erzählung, p. 49, on the side of Jonah revealed by the "Psalm", and Von Rad, Jona, p. 13f. c.f. Rauber, Jonah, p. 36.

35) Haller, Erzählung, p. 23.
36) See Psalm Section, page 132 n 61.
37) See section on The Power of God/The Freedom of Man.

38) For the problem of the position of 4:5, see discussion in the section on the Analysis of Structure, page 58.

39) See Psalm Section, page 45 f., 52.

40) This line of interpretation has led to the accusation of Jonah as "bloodthirsty" - Pfeiffer, Introduction, p. 588; waiting with "hate in his heart" - Robinson, Commentary, p. 125. Rauber, Jonah, p. 35, suggests that this is a mistake made by reading too realistically what is an "exaggerated comic mode." Jonah is "the man with the idée fixe, and the artist's emphasis is not upon blood but upon the absurdity of the situation and the bewildering paradox which has developed."

41) For these two explanations see Good, Irony, p. 51. c.f. Landes, Kerygma, p. 29.

42) Perhaps his sitting down miqqedem (to the East) of the city, in addition to its rhythmical and emphasising functions (Cohn, Erzählkunst, p. 68) also plays on the meaning of the root qdm. Just as he "anticipated" and fled to Tarshish (c.f. p. 79), so he "anticipates" again the fate of the city.

43) See discussion, page 107 ff.
44) See page 88   and the analysis of "knowing," page 26.
45) See page 52.
46) See section on the Analysis of Language, page 26 ff.
47) See section on the Growing Phrase, page 31 ff.
48) The purpose of the gourd is "to deliver him from his evil."
49) See page 31 ff.
50) See page 24.

51) For a different interpretation of the significance of אבד , see Trible, Studies, p. 195f, who puts emphasis on the theme of destruction implied in the repetitions rather than the specific relationship to Jonah.

52) See Analysis of Quotations, page 76 f. c.f. Kaiser, Wirklichkeit, p. 100.

146

53) For a discussion on the various interpretations of the book of Jonah in Midrash and the Church Fathers, see E.E. Urbach, "Teshuvat Anshey Nineveh," in Tarbiz 20 (1950), pp. 118-122; Wolf, Jona, p. 5ff. For a briefer treatment, see A.M. Goldberg, "Jonah in der jüdischen Schriftauslegung," BiKi, 1962, pp. 17-18.

54) See Analysis of Quotations, page 70.
55) See further discussion in Traditional Teaching/New Experience, page 103.
56) The incongruity of this is noted by Good, Irony, p. 44.

57) See page 142 n 12. One has sometimes the feeling that the author makes Jonah so bad that he is testing the reader's ability to feel pity for the prophet, just as Jonah was tested by Nineveh. (For a similar observation, see Scott, Sign, p. 24f.)

58) c.f. Haller, Erzählung, p. 28f; Cohen, Erzählkunst, p. 59; Rudolph, Jona, p. 234.

59) c.f. Goitein, Observations, p. 66.

60) Andrew, Gattung, p. 78f, tries to synthesise the work of Wolff and Keller in suggesting that the emphasis lies both on the character of Jonah and the action of God. But this is to ignore the well-developed "character" of the pagans.

61) See Analysis of Language and of Structure.
62) See page 19 f.
63) Cohn, Erzählkunst, p. 74. c.f. Wolff, Studien, p. 36.
64) See above, page 20 f.
65) See the Section Power of God/Freedom of Man, page 109 f.
66) See page 109.
67) Studien, p. 118.
68) See Psalm Section, page 41 ff.
69) c.f. Cohn, Erzählkunst, p. 70, and see the section on "Growing Phrase."

70) An interesting interpretation comes in Midrash Tehillim 9:16 (to Psalm 9:21b): "Let the nations know that they are but men." Whenever in Scripture you find the word "Adam," it means a man of low degree, e.g., Psalm 36:7, "Man and beast." i.e., a man whose understanding is like a beast.

71) c.f. Scott, Sign, p. 24. This is against the majority of commentators who base themselves on analogies with Deut 1:39 and Isaiah 7:15-16, etc. e.g. Gunkel, Jonabuch, Col. 639; Van Hoonacker, Commentary, p. 338; Lippl, Commentary, p. 175; Goitein, Observations, p. 76; Lanchester, Jonah, p. 31; Halévy, Recherches, p. 18. Most recently Kaiser, Wirklichkeit, p. 92n9. For another dissenting voice, see Burrows, Character, p. 83n5.

72) See page 33 ff.

73) That the sailors come even closer to Jonah's position of relationship to YHWH is underlined by the terms "sacrifice" and "vows"
used of both the sailors (1:16) and Jonah (2:10).

74) c.f. Orlinsky, Nationalism, p. 231.

75) See page 32 f.

76) For a more detailed discussion, see Analysis of Quotations, page 71.

77) See page 27.

78) This is frequently recognised as the central idea of the book - see,
for example, Kaufmann, Religion, p. 282ff; Loretz, Gotteswort,
p. 18. See also Dentan, Affinities, p. 50.

79) See discussion on "innocent blood," page 72ff. and "Hallel," page 70

80) See page 71 f.

81) See page 65 . While accepting Kaufmann's recognition that the evocation of Sodom is to show a new attitude to it (p. 385), we cannot accept that the main purpose is to demonstrate teshuvah. This is in
view of Kaufmann's dating (pre-exilic) of the book, and the fact of
the continuation of the book itself into the fourth chapter. Anyway,
Kaufmann's view would mean downgrading the significance of Nineveh which is mentioned in "Jonah," and upgrading disproportionately
the meaning of Sodom which is not mentioned in "Jonah."

82) Among the reminiscences which are harder to prove is the suggestion
of Baudissin, Einleitung, p. 596, that God's questions to Jonah in
Chapter 4 are modelled on God's question to Cain in Genesis 4:6-7.
c.f. W. Rudolph, Commentary, p. 328. This would give added dimensions to Jonah's selfishness, evoking the memory of Cain's
jealousy for Abel and thus suggesting the roots of Jonah's problem
with Nineveh (that was now favoured by God). Cohen, Tragedy, p. 171,
evokes this connection in developing his idea that חרה in both these
cases means despair (suggesting a depressive illness in Jonah). Unfortunately this does not account for all the uses of the word in "Jonah," and the depression has to disappear conveniently for Jonah to
make his proclamation. More significantly, since he has evoked Cain,
there is no suggestion of guilt-feelings in Jonah's death wish, which
one might have expected if such illness was being described.

83) See above, page 45.

84) See the discussion of "עברי", page 100f.

85) This gives us a basis for some evaluation of the idea that Jonah
"represents" Israel. Such suggestions are not usually tied too closely to the text itself. Perhaps this is understandable in the case of
attempts to allegorise (Jonah as Israel preferring to be a business
man visiting Tarshish than a prophet - P. Kleinert Obadiah, Jonah,
etc. (Die Heilige Schrift) Leipzig, 1868, p. 16f); but surprising

when the attempt is made to understand the more overt meaning of the book: e.g. Driver, Einleitung, p. 346; Cheyne, Study, p. 214; Bewer, Commentary, p. 64; Wolff, Jonabuch, Col. 854. For Jonah as the incarnation of "Jewish particularism", see Lods, Jonah, p. 584. c.f. Loretz, Buch, p. 34; McGowan, Jonah, p. 637; Feuillet, Sens, p. 346; of "prophetic discontent" see Halévy, Recherches, p. 42; as "the nation, insofar as it rejects its commission to be a light to the Gentiles," Smart, Jonah, p. 873. The most general significance given to Jonah's "particularism" is that of Napier, Song, p. 366, who sees the book as a "rebuke of all provincial pride, all arrogance born of parochialism...the...most timelessly pertinent repudiation of exclusivism - religious, theological, ethnic, political, national...." For a discussion on whether Jonah represents "man," "prophet" or "Israel," see J.H. Stek, "The Message of the Book of Jonah" CTJ 4 (1969) pp. 23-50, p. 38ff.

86) In a similar way the "suffering servant" passages present different interpretations as the perspective changes - the prophet himself or another, the future Messiah, Israel as a nation.

87) c.f. G. Von Rad, Old Testament Theology, Vol. 2 (Trans. D.G.M. Stalker), Edinburgh, 1965, p. 219f.

88) Ackroyd, Israel, p. 338.
89) Von Rad, Theology, p. 292.
90) Kaiser, Wirklichkeit, p. 92.

91) A remark by Loretz, Gotteswort, p. 35, gives a hint towards this in discussing Jonah's quotation in 4:2 which is an old traditional belief and no new creation. "Die Jona-Erzählung bemüht sich nun, deutlich zu machen, dass die Einstellung des Propheten Jona zu den Heiden im Widerspruch zur Überlieferung Israels steht."

92) c.f. Haller, Erzählung, p. 6.
93) c.f. De Boer, Jona, p. 101.
94) See above, page 62 f.
95) c.f. Abarbanel to 1:8, 9.

96) For a study on the development of this term, see L.I. Baeck, "Der Ibri," MGWJ 83 (1939) (N.F. 47 (1963)), pp. 66-80. For further literature, see Rudolph, Commentary, p. 342n8.

97) c.f. Keller, Commentary, p. 274. It becomes more paradoxical still when we recall that the accompanying title of YHWH as "God of the Heavens" is used almost exclusively with regards self-identification to foreigners in post-exilic times, most notably in II Chronicles and Nehemiah (and in Ezra and Daniel in aramaic). (c.f. Andrews, Yahweh; Bewer, Commentary, p. 12f; Haller, Erzählung, p. 21n33.)

98)   Keller, Commentary, p. 274.

99)   Jepsen, Anmerkungen, p. 300.

100)   c.f. Wolff, Studien, p. 37.

101)   See discussion on the Analysis of Structure, page 60 ff.

102)   More problematic is the evocation of Moses by Jonah's quotation of a form of the "Thirteen Attributes." Since variations on this formula occur several times, the specificity of the allusion to Moses here is somewhat weakened. We shall deal with this at the end of the section. See page 104 f.

103)   c.f. Cohn, Erzählkunst, p. 99n1; Good, Irony, p. 51; Kaiser, Wirklichkeit, p. 100; McGowan, Jonah, p. 636f.

104)   See Analysis of Quotations, page 67 ff.

105)   Reading God's command "Go, return on your way" (I Kings 19:15) as a formula of rejection - as it is later used by Elijah himself (with bitter irony) when Elisha delays following him. (I Kings 19:20.)

106)   At the same time the tragic struggle of Jeremiah and his suffering is also brought into mind. c.f. Rauber, Jonah, p. 33.

107)   c.f. Wolff, Studien, p. 17f.

108)   Sources, p. 174f.

109)   Keller, Portrait, p. 338f; Commentary, p. 268.

110)   See Analysis of Quotations, page 74 f.

111)   By this reading, יבשה is seen primarily in its "Reed Sea" context - the dry land on which the children of Israel walked in safety under God's protection. See discussion in the Analysis of Quotations, page 65 f.

112)   See Analysis of Quotations, page 75.

113)   c.f. Bewer, Commentary, p. 8; Burrows, Character, p. 103; Feuillet, Sources, p. 168; Rudolph, Commentary, p. 335; Ackroyd, Israel, p. 338; W. Scarlett Jonah (Int B Vol 6) New York, 1956, p. 876.

114)   Cohen, Tragedy, p. 174.

115)   H. Winckler, Altorientalische Forschungen, II Leipzig, 1898, pp. 260-265, p. 262 (an opinion later retracted, according to K. Budde, "Jonah," Jewish Encyclopaedia, Vol. 7, New York, 1916, pp. 225-226, p. 226); Gottwald, Light, p. 520.

116)   Bewer, Commentary, p. 8; Wolff, Gotteswort, p. 23; Ellul, Livre, p. 4; W.O.E. Oesterley and T.H. Robinson An Introduction to the Books of the Old Testament London, 1934, p. 377.

117) Good, Irony, pp. 41-42; c.f. König, Jonah, p. 746. Van Hoonacker, Commentary, p. 318, suggests that the author chose Nineveh as a symbol from the past of a wicked pagan city (so as not to upset contemporary sensitivities by suggesting that God's mercy extended to an existing enemy). Then he had to find a divine messenger from the Assyrian period - and hence chose Jonah. c.f. Oesterley and Robinson, Introduction, p. 376. Schildenberger, Sinn, p. 96ff, 100f, suggests conversely that Jonah's story was deliberately made so unlike anything that might have happened to the known historical Jonah that the reader at once knew he was supposed to understand it as a lesson for himself.

118) Budde, Jonah, pp. 227-230, suggests that this support by YHWH of Jeroboam despite his disloyalty, provides a model for the "midrash" of Jonah, which shows why God does not at once destroy the heathen, but gives them time to repent. For a survey of the "Jonah as Midrash" position, see Burrows, Character, p. 88f and the attempt to clarify the category "Midrash" by Wright, Midrash.

119) For the idea that the forty days warning is an implicit call to do repentance, see W. Zimmerli, "Promise and Fulfillment," Interpretation 15 (1961), pp. 310-338, p. 321. c.f. Stek, Message, p. 32. Bickerman, Strange, p. 32, gives early traditional Christian views for and against this reading.

120) An allusion to the exile has been seen by Smart, Jonah, p. 886, in the quotation from Psalm 42:7 in Jonah's "Psalm." c.f. the cautious statement of P.R. Ackroyd, Exile and Restoration (OTL), London, 1968, p. 245.

121) In line with this is the suggestion of Sellin, Das Zwölfprophetenbuch (KAT) (2nd and 3rd Ed.) 1929, p. 285f, of a folk literature concerning the disobedience of prophets against God's mission, thus "compensating" for the hard words of the prophets against them. Into such a category come the Elijah tales, the story of Gehazi and of Bileam - tales which are notable for their wider horizons and international stress. This is valuable for its recognition of a critical element in these legends and accords with the humorous quality of "Jonah," which may thus represent the culmination of such a tradition.

122) See Analysis of Quotations, page 69.

123) As with all the categories we have examined, this further level of interpretation in no way contradicts the "simple meaning of the text," but rather serves to reinforce it, helping to fill out the character, and thus explain the motives and actions of Jonah.

124) c.f. Von Rad, Theology, p. 292. "Yet the prophetic proclivity for self-questioning - one of the best aspects of its spirit - once again sprang to life in this little book. It is worth noticing that one of the last utterances of Israelite prophecy is so devastatingly self-critical."

125) See above, page 102.

126) c.f. Feuillet, Sources, p. 171, 173, and especially Kessler, Form, p. 390f.

127) c.f. Haller, Erzählung, p. 28n36.

128) Feuillet, Sources, p. 169, recognises that "Jonah" expands upon the Elijah events without drawing any conclusion from this.

129) This would accord with the critical line running through the Old Testament with regard to miracles - not as to their existence, but as to their relevance. c.f. Ellul, Livre, p. 1. God's signs for Moses (Exodus 4:1-10) are a concession to the people's need of proof that he is God's messenger; God himself laments that despite all the wonders they still do not believe Him (Numbers 14:11); Elijah is unsuccessful despite the spectacular miracle before the prophets of Baal, and most significantly in our context, God is not to be found in the wind, earthquake and fire, but in the "still, small voice." c.f. Leibovitz, Iyunim, p. 121ff.

130) Significantly Jonah is never called "prophet" in the book. c.f. Wolff, Jonabuch, col. 855; Gotteswort, p. 23.

131) A number of problems are usually discussed in the literature which come into this category:
(a) That God's word is always fulfilled despite the unwillingness/opposition of his prophets/of man. c.f. Andrew, Gattung, p. 14; Delcor, Jonas, p. 276.
(b) That God's mercy is greater than His justice. c.f. G. Cohn, "Jonah, Book of," Encyclopaedia Judaica, Vol. 10, Jerusalem, 1972, col. 169-173, col. 172; Jepsen, Anmerkungen, p. 299. Goitein, Observations, p. 76, expresses it: "God's pity with man is in the last instance not determined by man's behaviour, but by far more constant factors. Better said, between man's atonement and God's grace there is an interdependence which is veiled from human comprehension."
(c) A combination of the above two is suggested by Van Hoonacker, Commentary, p. 317, one proposition found in each of the two parts of the book (Chapters 1-2/3-4).
(d) The theme of the mercy of God overcoming His judgement is sometimes coupled with the particularist/universalist argument - that God's mercy extends to all nations: "Die Allgemeinheit der

göttlichen Gnade, gegenüber menschlichen aus Eigenwillen und Stolz hervorgehenden Particularismus - das ist das Thema." Delitzsch, Etwas, p. 120. See also Bewer, Commentary, p. 7; Andrew, Gattung, p. 85; Rudolph, Commentary, p. 368.

(e) A variation on the mercy/justice theme is a more direct concern with the problem of the non-fulfillment of prophecies of destruction. c.f. Bickerman, Strange, p. 38; Budde, Jonah, p. 229; Wellhausen, Propheten, p. 222; Schildenberger, Sinn, p. 100; Feuillet, Sens, p. 345, who also tackles the problem of the true and false prophet.

132) c.f. Rauber, Jonah, p. 32. Rudolph's assertion (Commentary, p. 326), that something has happened which he wished to prevent by his flight, namely that pagans find their way to God, is reading more into Jonah's motivations than his quite specific reluctance to preach against Nineveh would suggest.

133) That Jonah must now obey is underlined by the change in the final part of the sentence:

(1:2 וקרא עליה כי עלתה רעתם לפני
(3:2 וקרא אליה את הקריאה אשר אנכי דבר אליך

The latter part of 1:2 may mean "cry against her because their evil has come up before me" or "that their evil has come up before me." i.e., in either case Jonah is given a free hand to make his prophetic statement. In 3:2 he may only "cry to her" the particular preaching God gives (c.f. Haller, Erzählung, p. 31). Though על and אל may be similar in meaning, the change suggests also the change in his prophetic status. That the final part of 3:2 is identical with Exodus 6:29b (where God speaks to Moses) reminds us that Moses too was unwilling to go on a mission - though he did not need such drastic persuasion as Jonah.

134) Jepsen, Anmerkungen, p. 239.

135) c.f. Wolff, Studien, p. 33, and the critique by Andrew, Gattung, p. 79.

136) c.f. Möllerfeld, Du bist, p. 329f. To this point we have also been led by our analysis of the different usage of the names of God through Chapters 1-3 and in Chapter 4. See page 37.

137) See fuller account in the Analysis of Language, page 30 f.

138) The contrast is most clearly seen by comparison with 1:3b where another series of actions by Jonah is recorded.

139) See Analysis of Language, page 29 f.

140) Good, Irony, p. 48f. See König, Jonah, p. 745, who argues against Wolf, Jona, p. 21f, that this word was used "with intentional ambiguity."

NOTES to Chapter V

141)   See Psalm Section, page 41.

142)   c.f. page 20f. Also the symmetrical structure of Chapter 4 (see
         page 56 and diagram 4b) which sets the two in exactly balanced
         opposition to each other. Despite the ironic overtones, the extent
         of man's freedom is not underestimated here. A further structural
         element is also of significance. Chapters 1 and 3 parallel each
         other, showing two different reactions of Jonah to the same call
         of God. In Chapter 1 where he rebels, the whole chapter has to
         deal with all the consequences, dangers and confusions caused by
         his flight, with everything continually revolving round the figure
         of the prophet. In Chapter 3 when he obeys and allows God's words
         to speak through him, he quite literally disappears from the scene,
         only reappearing at the very end, his personality no longer intruding
         into the direct effect produced by the words of God.

143)   c.f. Wolff, Studien, p. 37; Lohfink, Jona, p. 197n40.
144)   See discussion, page 91.

145)   Andrew in emphasising the reader involvement concludes with the
         idea: "But the fact that the book is first of all about Yahweh and
         Jonah, and even about Yahweh and the reader, before it is about
         Jonah and the peoples, means this: that no one can hope to establish
         a relation with the peoples as real people and not just as "types"
         before he has recognised that he would actually prefer to see them
         destroyed and, through this radical admission, has fully accepted
         God's mercy towards them." Gattung, p. 85.

146)   B.D. Eerdmans, The Religion of Israel, Leiden, 1947, p. 176.
         c.f. F. Dykema, "Het Boek Jona," N.Th.T. 25 (1936), pp. 338-347,
         p. 338. c.f. Baudissin, Einleitung, p. 598, who suggests that Nine-
         veh stands here for Babel. For the answer of Rudolph to Eerdmans,
         see Commentary, p. 329.

147)   c.f. Targum to Nahum 1:1.
148)   c.f. page 118 n 36.

149)   c.f. Napier, Song, p. 367. "To the pious protest of orthodox in-
         stitutionalism that God is architecturally contained, Jonah's
         author simply laughs. 'Don't be ridiculous...here God is now re-
         ceiving praise in the most incongruous of all places, the belly of
         a great fish...'
         "To all claims of God's exclusive love and concern for one people...
         this preaching story-teller replies in effect. 'Don't be ridiculous,
         for here He is now loving the most incongruous, the most improb-
         able, of all people, the Assyrians...'"

BIBLIOGRAPHY

AALDERS, G.Ch. The Problem of the Book of Jonah. London, 1948

ABEL, E. and others. Überall ist Ninive. Das Buch Jona. (Arbeitshefte zur Bibelwoche und für Gruppenarbeit 8) Stuttgart, 1972.

ABEL, F.M. "Le Culte de Jonas en Palestine" JPOS 2. 1922, pp. 175 - 183.

ABRABANEL, I. Peruš 'Al N'bi' im Uk'tubim. Warsaw, 1862.

ABRAMSKI, S. "Jonah Ben 'Amittai" Gazit 17. 1959, pp. 5 - 10.

ACKROYD, P.R. Exile and Restoration (OTL). London, 1968.

ACKROYD, P.R. Israel under Babylon and Persia. (New Clarendon Bible) London, 1970.

ADAR, Z. The Biblical Narrative. Jerusalem, 1959.

ALONZO DIAZ, J. "Paralelos entre la Narracion del Libro de Jonas y la Parabola del Hijo Prodigo" Biblica 40. 1959, pp. 632 - 648.

ALONZO DIAZ, J. "Difficultades que plantea la interpretación de la narración de Jonás como puramente didáctica y soluciones que ne suelen dar." EstB. 1959, pp. 351 - 374.

ALONZO, J. "Leccion teologica del libro de Jonas" Miscelanea Antonio Perez Goyena. (Estudios Ecclesiasticos. Numero Extraordinario Vol. 35) Madrid, 1960, pp. 79 - 93.

ALONSO-SCHÖKEL, L. "Die stilistische Analyse bei den Propheten" VT.S 7. 1959. pp. 154 - 164.

ALONSO-SCHÖKEL, L. "Erzählkunst im Buche der Richter" Biblica 42. 1962, pp. 143 - 172.

ANDREW, M.E. "Gattung and Intention of the Book of Jonah" Orita 1. Ibadan, Nigeria, 1967, pp. 13 - 18, 78 - 85.

ANDREWS, D.K. "Yahweh the God of the Heavens" Essays in Honour of T.J. Meek. Toronto, 1964, pp. 45 - 57.

ANTIN, P. "Saint Cyprien et Jonas" RB 68. 1961, pp. 412 - 414.

ARPALI, B. "Caution: A Biblical Story" Hasifrut. 2. 1970, pp. 580 - 597 (Hebrew) (English Summary, pages 684 - 686).

AUERBACH, E. Mimesis. (Trans. W.R. Trask) Princeton, 1953 (= Mimesis, Berne 1946).

AUGÉ, R. Profetes Menors. (La Biblia XVI) Montserrat, 1957.

BACHARACH, J. Jonah Ben 'Amittai W''Eliyahu. Jerusalem, 1959.

BACHYA BEN ASHER. Kithbey Rabbenu Bachya. A. Shaval (ed.). Jerusalem, 1970.

BAECK, L.I. "Der Ibri" MGWJ 83. (N.F. 47) (1939/1963), pp. 66 - 80.

BALSCHEIT, B. Der Gottesbund. Einführung in das Alte Testament. Zurich, 1943.

BARTH, C. Die Errettung vom Tode in den individuellen Klage- und Dankliedern des Alten Testaments. Zollikon, 1947.

BAUDISSIN, W.v. Einleitung in die Bücher des Alten Testaments. Leipzig, 1901.

BAUER, J.B. "Drei Tage" Biblica 39. 1958, pp. 354 - 358.

BAUMGARTEN, W. "Ein Kapitel vom hebräischen Erzählungsstil" FRLANT N.F. 19. 1923, pp. 145 - 157.

BEN CHORIN, S. Die Antwort des Jona. Zum Gestaltwandel Israels. Hamburg-Volksdorf, 1956.

BENTZEN, A. Introduction to the Old Testament. 2d Ed. Copenhagen, 1952.

BEWER, J.A. A Critical and Exegetical Commentary on Joel. (ICC) Edinburgh, 1911.

BEWER, J.A. A Critical and Exegetical Commentary on Jonah. (ICC) Edinburgh, 1912.

BICKERMAN, E.J. Four Strange Books of the Bible. New York, 1967.

BIRD, T.E. The Book of Jona. (The Westminster Version of the Sacred Scriptures. The Old Testament) London, 1938.

BISER, E. "Zum frühchristlichen Verständnis des Buches Jonas" BiKi 1962, pp. 19 - 21.

BLANK, S.H. "'Doest Thou Well To Be Angry?' A Study in Self-Pity" HUCA 26. 1925, pp. 29 - 41.

BÖHL, F.M.T. "Wortspiele im Alten Testament" JPOS 6. 1926, pp. 196 - 212.

BÖHME, W. "Die Komposition des Buches Jona" ZAW 7, 1887, pp. 224 - 284.

BOMAN, A.T. "Jahve og Elohim i Jonaboken" NTT 1936, pp. 159 - 168.

BRIGGS, C.A. A Critical and Exegetical Commentary on the Book of Psalms. (ICC) 2 Vols. Edinburgh, 1907.

BRIGHT, J. Jeremiah. (AncB) New York, 1965.

BUBER, M. The Prophetic Faith. New York, 1949.

BUBER, M. and ROSENZWEIG, F. Die Schrift und ihre Verdeutschung. Berlin, 1936.

BUBER, M. and ROSENZWEIG, F. Bücher der Kündung. Köln, 1958.

BUDDE, K. "Vermutungen zum 'Midrasch des Buches der Könige'" ZAW 12. 1892, pp. 37 - 51

BUDDE, K. "Jonah", "Jonah, Book of" Jewish Encyclopaedia. Vol 7. New York, 1916, pp. 225 - 230.

BUNSEN, C.C.J. Gott in der Geschichte. Vol 1. Leipzig 1857.

BURROWS, M. "The Literary Category of the Book of Jonah" Translation and Understanding the Old Testament (Essays in Honour of H.G. May). New York, 1970, pp. 80 - 107.

CAMPBELL, J. The Hero With a Thousand Faces. New York, 1949.

CASANOWICZ, I.M. "Paranomasia in the Old Testament" JBL 11. 1892, pp. 105 - 167.

CASSUTO, U. "Jona" Encyclopaedia Judaica. Vol 9. Berlin, 1932, Col. 268 - 272.

CASSUTO, U. A Commentary on the Book of Exodus (Trans. I. Abrahams). Jerusalem, 1967.

CHEYNE, T.K. "Jonah, A Study in Jewish Folklore and Religion" Theological Review. London 14, 1877, pp. 211 - 219.

CHEYNE, T.K. "Jonah (Book)" Encyclopaedia Biblica. London, 1901, Col. 2565 - 2571.

CHILDS, B.S. "Jonah, A Study in Old Testament Hermeneutics" SJTh 11. 1958, pp. 53 - 61.

COHEN, A.H. "The Tragedy of Jonah" Judaism 21. 1972, pp. 164 - 175.

COHN, G.H. Das Buch Jona im Lichte der biblischen Erzählkunst (Studia Semitica Neerlandica 12). Assen, 1969.

COHN, G.H. "Jonah, Book of" Encyclopaedia Judaica. Vol 10. Jerusalem, 1971, Col. 169 - 173.

CORNILL, C.H. Einleitung in die kanonischen Bücher des Alten Testaments. Tübingen, 1913.

COUTURIER, G.P. Jeremiah (Jerome Biblical Commentary). London, 1968, pp. 306 - 336.

DAHOOD, M. Psalms III. (AncB) New York, 1970.

DE BOER, P.A.H. "Jona" Zoals er gezegd is over Jeremia. (Phoenix Bijbel Pockets) Antwerp, 1964, pp. 93 - 102.

DEDEN, D. "Jonas (Buch)" Bibel Lexikon 2d Ed. Tübingen, 1968, Col. 876 - 877.

DELCOR, M. Les Petits Prophètes. Joel, Jonas, etc. (La Sainte
    Bible) Paris, 1961.

DELITZSCH, F. "Etwas über das Buch Jona" Zeitschrift für die Ge-
    sammte Lutherische Theologie und Kirche 1. 1840, pp. 112 - 126.

DELL'OCA, R. "El libro de Jonas" Revista Biblica. 26. 1964, pp. 129 -
    139.

DENTAN, R.C. "The Literary Affinities of Exodus 34, 6f" VT 13. 1963,
    pp. 34 - 51.

DIGGES, M.L. "Jona The Reluctant Prophet" Worship 36. 1962, pp. 321 -
    326.

DIJKEMA, F. "Het Boek Jona" NThT 25. 1936, pp. 338 - 347.

DRIVER, S.R. Einleitung in die Literatur des alten Testaments. Berlin,
    1896.

DUHM, B. "Anmerkungen zu den Zwölf Propheten XIV Buch Jona" ZAW
    1911, pp. 200 - 204.

EERDMANS, B.D. The Religion of Israel. Leiden, 1947.

EHRLICH, A.B. Randglossen zur hebräischen Bibel. Vol. 5. Leipzig,
    1912.

EISSFELDT, O. "Amos und Jona in volkstümlicher Überlieferung"
    ....und fragten nach Jesus. Beiträge aus Theologie, Kirche
    und Geschichte. Festschrift für Ernst Barnikol. Berlin, 1964,
    pp. 9 - 13.

EISSFELDT, O. The Old Testament. An Introduction (Trans. P.R. Ack-
    royd). Oxford, 1965. (= Einleitung in das Alte Testament (3rd
    Ed.) Tübingen, 1964).

EITAN, I. "La Repetition de la Racine en Hebreu" JPOS 1. 1921,
    pp. 171 - 186.

ELLIGER, K. Liber XII Prophetarum (Biblia Hebraica Stuttgartensia).
    Stuttgart, 1970.

ELLUL, J. "Le Livre de Jonas" Cahiers Bibliques de "Foi et Vie."
    1952.

EMPSON, W. Seven Types of Ambiguity. (2nd Ed.) London, 1947.

ENGNELL, I. Critical Essays on the Old Testament. London, 1970.

ERBT, W. Elia, Elisa, Jona (Untersuchungen zur Geschichte der He-
    bräer I). Leipzig, 1907.

EWALD, H. Die Propheten des Alten Bundes (Vol. 2). Stuttgart, 1840.

FEUILLET, A. "Les Sources du livre de Jonas" RB 54. 1947, pp. 161
    - 186.

FEUILLET, A. "Le Sens du livre de Jonas" RB 54. 1947, pp. 340 - 361.

FEUILLET, A. "Jonas (Le Livre de)" Dictionnaire de la Bible Supplément (Vol. 4). Paris, 1949, col. 1104 - 1131.

FEUILLET, A. Le Livre de Jonas (La Sainte Bible). Paris, 1966.

FINGERT, H.H. "Psychoanalytic Study of the Minor Prophet, Jonah" PR 1954, pp. 55 - 65.

FISH, H. "The Analogy of Nature: A Note on the Structure of Old Testament Imagery" JThS 1955, pp. 161 - 173.

FLANAGAN, J.W. "Court History or Succession Document? A Study of 2 Samuel 9 - 20 and 1 Kings 1 - 2" JBL 91. 1972, pp. 172 - 181.

FOHRER, G. Introduction to the Old Testament. (Tr. D. Green) London, 1970. (= E. Sellin - G. Fohrer Einleitung in das Alte Testament (10th Ed.) Heidelberg, 1965)

FRÄNKEL, L. "W'raḥamaw 'Al Kol Ma' 'assaw" Ma' ayanot 9. Jerusalem, 1967, pp. 193 - 207.

FRÄNKEL, L. "Ha' antitezah k'yesod siphruti b'miqra'" Hammiqra' w'toldot yisra' el. Jerusalem, 1972, pp. 129 - 146.

FRANSEN, I. "Le Livre de Jonas" Bible et Vie Chretienne. 1961, pp. 33 - 39.

FREEDMAN, D.N. "Jonah 1 : 4b" JBL 77. 1958, pp. 161 - 162.

FROMM, E. You Shall Be As Gods. New York, 1966.

GAUTIER, L. Introduction à l'Ancien Testament. Paris, 1914.

GINZBERG, L. The Legends of the Jews (6th Ed.) Vol. 4. Philadelphia, 1954.

GOITEIN, S.D. "Some Observations on Jonah" JPOS 17. 1937, pp. 63 - 77.

GOITEIN, S.D. ⟨Iyunim Bammiqra⟩. Tel Aviv, 1957.

GOLDBERG, A.M. Das Buch Jonas. Freiburg, 1959.

GOLDBERG, A.M. "Jonas in der jüdischen Schriftauslegung" BiKi 1962, pp. 17 - 18.

GOLDMAN, M.D. "The Root 'NQY'" ABR 4. 1954-5, pp. 51-55.

GOLDMAN, S. "Jonah, Introduction and Commentary" The Twelve Prophets (Soncino Books of the Bible). Ed. A. Cohen. London, 1948.

GOOD, E.M. Irony in the Old Testament. Philadelphia, 1965. [Repr. Sheffield: Almond, 1981]

GORDIS, R. Poets, Prophets and Sages. Indiana, 1971.

GOTTWALD, N.K. A Light To The Nations. New York, 1959.

GREENBERG, H. "Go To Nineveh" The Inner Eye. New York, 1953, pp. 57-61.

GREENBERG, M. "The Biblical Conception of Asylum" JBL 78. 1959, pp. 125 - 132.

GRÜNEWALD, H. I. "Das Buch Jona" Udim 2. 1971. (Zeitschrift der Rabbinerkonferenz in der Bundesrepublik Deutschland.) pp. 69 - 88.

GUILLAUME, A. "Paranomasia in the Old Testament" JSSt 9. 1964, pp. 282 - 290

GUNKEL, H. Ausgewählte Psalmen (3rd Ed.). Göttingen, 1911.

GUNKEL, H. "Jonabuch" RGG (2nd Ed.) Vol. 3. Tübingen, 1929, Col. 638 - 643.

GUNKEL, H. "The Poetry of the Psalms" Old Testament Essays. London, 1927, pp. 118 - 142.

GUNKEL, H. and BEGRICH, J. Einleitung in die Psalmen. Göttingen, 1933. (2nd Ed. Göttingen 1966)

GUNKEL, H. Genesis. (HK I, 1) (6th Ed.) Göttingen, 1964.

HAARBECK, A. Unterwegs nach Ninive. (Der Gemeinde zur Bibelwoche 1972/73.) Berlin, 1972.

HALÉVY, J. "Recherches Bibliques. Le Livre de Jonas" RSEHA 14. 1906, pp. 1 - 49.

HALLER, E. "Die Erzählung von dem Propheten Jona" TEH N.V. 65. München, 1958.

HARRISON, R. K. Introduction To The Old Testament. London, 1970.

HEINRICH, K. Parmenides und Jona. Frankfurt, 1966.

HERTZ, J. H. The Pentateuch and Haftorahs (2nd Ed.). London, 1960.

HESCHEL, A. The Prophets. New York, 1955.

HEUSCHEN, J. "L'interprétation du Livre de Jonas" Revue Ecclésiastique de Liège 35. 1948, pp. 141 - 159, 295 - 309.

HOLLADAY, W. L. "Prototype and Copies: A New Approach to the Poetry-Prose Problem in the Book of Jeremiah" JBL 79. 1960, pp. 351 - 367.

HOLLADAY, W. L. "The Background of Jeremiah's Self-Understanding" JBL 83. 1964, pp. 153 - 164.

HOLMAN, J. "Analysis of the text of Psalm 139" BZ 14. 1970, pp. 37 - 71, 198 - 227.

HOONACKER, A. Van. Les Douze Petits Prophètes (Etudes Bibliques). Paris, 1908.

HORST, F. "Die Kennzeichen der hebräischen Poesie" ThR 21. 1953,
    pp. 97 - 121, 485 - 492.

HYATT, J. P. Jeremiah. (IntB Vol. 5.) New York, 1956.

HYMAN, S. E. The Armed Vision. New York, 1948.

IBN EZRA, A. Commentary. (MG) Warsaw, 1869 - 64.

JACOB, E. "Sagen und Legenden in A. T." RGG (3rd Ed.) Vol. 5.
    Göttingen, 1959, Col. 1302 - 1308.

JACOB, E. L'Ancien Testament. (Que Sais-je?) Paris, 1970.

JACOBSON, Y. (BS) Hazon Hammiqra'. (Vol. 2.) Tel Aviv, 1959.

JACOBSON, B. S. Meditations on the Torah. Tel Aviv, 1959.

JEPSEN, A. "Anmerkungen zum Buch Jona" Wort-Gebot-Glaube.
    Beiträge zur Theologie des Alten Testaments. Walter Eichrodt
    zum 80. Geburtstag. (AThANT 59), 1970.

JEREMIAS, J. 'Iwvas "Der Prophet Jonas" Theologisches Wörterbuch
    zum Neuen Testament. (Vol. 3.) Stuttgart, 1967, pp. 410 - 413.

JOHNSON, A. R. "Jonah 2:3-10. A Study in Cultic Phantasy" Studies in
    Old Testament Prophecy. Ed. H. H. Rowley. Edinburgh, 1946.

JONES, A. Unless Some Man Show Me. London, 1951.

JUNKER, H. "Die religiöse Bedeutung des Buches Jonas" PastB 51.
    1940, pp. 108 - 114.

KAISER, O. Einleitung in das Alte Testament. (2nd Ed.) Gütersloh,
    1970.

KAISER, O. "Wirklichkeit, Möglichkeit und Vorurteil. Ein Beitrag zum
    Verständnis des Buches Jona" EvTh 33. 1973, pp. 91 - 103.

KAUFMANN, W. A. Critique of Religion and Philosophy. New York, 1958.

KAUFMANN, Y. The Religion of Israel. (Trans. and Abridged by
    M. Greenberg.) Chicago, 1960.

KELLER, C. A. "Jonas. Le portrait d'un Prophète" ThZ 21. 1965,
    pp. 329 - 340.

KELLER, C. A. Jonas. (Commentaire de l'ancien testament XIa.)
    Neuchâtel, 1965.

KESSLER, M. "Form-Critical Suggestions on Jer 36" CBQ 28. 1966,
    pp. 389 - 401.

KESSLER, M. "The Significance of Jer 36" ZAW 81. 1969, pp. 381 - 383.

KLEINERT, P. Obadiah, Jonah, etc. (Die Heilige Schrift.) Leipzig,
    1868.

KNOBEL, A. Der Prophetismus der Hebräer (Vol. 2.) Breslau, 1837.

KNOCH, O. "Das Zeichen des Jonas" BiKi 1962, pp. 15 - 16.

KOCH, K. The Growth of the Biblical Tradition. (Trans. S. M. Cupitt.)
     London, 1969 (=Was ist Formgeschichte? Neue Wege der Bibel-
     exegese (2nd Ed.) Neukirchen, 1967).

KOCH, K. "Der Spruch 'Sein Blut bleibe auf seinem Haupt' und die Isra-
     elitische Auffassung vom vergossenen Blut". VT 12. 1962,
     pp. 396 - 416. (=Um das Prinzip der Vergeltung in Religion und
     Recht des Alten Testaments, Ed. K. Koch,Darmstadt,1971, pp. 412 - 431).

KOEHLER, K. "The Original Form of the Book of Jonah" Theological
     Review. 16. London, 1879, pp. 139 - 144.

KOENIG, E. "Jonah" Dictionary of the Bible. New York, 1911, pp. 744 -
     753.

KRAUS, H. J. Psalmen II.(BK.AT XV/2) Neukirchen, 1960

KUHL, C. "Die 'Wiederaufnahme' - ein literar kritisches Prinzip?"
     ZAW 64. 1952, pp. 1 - 11.

KUHL, C. Die Entstehung des Alten Testament. München, 1953.

LANCHESTER, H. C. O. Obadiah and Jonah. (The Cambridge Bible.)
     Cambridge, 1918.

LANDES, G. M. "The 'Three Days and Three Nights' Motif in Jonah 2:1"
     JBL 86. 1967, pp. 446 - 450.

LANDES, G. M. "The Kerygma of the Book of Jonah" Interpretation 21.
     1967, pp. 3 - 31.

LAWRENCE, M. "Ships, Monsters and Jonah" AJA 66. 1962, pp. 289 -
     296.

LEIBOVITZ, N. ʿIyunim Ḥadašim Bʾsepher Šʾmot. Jerusalem, 1970.

LEWIS, C. "Jonah, A Parable For Our Time" Judaism 21. 1972,
     pp. 159 - 163.

LICHT, J. S. "Sepher Jonah" Ensiqlopediyah Miqraʾit. (Vol. 3.)
     Jerusalem, 1958, pp. 608 - 613.

LINDBLOM, J. "Lot-Casting in the Old Testament" VT 12. 1962,
     pp. 164 - 178.

LIPPL, J. Die zwölf kleinen Propheten I. (HSAT VIII, 3) Bonn, 1937.

LODS, A. Histoire de la Littérature Hebraique et Juive. Paris, 1950.

LOEWENSTAMM, S. E. "Law" The World History of the Jewish People
     Vol. 3. Judges. Tel Aviv, 1971, pp 231 - 267.

LOHFINK, N. "Und Jona ging zur Stadt hinaus (Jona 4:5)" BZ 5. 1961,
    pp. 185 - 203.

LORETZ, O. "Herkunft und Sinn der Jona-Erzählung" BZ 5. 1961,
    pp. 18 - 29.

LORETZ, O. Gotteswort und menschliche Erfahrung. Freiburg, 1963.

MAGNUS, P. "The Book of Jonah" The Hibbert Journal 16. 1918,
    pp. 429 - 442.

MAGONET, J. D. "Jüdisch-theologische Beobachtungen zum Buch Jonas"
    BiLe 13. 1972, pp. 153 - 172.

MALBIM, M. L. Commentary. Warsaw, 1866 - 68.

MARMORSTEIN, A. The Old Rabbinic Doctrine of God. London,1927.

MARTI, K. Das Dodekapropheton. (KHC XIII.) Tübingen, 1904.

MARTIN-ACHARD, R. "Israel et les Nations. La perspective missionaire
    de l'ancien Testament" CTh 42. 1959.

McCULLOUGH, W. S. The Book of Psalms. (IntB Vol. 4.) New York,
    1955.

McGOWAN, J. C. Jonah. (Jerome Biblical Commentary.) London, 1968,
    pp. 633 - 637.

MEVES, C. "Die zeitlose Wahrheit der Jonas-Geschichte" Die Bibel ant-
    wortet uns in Bildern. Freiburg, 1973, pp. 42 - 54.

MISKOTTE, K. H. Wenn die Götter schweigen. Vom Sinn des Alten
    Testaments. München, 1963.

MÖLLER, W. Einleitung in das Alte Testament. Zwickau, 1934.

MÖLLERFELD, J. "'Du bist ein gnädiger und barmherziger Gott'
    (Jonas 4:2)" GuL 33. 1960, pp. 324 - 333.

MORE, J. "The Prophet Jonah: The Story of an Intrapsychic Process"
    American Imago. 1970, pp. 3 - 11.

MOWINCKEL, S. "Efterskrift til pastor Th. Bowmans artikel" NTT
    1963, pp. 164 - 168.

MOWINCKEL, S. The Psalms in Israel's Worship. (2 Vols.) (Tr.D.R.
    Ap-Thomas) Oxford, 1962.

MUILENBURG, J. "A Study in Hebrew Rhetoric: Repetition and Style"
    VT.S 1. 1953, pp. 97 - 111.

MUILENBURG, J. "Form Criticism and Beyond" JBL 88. 1969,
    pp. 1 - 18.

MUILENBURG, J. "Biblical Poetry" Encyclopaedia Judaica. (Vol. 13.)
    Jerusalem, 1971, Col. 671 - 693.

NAPIER, B. D. Song of the Vineyard. New York, 1962.

NEHER, A. L'essence du prophétisme. (2nd Ed.) Paris, 1972.

NEIL, W. "Jonah, Book of" IDB (Vol. 2.) Nashville, 1962, pp. 964 - 967.

NEIL, W. "Joel, Book of" IDB (Vol. 2.) Nashville, 1962, pp. 926 - 929.

NÖTSCHER, F. Zwölfprophetenbuch. (Echter Bibel IV) Würzburg, 1948.

NÖTSCHER, F. "Zur Auferstehung nach drei Tagen" Biblica 35. 1954,
      pp. 313 - 319.

NOWACK, D. W. Die kleinen Propheten. (HK III, 4.) (3rd Ed.) Göttingen,
      1922.

OESTERLEY, W. O. E. and ROBINSON, T. H. An Introduction to the
      Books of the Old Testament. London, 1934.

ORELLI, C. v. Die zwölf kleinen Propheten. (KK) München, 1891.

ORLINSKY, H. M. "Nationalism-Universalism and Internationalism in
      Ancient Israel" Translating and Understanding the Old Testament
      (Essays in honour of H. G. May). New York, 1970, pp. 206 - 236.

PARROT, A. Nineveh and the Old Testament. London, 1955.

PEDERSEN, J. P. E. Israel. Its Life and Culture I-II. Oxford, 1926.

PERRY, M. and STEINBERG, M. "The King through Ironic Eyes: The
      Narrator's Devices in the Biblical Story of David and Bathsheba
      and two excurses on the Theory of the Narrative Text." Hasifrut 1.
      1968, pp. 263 - 292 (Hebrew) (English summary, pp. 449 - 452.)

PERRY, M. and STEINBERG, M. "Caution: A literary Text" Hasifrut 2.
      1970, pp. 608 - 663 (Hebrew) (English summary, pp. 679 - 682.)

PESCH, R. "Zur konzentrischen Struktur von Jona 1" Biblica 47. 1966,
      pp. 577 - 581.

PFEIFFER, R. Introduction to the Old Testament. (2nd Ed.) New York,
      1948.

RAD, G. v. Der Prophet Jona. Nürnberg, 1950.

RAD, G. v. Old Testament Theology. Vol. 2. (Trans. D. G. M. Stalker.)
      Edinburgh, 1965. (=Theologie des Alten Testaments Bd II (5th Ed.)
      Göttingen, 1968).

RAD, G. v. Deuteronomy. (OTL) (Trans. D. Barton.) London, 1966.
      (=Das fünfte Buch Mose: Deuteronomium (ATD, 8) Göttingen,
      1964).

RASHI. Commentary (MG) Warsaw, 1860 - 1864.

RAUBER, D. F "Jonah--The Prophet as Shlemiel" BiTod 49. 1970,
      pp. 29 - 37.

RAUBER, D. F. "Literary Values in the Bible: The Book of Ruth" JBL 89. 1970, pp. 27 - 37.

RAUBER, D. F. "Regii Sanguinis Clamor Ad Coelum: The Condition of Modern Biblical Translations" CBQ 32. 1970, pp. 25 - 40.

REDAK. Commentary (MG) Warsaw, 1860 - 1864.

RENDTORFF, R. "Botenformel und Botenspruch" ZAW 74. 1962, pp. 165 - 177.

REVENTLOW, H. Graf. "'Sein Blut komme über sein Haupt'" VT 10. 1960, pp. 311 - 327. (=Um das Prinzip der Vergeltung in Religion und Recht des Alten Testaments. Ed. K. Koch, Darmstadt, 1972, pp. 412 - 431).

RIDDERBOS, N. H. Die Psalmen (BZAW 117) 1972.

RIDDERBOS, N. H. "The Psalms: Style-Figures and Structure" Studies on Psalms. (Oudtestamentische Studien 13.) Ed. P.A.H.De Boer, Leiden, 1963, pp. 43 - 76

ROBERT, A. and FEUILLET, A. Einleitung in die Heilige Schrift. (Vol. 1.) Wien, 1963.

ROBINSON, T. H. Die zwölf kleinen Propheten. (HAT) Tübingen, 1938.

ROFÉ, A. "The Classification of the Prophetical Stories" JBL 89. 1970, pp. 427 - 440.

ROSENZWEIG, F. Kleinere Schriften. Berlin, 1937.

ROSIN, H. The Lord is God. La Haye, 1955.

ROWLEY, H. H. "The Prophet Jeremiah and the Book of Jeremiah" Studies in Old Testament Prophecy. Edinburgh, 1946, pp. 157 - 174.

ROWLEY, H. H. The Missionary Message of the Old Testament. London, 1955.

RUDOLPH, W. "Jona" Archäologie und Altes Testament (Festschrift für Kurt Galling). Tübingen, 1970, pp. 233 - 239.

RUDOLPH, W. Joel-Amos-Obadia-Jona. (KAT XIII 2). Gütersloh, 1971.

SADEH, P. Life as a Parable. London, 1966.

SANDMEL, S. "Parallelomania" JBL 81. 1962, pp. 1 - 13.

SANDMEL, S. The Hebrew Scriptures. New York, 1963.

SANDS, P. C. Literary Genius of the Old Testament. Oxford, 1924.

SCARLETT, W. Jonah. (IntB Vol. 6.) New York, 1956.

SCHARBERT, J. "Formgeschichte und Exegese von Ex 34:6f und seiner Parallelen" Biblica 38. 1957, pp. 130 - 150.

SCHILDENBERGER, J. "Der Sinn des Buches Jonas" EuA N.F.38. 1962, pp. 93 - 102.

SCHMIDT, H. "Die Komposition des Buches Jona" ZAW 25. 1905, pp. 285 - 310.

SCHMIDT, H. "Absicht und Entstehungszeit des Buches Jona" ThStK 79. 1906, pp. 180 - 199.

SCHMIDT, H. Jona--eine Untersuchung zur vergleichenden Religionsgeschichte. Göttingen, 1907.

SCHMIDT, H. Die Grossen Propheten. (Die Schriften des Alten Testament.) Göttingen, 1915. (2nd Ed., 1923).

SCHOLEM, G. Zohar--Basic Readings from the Kabbalah. New York, 1963.

SCHREINER, J. "Eigenart, Aufbau, Inhalt und Botschaft des Buches Jonas" BiKi 1962, pp. 8 - 14.

SCOTT, R. B. Y. "The Sign of Jonah" Interpretation. 19. 1965, pp. 16 - 25.

SEGAL, J. D. "Numerals in the Old Testament" JSSt 10. 1965, pp. 2 - 20.

SEGAL, M. H. "The Use of the Divine Names in the Hebrew Bible" The Pentateuch. Jerusalem, 1967, pp. 103 - 123.

SEGAL, M. H. Mavoʾ Hammiqraʾ. Jerusalem, 1967.

SEGERT, S. "Problems of Hebrew Prosody" VT.S 7. 1959, pp. 283 - 291.

SELLIN, E. Das Zwölfprophetenbuch. (KAT) (2nd and 3rd Ed.) Leipzig, 1929.

SEYDL, E. "Das Jonalied" ZKTh 24. 1900, pp. 187 - 193.

SIEVERS, E. Metrische Studien I. Leipzig, 1901.

SIMON, E. "Flight from God--and Return" Commentary 16. 1953, pp. 214 - 218.

SIMON, U. "An Ironic Approach to a Bible Story" Hasifrut 2. 1970. pp. 598 - 607 (Hebrew) (English summary pp. 683 - 4).

SMART, J. D. Jonah. (IntB Vol. 6.) New York, 1956.

SNAITH, N. H. The Distinctive Ideas of the Old Testament. London, 1945.

SNAITH, N. H. Notes on the Hebrew Text of the Book of Jonah. (Study Notes on Bible Books.) London, 1945.

SNAITH, N. H. "The Meaning of the Hebrew ʾak" VT 14. 1964, pp. 221 - 225.

STÄRK, W. "Die Lyrik des Alten Testaments" Die Schriften des Alten
     Testaments. Göttingen, 1911, pp. 97 - 100.

STANTON, G. B. "The Prophet Jonah and his Message" BS 1951,
     pp. 237 - 249, 363 - 376.

STEFFEN, U. Das Mysterium von Tod und Auferstehung. Göttingen,
     1963.

STEIF, M. "Einige besondere Wortspiele im Pentateuch" MGWJ 69.
     1925, pp. 446 - 448.

STEIF, M. "Wortspiele im Pentateuch II" MGWJ 74. 1930, pp. 194 - 199.

STEK, J. H. "The Message of the Book of Jonah" CTJ 4. 1969, pp. 23 -
     50.

STENZEL, M. "Zum Vulgatatext des Canticum Jonae" Biblica 33.
     1952, pp. 356 - 362.

STINESPRING, W. F. "Irony and Satire" IDB (Vol. 4.) Nashville, 1962,
     pp. 726 - 728.

STOLLBERG, L. C. Jona. (Theological Dissertation.) Halle, 1927.

STOMMEL, E. "Zum Problem der Frühchristlichen Jonasdarstellungen"
     Jahrbuch für Antike und Christentum 1. 1958, pp. 112-115.

STRACK, H. L. Einleitung in das Alte Testament. München, 1898.

STRAUSS, L. B'darkey Hassiphrut. Jerusalem, 1959.

THOMA, A. "Entstehung des Büchleins Jona" ThStKr 84. 1911, pp. 479 -
     502.

THOMAS, D. W. "A consideration of some unusual ways of expressing
     the superlative in Hebrew" VT 3. 1953, pp. 209 - 224.

THOMPSON, J. A. Joel. (IntB Vol. 6.) New York, 1956.

TREPANIER, B. "The Story of Jonas" CBQ 13. 1951, pp. 8 - 16.

TRIBLE, P. L. Studies in the Book of Jonah. (Unpublished Doctoral
     Dissertation.) Columbia, 1963.

TURNBULL, H. C. "Jonah in Nineveh" JBL 11 - 12. 1892 - 3, pp. 53 -
     60.

URBACH, E. E. "T'šubat 'Anšey Ninbeh W'hawwikuah Hayy'hudi -Nosri"
     Tarbiz 20. 1950, pp. 118 - 122.

URBACH, E. E. Hazal (2nd Ed.). Jerusalem, 1971.

VACCARI, P. A. "Il genere letterario del libro di Giona in recenti
     pubblicazioni" Divinitas 6. 1962, pp. 231 - 256.

VISCHER, W. "L'Evangelo secondo il Profeta Giona" Protestantesimo 16.
     1961, pp. 193 - 204.

VOLLERS, K. "Das Dodekapropheton der Alexandriner" ZAW 1883, pp. 18 - 20.

WADE, G. W. Micah, Obadiah, Joel and Jonah. (Westminster Commentaries.) London, 1925.

WANKE, G. Untersuchungen zur sog. Baruchschrift (BZAW 122) 1971.

WEINREB, F. Das Buch Jonah. Der Sinn des Buches Jonah nach der ältesten jüdischen Überlieferung. Zürich, 1970.

WEISER, A. Einleitung in das Alte Testament. (5th Ed.) Göttingen, 1963.

WEISER, A. Psalmen (ATD 14 - 15) (6th Ed.) Göttingen,1963.

WEISS, M. Hammiqra⁷ Kidmuto. Jerusalem, 1962.

WEISS. M. "Einiges über die Bauformen des Erzählens in der Bibel" VT 12. 1963, pp. 456 - 475.

WEISS, M. "Weiteres über die Bauformen des Erzählens in der Bibel" Biblica 46. 1965, pp. 181 - 206.

WELLHAUSEN, J. Die kleinen Propheten übersetzt und erklärt. (3rd Ed.) 1892. (4th Ed. 1963).

WESTERMANN, C. Das Loben Gottes in den Psalmen. (4th Ed.) Göttingen, 1968.

WILSON, R. D. "The Authenticity of Jonah" PTR 16. 1918, pp. 280 - 298, 430 - 456.

WILSON, R. D. " מנה 'To Appoint' in the Old Testament" PTR 16. 1918, pp. 645 - 654.

WINCKLER, H. Altorientalische Forschungen II. Leipzig, 1898.

WOLF, B. Die Geschichte des Propheten Jona. Nach einer karschunischen Handschrift. Berlin, 1897.

WOLFF, H. W. Die Bibel--Gotteswort oder Menschenwort? Neukirchen, 1959.

WOLFF, H. W. "Jonabuch" RGG (3rd. Ed.) Vol. 3. Tübingen, 1959, Col. 853 - 856.

WOLFF, H. W. Studien zum Jonabuch. Köln, 1965.

WOLFF, H. W. Der Prophet Joel. (BK.AT Dodekapropheton II.) Neukirchen-Vluyn, 1969.

WOOD, G. F. Joel, Obadiah. (Jerome Biblical Commentary.) London, 1968, pp. 439 - 445.

WRIGHT, A. G. "The Literary Genre Midrash" CBQ 28. 1966, pp. 105 - 138, 417 - 457.

WRIGHT, A. G. "The Riddle of the Sphinx: The Structure of the Book of Qohelet" CBQ 30. 1968, pp. 313 - 334.

WRIGHT, G. E. and FULLER, R. The Book of the Acts of God. London, 1965.

WRIGLEY, J. E. "An Old Testament Ecumenical Message" BiTod 25. 1961, pp. 1763 - 1769.

ZIEGLER. "Zur Einleitung in das Alte Testament" BZ 4. 1960, pp. 137 - 154.

ZIMMERLI, W. "Promise and Fulfillment" Interpretation 15. 1961, pp. 310 - 338 (=Verheißung und Erfüllung" EvT 12. 1952 - 3, pp. 34 - 59 = Probleme Alttestamentlicher Hermeneutik Ed. C. Westermann. München, 1960, pp 69 - 101.

ZOLLER, I. "Considerazioni Storico-Religiose sul Libro di Giona" Studi e Materiali di Storia Delle Religioni 7. 1931, pp. 48 - 58.

BIBLIOGRAPHY - A SELECTIVE SUPPLEMENT (1983)

ACKERMAN, James S. "Satire and Symbolism in the Song of Jonah" in: B. Halpern & J. D. Levenson, eds. Traditions in Transformation. Winona Lake, IN: Eisenbrauns, 1981, pp. 213-46.

ALLEN, Leslie C. "The Book of Jonah" in: The Books of Joel, Obadiah, Jonah and Micah. Grand Rapids: Eerdmans, 1976, pp. 173-235.

BARILIER, Roger "Jonas lu pour aujourd'hui" La Revue Reformée [Aix en Provence] 32. 1981, pp. 49-87.

BEN MENACHEM, E. "Sefer Yona" Trei ᶜAsar I (Daᶜat Miqraʾ) Jerusalem, 1973.

BICKERMAN, Elias "Les deux erreurs de Prophète Jonas" Revue d'Histoire et de Philosophie Religieuses 45. 1965, pp. 232-64.

CLEMENTS, R. E. "The Purpose of the Book of Jonah" Supplements to Vetus Testamentum 28. 1975, pp. 16-28.

CRAGHAN, John Esther, Judith, Tobit, Jonah, Ruth (OT Message, 16). Wilmington, DE: Michael Glazier, 1982.

ELLUL, Jacques "Le Livre de Jonas" Cahiers Bibliques de "Foi et Vie" 50. 1952, pp. 81-184. Eng. trans.: The Judgment of Jonah. Grand Rapids: Eerdmans, 1971.

EMMERSON, Grace I. "Another Look at the Book of Jonah" Expository Times 88. 1976-7, pp. 86ff.

FRETHEIM, Terence E. The Message of Jonah. A Theological Commentary. Minneapolis: Augsburg Pub., 1977.

FRETHEIM, Terence E. "Jonah and Theodicy" ZAW 90. 1978, pp. 227-37.

GEVARYAHU, Haim "The Universalism of the Book of Jonah" Dor leDor [Jerusalem] 10. 1981, 20-7.

HOLBERT, John C. "'Deliverance Belongs to Yahweh!' Satire in the Book of Jonah" Journal for the Study of the Old Testament 21. 1981, 59-81.

LACOCQUE, André and LACOCQUE, Pierre-Emmanuel The Jonah Complex. Atlanta: John Knox, 1981.

LANDES, George M. "Jonah, Book of" IDB Supplementary Volume. Nashville: Abingdon, 1976, pp. 488-91.

LANDES, George M. "Jonah: A māšāl?" in: J. G. Gammie et al., eds. Israelite Wisdom. Missoula: Scholars, 1978, pp. 137-158.

MILES, J. A. "Laughing at the Bible: Jonah as Parody" Jewish Quarterly Review 65. 1974-5, pp. 168-81.

MORA, Vincent "Jonas" Cahiers Évangile 36. 1981.

PAYNE, David F. "Jonah from the Perspective of its Audience" Journal for the Study of the Old Testament 13. 1979, pp. 3-12.

PELLI, Moshe "The Literary Art of Jonah" Hebrew Studies [Univ. of Wisconsin] 20-21. 1979-80, pp. 18-28.

PRICE, Brynmor F. and NIDA, Eugene A. A Translator's Handbook on the Book of Jonah (Helps for Translators, Vol. XXI). Stuttgart, 1978.

SCHMIDT, Ludwig "De Deo". Studien zur Literarkritik und Theologie des Buches Jona, des Gesprächs zwischen Abraham und Jahwe in Gen. xviii 22ff. und von Hi.i (BZAW 143). Berlin: de Gruyter, 1976.

STEFFAN, U. Jona und der Fisch: Der Mythos von Tod und Wiedergeburt. Stuttgart: Kreuz, 1982.

STRIKOVSKY, Aryeh "Divine Nomenclature in Jonah" Niv. A Journal Devoted to Halacha, Jewish Thought and Education 1976/7 (pub. by Friends of the Midrashia in Israel).

WALSH, Jerome T. "Jonah 2,3-10: A Rhetorical Critical Study" Biblica 63. 1982, pp. 219-229.

WATTS, J. D. W. The Books of Joel, Obadiah, Jonah, Nahum, Habakkuk and Zephania. Cambridge: C.U.P., 1975, pp. 72-97.

WIESEL, Elie. "Jonah" in: Five Biblical Portraits. Notre Dame & London: Univ. of Notre Dame, 1981, pp. 129-155.

WOLFF, H. W. Obadja und Jona (BKAT 14/3) Neukirchen: Neukirchener, 1977.

WOLFF, H. W. Studien zum Jonabuch. Neukirchen: Neukirchener, 1965. The last three chapters are now in Eng. trans. in: Currents in Theology and Mission 3. 1976, pp. 4-19, 86-97, 141-50.

POSTSCRIPT

KING ALFRED'S COLLEGE
LIBRARY

Chapter VI - Postscript

"WHITHER SHALL I GO FROM YOUR SPIRIT?"

The Zohar speaks of Jonah as follows:

"In the story of Jonah we see the whole of a man's experience in this world. Jonah descending into the ship is like a man's soul that descends into the world as it enters his body. Why is it called "Jonah", troubled? Because as soon as it becomes a partner with the body in this world it finds itself full of troubles. For man is in this world as in a ship that is crossing the great ocean and seems to be breaking up."

This troubled and tormented soul on its brief journey through the world is a favoured image of the mediaeval Jewish thinkers. The image begins in the Sayings of the Fathers (4:21):

"The world is like a corridor to the world to come. Prepare yourself in the corridor so that you may enter the inner chamber."

And it finds one of its most unnerving expressions in the words of the thirteenth century philosopher, Jedaiah of Beziers:

"The world is a tempestuous sea of immense depth and breadth, and time is a frail bridge constructed over it. The beginning of it is fastened with the cords of chaos that preceded existence, while the end of it is to see eternal bliss, and to be enlightened with the light of the King's countenance. The width of the bridge is the width of a man, and it has no handrail. And you, son of man, against your will are living, and are continually travelling over it, since the day you became a man."

Beyond the world of physical dangers, where life itself is constantly threatened, there lies the world of the journey of the spirit - a world no less tricky to pass through unharmed. And the soul and body in uneasy alliance must pick their careful way through the two, always running the risk of confusing one with the other or of paying insufficient attention to the legitimate needs and challenges of each. In his book Awakenings (Penguin Books, rev. edn. 1976), Dr Oliver Sacks points to one way in which our confusion may arise:

"There is, of course, an ordinary medicine, an everyday medicine, humdrum, prosaic, a medicine for stubbed toes, quinsies, bunions and boils; but all of us entertain the idea of another sort of medicine, of a wholly different kind: something deeper, older, extraordinary, almost sacred, which will restore to us our lost health and wholeness, and give us a sense of perfect well-being.

"For all of us have a basic, intuitive feeling that once we were whole and well; at ease, at peace, at home in the world; totally united with the grounds of our being; and that then we lost this primal, happy, innocent state, and fell into our present sickness and suffering. We had something of infinite beauty and preciousness - and we lost it; we spend our lives searching for what we have lost; and one day, perhaps, we will suddenly find it. And this will be the miracle, the millenium!

"We may expect to find such ideas most intense in those who are enduring extremities of suffering, sickness, and anguish, in those who are consumed by the sense of what they have lost, or wasted, and by the urgency of recouping before it is to late. Such people, or patients, come to priests or physicians in desperations of yearning, prepared to believe anything for a reprieve, a rescue, a regeneration, a redemption. They are credulous in proportion to their desperation – the predestined victims of quacks and enthusiasts.

"This sense of what is lost, and what must be found, is essentially a metaphysical one. If we arrest the patient in his metaphysical search, and ask him what it is that he wishes or seeks, he will not give us a tabulated list of items, but will say, simply, 'My happiness', 'My lost health', 'My former condition', 'A sense of reality', 'Feeling fully alive', etc. He does not long for this thing or that; he longs for a general change in the complexion of things for everything to be all right once again, unblemished, the way it once was. And it is at this point, when he is searching, here and there, with so painful an urgency, that he may be led into a sudden grotesque mistake; that he may (in Donne's words) mistake 'the Apothe-caryes shop' for 'the Metaphoricall Deity': a mistake which the apothecary or physician may be tempted to encourage."

For us the search for the "Metaphoricall Deity" may seem all too often a confused and disturbing task, one full of traps no less dangerous than those awaiting us in the "Apothecaryes shop". A multiplicity of objections, intellectual and emotional, warn us against the very validity of such a search; and a writer like C. S. Lewis, in The Screwtape Letters, has shown us the unengaging realities of organised religious life that may lead us to reject the very communities, and their spiritual leaders, who should be offering us a home in which to make such an exploration. Something stands in the way - and whether we characterise it as the materialism of the times we live in, or the workings of some element of our subconscious, or ascribe it to some externalised principle of evil - all too often we give up on the threshold, and settle for the security of a familiar unease, perhaps because we are somehow aware of the risks we run in taking a further step.

This hesitancy is expressed vividly in the Hebrew Bible in stories about the call of prophets to serve God. For them, at least, the source of the call is not questioned and for one of them, Abraham, the response seems to be immediate acquiescence. Yet for others there is a moment of hesitancy, expressed in different ways: Moses has a whole string of objections: Who am I to rescue the children of Israel? Anyway they'll never believe You sent me! Anyway I cannot speak adequately! In the end he seems to become quite peevish: "Oh! send whoever You want!" - anyone, that is, but me. And yet the anger, and perhaps God's anger in reply, is only because he knows that he has swallowed the bait and accepted. Jeremiah says he is too young. Isaiah feels himself impure. Amos probably complained that he was not professionally qualified. Yet in the end, they all had to go. Leon Roth expressed it well:

"It has become fashionable to talk of the relationship between God and man as that of a dialogue. That is as may be; but it should at least be noted that the dialogue involved is not a tea-table conversation. It is rather a call, even a calling to account; and it is curious to observe from the record how some of those called upon found in it terror and suffering and how some, for varying reasons, tried to evade it" (God and Man in the Old Testament [Allen & Unwin, 1955] p. 19).

In such a context there is an inevitablity to the creation of the Book of Jonah, the story of the prophet who not only refused the call, but went to enormous extremes, to the very brink of death itself, so as to run away from it. Nor do we really know why he refused, for in the typical manner of Biblical narratives, we are given a description of events but very little in the way of overt evaluation of why things happened. We, the reader, must follow Jonah on his journey, picking up such clues as we can from what occurs, but ultimately investing the story with our own insights and, inevitably, our own experience and private fears.

The call of God is clear and precise, another task set for one who is used to such things: "Rise, go to Nineveh and call out to them that their evil has come up before Me! (1.2) We know that Jonah is a prophet because he is called such elsewhere in the Bible (2 Kings 14:25). But he is not named as one in our book, and in fact the whole tenor of the story is to make him into an everyman, not bound by time or space. Yet Nineveh is a real place - the capital of the Assyrian Empire, a military power that cast its shadow of fear across the entire Near East. To the Assyrians goes the credit of inventing the military tactic of uprooting entire populations, settling them elsewhere and replacing them with other defeated peoples. The tactic was to prove successful in destroying the Northern Kingdom of Israel, and leading, incidently, to the legend-inspiring ten lost tribes. Nineveh, for Jonah, was the Berlin of the Third Reich. To Nineveh he is sent, but to Tarshish he flees. If we can identify the place accurately it is somewhere at the southern tip of Spain, that is to say not merely in the diametrically opposite direction from Nineveh, but literally across the sea at the other end of the world. Not only is it a journey into the unknown, and into considerable danger, but the economics of it must have presented a problem! Certainly on the basis of this account the Rabbis assumed that the prophets must have been wealthy, arguing that Jonah hired the whole boat for his use. To flee from God, Jonah must have sold up his home, left everything behind and set off at the risk of his life. To flee from God, he reproduces the experience of the patriarchs, of ancient Israel and of the Jewish people, of going into exile, but this time against the will of God. Yet the author hints that his flight is more than just an attempt to escape the immediate task. Three times the hebrew verb for "going down" (yarad) occurs in the first chapter - as Jonah goes down to Jaffa, down into the ship, down into the bowels of the ship - and then a fourth time, because of a pun, when he goes down into a deep sleep. There is a direction to his journey - into unconsciousness as he sleeps through the storm, and ultimately into oblivion, as he asks to be thrown overboard. Jonah in flight is on a journey away from God, on a journey towards death.

But the prophet is not alone on his travels. Others are borne along, and others are thus exposed to the danger he seems to think is merely his private concern. The sailors are characterised as people of remarkable sensitivity and generosity. When the storm threatens to destroy them, they pray to their respective gods. They then apply standard "technological" ploys to discover the culprit, by casting lots and the lot falls on Jonah. Instead of throwing him overboard at once, they open up a court of law and ply Jonah with questions, trying to establish his identity, what is be running from? of what is he guilty? When Jonah, having admitted his responsibility, is asked what should be done - he has the chance to ask to be taken back, but he refuses - so the sailors try to row him back, but no one can make that return on behalf of another. When finally defeated, they turn to God: We beg you, Lord, let us not perish for this man's life, and do not hold us guilty of shedding innocent blood, for You are the Lord, as You will it, so You act." (1:14). They are trapped in a double bind: to do nothing means they will drown with Jonah; to throw him overboard means they are guilty of murder and thus condemned to death. Only God can untangle such a paradox. So Jonah's solution of self-immolation is not a generous gesture to save the lives of his fellows but merely the logical conclusion of his flight, and the sailors seem to count for very little; they can only be on the periphery of his concerns. The Rabbis, however, recognized their worth, and portrayed them as making yet one more bid to save the prophet. First they lowered him till his feet entered the water. At once the sea calmed down - so they hauled him back aboard, but the storm raged again. Again they lowered him to his waist, again calm and again they pulled him back. But the storm returned. The third time he went in up to his neck before the cycle was repeated. In the end they had no choice and threw him in. The author has twice recorded their growing fear as the storm increased against them (1:5, 10). But their fear is now greatest with the calm that descends - for their fear has become the fear and awe of God. (1:16). They made sacrifices and vowed vows - and the Rabbis had them returning to Jerusalem where they converted to the faith in the one God. Even on his flight, Jonah serves God's purposes.

We may also read this story inside out - for how do we come to recognise that our journey is actually a flight? Perhaps in the damage we do to others on the way, if the realization ever penetrates to our awareness. Certainly for Jonah other messages were continually coming through. In one of the most subtle ploys of the author, the words of the captain to Jonah when he asks him to rise up and call on his God (1:6) are identical with the words describing God's call. For the captain they merely mean: Wake up and pray! for Jonah the words of God echo in the air waiting for him to respond. Thus the captain becomes the unconscious messenger of God's word, and indeed the wind, the storm, as later on the fish, the gourd, the worm, all of nature, become the agents of God, bringing His word to the recalcitrant prophet. The verse from Psalm 139 (v.7) that forms the title of this paper: "Whither can I go from Your spirit (ruach)" can also be translated literally as "Whither can I go from Your wind" - the wind that brings the storm to the sea, the wind that will affect Jonah sitting beneath the remains of his hut, the wind that is part of a creation faithfully serving its master. Or is this just the nightmare in which Jonah finds himself trapped, a paranoid universe in which every person, every sound, each breath of wind closes in on him with some message he does not wish to hear. For Jonah in flight, even death seems to be the better option than living with the God who haunts him. But even the luxury of death is not permitted him - waiting in the wings is the fish.

A century ago, scholars still tried to identify the precise fish that swallowed Jonah - not a whale but some sort of shark seems to have been favoured. Today it is hard to discuss the remarkable creature as anything but a womb. And yet it is worth noting the function it plays for the author. Most obviously it gets Jonah out of the sea and back to dry land. It also provides him a home for three days in which to reassess his situation. Despite the resurrection echo this three day period must have for the Christians, the Rabbis were rather annoyed at Jonah for taking so long to come out with his prayer. On the basis of a change in the grammatical form of the word for fish, which could also be interpreted as a change from a male to a female fish, they constructed a long underwater voyage taken by Jonah in which he visited the foundations of the earth, the path through the Reed Sea taken by the children of Israel on leaving Egypt - and generally exploring significant moments in Israel's divine history. God grew so impatient at this Cook's tour that he sent a female fish to threaten Jonah's male transporter, and the latter vomited Jonah out into the jaws of the former. It was only in the discomfort of his new accomodation, jostled on all sides by embryo fish, that Jonah finally felt the need to pray to God. And even then the Rabbis were not satisfied with his prayer as recorded in the Bible because there is no hint in it of Jonah repenting or otherwise apologising for his flight from God in the first place.

Was Jonah's time in the fish one of those transforming experiences? Did he emerge with a new heightened consciousness or at least a greater insight into his situation and his nature? Again, conventional psychology would probably say yes - surely such an experience - a regression to the womb, the dark night of the soul, sensory deprivation - must have done something to him. And yet - there is a stubborn obliviousness about Jonah that is hearteningly consistent. True, he prays. But the psalm he recites (taken as an integral part of the book - see above, ch. II) is remarkable for all that is left out. In its outer edges it says quite bluntly to God - You threw me in and You drew me out, with not a word about how this came about. More sensitive is the play on Jonah's gradual physical descent (The waters closed in over me; the deep was round about me, weeds wrapped over my head, I went down to the base of the mountains...) which is matched by a spiritual rise. Whereas at the beginning he says: "I am driven out of Your sight, yet still I will look to Your holy Temple.", at the end, when he again speaks of God's holy Temple, the wording is quite different. "When my soul was fainting within me, it was the Lord that I remembered, and my prayer reached out to You, to Your holy Temple." What gets lost in the translation is the emphatic "I" that comes to the fore in the hebrew of Jonah's psalm. In verse 5 it is a strong: "And as for me, I said ..." with the implications that Jonah considered himself still the master of the situation. Yet as he sinks lower and lower into the depths (another phase of the descent that began in chapter one) something happens to him. In the matching first person statement in verse 8, as he faints away, the "I" disappears completely, and a disembodied prayer manages to reach the Temple of God, stripped of all pride and egoism. Jonah has indeed undergone some change of perspective - for one brief moment his centre has moved outside his limited self and located itself within the Temple of God. But it becomes rapidly reconstituted two verses later at the conclusion (v. 10) where, in an echo of a standard thanksgiving psalm, Jonah says: "And as for me, I will sacrifice to You with thankful voice, what I have vowed I will fulfill." The "I" is restored, as indeed it must be, as Jonah moves back from the fish to the outer world. And yet what has really changed? There is a puzzling beginning to chapter three where we read: "The word of the Lord came to Jonah a second time." There then follows virtually the identical message (certainly the three words of his call reappear) as we had in chapter one. Why must God repeat his command if Jonah has now become reconciled to his task? Presumably the answer lies in the closing statement of Jonah's prayer that we have just read. For in his moment of dutiful piety, Jonah has just made an oath to head for Jerusalem and make sacrifices and fulfill vows, presumably intoning the words of the thanksgiving psalm he has just composed. Surely this is the pious step he should now undertake. No! says God. There is still a task awaiting you in Nineveh, and that is where you should be heading! For Jonah the retreat into piety is yet another evasion of the call from God - when flight from God did not work, there is always flight to God, or to that convenient God who makes no demands beyond those the worshipper can comfortably offer. This evaluation of Jonah's piety may seem harsh - but it may be backed by one other ironic touch that underlies the same theme. Jonah ends his prayer on a triumphant note: "yeshuatah ladonay" "Salvation belongs to the Lord!" For God has heard his prayer and God has saved him. And indeed God hears, and speaks to the fish, and with a fine sensitivity to the ambiguity of Jonah's confession of faith, the fish vomits him out!

In chapter three, after bringing Jonah reluctantly into Nineveh - it takes three days to cover the city, Jonah travels for only one day - the story turns to the actions of the Ninevites. It starts with a gound swell of public feeling, the people fast and put on sackcloth and ashes, the traditional response to threatened disaster. The news reaches the king who in turn removes his robes, dons sackcloth and sits in ashes. Finally, by decree of the king, all are commanded to fast and don sackcloth, human beings and animals alike. There would seem to be here a certain degree of repetition and, indeed, redundancy, in this threefold description of sackcloth and fasting. However the author has been building a rising tide of activity as a jumping off point for the king's final command. For till now these actions are part of a conventional response to danger. With the king's closing words we leap into a totally new dimension: "And let every man turn from his evil way, and from the violence of his hands. Who knows, God may turn and relent, and turn back from His fiery anger, so that we perish not." With these words, borrowed from the Book of Jeremiah, and thus bearing an added ironic edge in the mouth of a pagan king, the response of the people moves out of the area of fatalism into the realm of moral choice. Indeed, as the Rabbis pointed out, God does not respond in the story to their sackcloth and ashes but instead: "And God saw their actions, how they turned from their evil ways, and God relented of the evil He had said He would do to them." (3:10). As the chapter is constructed, we have here a stepwise build-up of activity ending with the breakthrough to the new dimension of religious hope - and there at the peak, God is waiting. In our previous chapter, as Jonah sinks lower and lower, he too breaks through to a new experience of God - there at the lowest reach of hopelessness and despair, God is waiting to meet him. The two chapters form mirror images of each other, and yet again we are reminded of the lines of Psalm 139:

"If I rise up to heaven - there, You!
If I make the underworld my bed - behold, You!" (v.8)

In this joyful affirmation that God is there to be found, even at the very extremes of existence, in exaltation or in despair, there comes to mind the fames song of the chasidic master Levi Yitzchak of Berditchev - the "Dudele":

Where I wander - You!
Where I ponder - You!
Only You, You again, always You!
You! You! You!
When I am gladdened - You!
When I am saddened - You!
Only You, You again, always You!
You! You! You!

Sky is You, earth is You!
You above! You below!
In every trend, at every end,
Only You, You again, always You!
You! You! You!

So the centre of our book pivots around this ladder leading into the depths and the heights. In chapter one we have had enormous activity as Jonah fled; in the closing chapter, on the surface at least, we have a moment of stillness - for Jonah sits and sits and sits. He takes his place outside Nineveh, knowing that the people have repented, yet nevertheless hoping for, and indeed willing, God to destroy it anyway. But his is not the stillness of acceptance, of harmony, of reconciliation, for Jonah rages. There is even an ironic overtone to the picture of Jonah's position. For within the city the king in sackcloth sits in ashes in great discomfort praying for the city to be saved; while without, Jonah sits in reasonable comfort beneath his shelter, praying for the city to be destroyed.

Why is Jonah angry? First we should note another exquisite touch of the author in presenting Jonah's second prayer in the book (4:2-3). Jonah begins with the conventional terminology of prayer - the same, in fact, used by the sailors in chapter One. "I beg You, Lord ..." And at the end he will use the same form of request - an imperative softened by the added "I beg You": "So now, O Lord, I beg You, take my life from me, for it is better for me to die than to live." But between these two expressions there bursts through all the resentment he has bottled up inside him since the beginning of this absurd mission: "Did I not say just this while I was still on my own land? That is why I tried first to flee to Tarshish, for I know that You are a gracious and merciful God, slow to anger, generous in love, who relents from punishing!" Jonah is here quoting the list of God's qualities first revealed to Moses, His compassion and mercy, His love for humanity and His enduring patience in the face of their wrongdoing - and spitting them into God's face - I knew You'd end up forgiving them, and You shouldn't!

That, at least, is Jonah's overt argument. But what he actually objects to is still a matter of conjecture. Some feel that Jonah is a nationalist who does not wish to see the enemy Nineveh go unpunished - perhaps in anticipation of the destruction they will bring to the Northern Kingdom. Others extend this and see in Jonah an expression of a narrow particularism that resented the idea that God's love could be extended to people beyond Israel's borders. Others see Jonah as a champion of rigid justice offended by God's softness on evildoers. One might go further and see Jonah as someone who wishes the universe to be governed by clear, unambiguous rules, wherein there is the security of knowing that action "A" will lead to consequence "B" with no random factor, like God's seemingly anarchic love, to confuse the system. All these are possible elements in Jonah's viewpoint, and yet behind them there remains the deeper question of the tension between the private limited ego of man and the will of God, in whatever form and with whatever terminology we envisage this interaction. Throughout the story we have seen this confrontation: God hurled a wind onto the sea; Jonah went down to sleep through the subsequent storm. God says Nineveh will not be destroyed; Jonah wills that it should be. In this final chapter, the author even organises his chapter so that words match words, actions match actions as the two protagonists confront each other. In the Hebrew text the identical number of words are given to Jonah's great speech of complaint at the beginning and God's long speech of explanation at the end. And God finally spells it out in His last words, again by using an emphatic form of expression: "As for you, you felt pity for the gourd ... As for me, should I not feel pity for Ninevah ..." Again, as Leon Roth put it, the call of God is a calling to account. The God from whom Jonah cannot flee demands that he confront the very problem he wishes to avoid.

There follows in the rest of the story more magical stage effects. The great fish gives way in turn to a magical plant, a destructive worm and a harsh wind. The violence of the storm is replaced by the violence of nature, creation and destruction, growth and struggle. And the outer violence is matched by a whole range of inner emotions that grip Jonah. Leaving the city he rages; under the shade of God's plant he rejoices greatly, both for the shade and the evidence of God's favour; then the sun beats upon his head, as he too experiences the destructive power he would so happily have unleashed on Nineveh, and in despair he asks for death. Again the author uses the device of repetition to indicate a change in perspective. Early in the chapter he wished to die in angry defence of his attitude to God's unacceptable behaviour - he would give his life for a principle. But at the end it is the physical discomfort that again leads him to make the same request, and here we have a clue to the whole curious episode with the gourd.

In God's final challenge He asks about Jonah's feelings for the gourd: "though you neither laboured over it nor made it grow." The gourd served Jonah, he had some relationship to it - though perhaps God is being ironic in sugesting he felt pity for it. But God could equally have used a pet animal or any other creature for his illustration if the only point to be made here was that Jonah could feel something for another part of creation. Why the gourd? The answer lies in the solution to another problem that has worried scholars. If Jonah has already built himself a booth beneath which to shelter from the sun, what is the purpose of the gourd, and indeed what happens to the booth. Presumably both are swept away by the wind, leaving Jonah exposed, but why this seeming repetition? While Jonah is angry with God and enters into a theological debate about the nature of God's qualities, he has incidently done something else. In verse 5 Jonah has gone out of the city and sat down to await events. But the sentence then adds that he got up again and built himself a shelter and sat again beneath it so as to watch the imminent hoped-for destruction in comfort. It is at this point that God, as if saying; "we have run out of words with which to talk to each other", picks up Jonah's action and responds with actions of His own. It is as if He is saying: "As well as your righteous anger, and perhaps really at the heart of the matter, is your concern for your own comfort. Very well if it is shade that you wish, shade I will give you, the most wondrous shade you could imagine - and with that physical aspect we shall continue our debate." So the gourd becomes the logical element which God brings to bear, and with which He will make his final point.

Ninevah is saved because of God's patience. No less wondrous is His patience with his reluctant prophet, a patience that goes beyond the confines of the book. For though the religious traditions try to supply an affirmative answer to God's final question to Jonah, the Bible wisely ends without it. We do not know if Jonah has a change of heart, if he is convinced by God's argument. We do not even know if this extraordinary man who has been subjected to the most intensive series of experiences, emerges at the end any different from before. We want to think he has, because religious and healing professions alike need the myth that human nature is changeable; that repentance, insight, growth, whatever terminology we use, are available and that we, the practitioners, can somehow help bring them about. But perhaps it is refreshingly necessary to encounter a Jonah once in a while, who asserts the right to remain stiffnecked, blind and wilfull despite the most frenzied efforts of others to persuade or even to force him to change. But that is a whimsical aside. For whether Jonah changes or not, it seems that he cannot ever escape the call to change that set him off on his adventures in the first place.

For the psalmist the universal presence of God is a matter of wonder; for Levi Yitzchak of Berditchev a source of joy; for Jonah a paranoiac's nightmare. Whatever our response, there is no neutral ground.

On the Jewish Day of Atonement, the Book of Jonah is read during the afternoon. Partly because of its reference to the repentance of the people of Nineveh, and hence their lesson for us, and partly perhaps because its universal theme prepares us for our re-entry into the world as the end of the day approaches. The concluding service is called Neilah which refers to the closing of the gates of repentance at the end of this penitential period. It is the time for final reconciliation with God. In this context a passage has been composed for the new edition of the High Holyday Prayerbook of the Reform Synagogues of Great Britain which gathers together a number of Biblical passages that relate to the theme of the relationship between God and man through the stages of life. It requires two voices, as each in turn speak.

The word of the Lord came to me, saying:
Before I formed you in the womb I knew you,
before you were born I set you apart. [Jeremiah 1:4-5]

        You have taken me from the womb,
        carried me safely on my mother's breasts ...
        do not be far from me. [Psalm 22:10, 12]

Like a man whose mother comforts him
so will I comfort you. [Isaiah 66:13]

        Do not remember the sins of my youth and my rebellion,
        remember me instead with Your love. [Psalm 25:7]

I remember the devotion of your youth,
the love of your bridal days,
when you went after Me into the desert,
to a land unsown. [Jeremiah 2:2]

        Whom have I in heaven but You?
        Beside You, I have nothing on earth.
        My flesh and my heart may fail
        but God is the rock of my heart
        and my portion forever. [Psalm 73:25-26]

I betroth you to Me forever.
I betroth you to Me with integrity and justice,
with tenderness and love.
I betroth you to Me with faithfulness
and you will know the Lord. [Hosea 2:21-22]

> Where could I go from Your spirit,
> or where could I flee from Your presence?
> If I climb to heaven, You are there,
> there too, if I lie in the depths. [Psalm 139:7-8]

I was ready to be sought by those who did not ask.
I was ready to be found by those who did not seek.
I said "Here am I", "Here am I"
to a nation that did not call on My name. [Isaiah 65:1]

> So I looked for You in the holy place,
> to see Your power and glory.
> My soul is thirsty for You,
> my flesh is pining for You. [Psalm 63:3, 2]

When you call Me and come to pray to Me,
I will hear you.
When you seek Me, you will find Me,
if you search for Me with all your heart.
I shall let you find me. [Jeremiah 29:12-14]

> Do not reject me in old age;
> when my strength is feeble, do not abandon me. [Psalm 71:9]

When you are old I am the same,
and when your hair turns grey I will support you;
I have made and I will bear;
I will support and I will save. [Isaiah 46:4]

> Yet I am always with You.
> You have grasped me by the hand.
> You will guide me with Your counsel
> and afterwards receive me with glory. [Psalm 73:23-24]

"For man is in this world as in a ship that is crossing the great ocean and seems to be breaking up." For Jonah, the search for security leads him to close off this threatening outside world, with its peoples, friend and foe alike, and its multiplicity of creatures all of which demand his attention and concern. But God would have him meet the other, perhaps because the security Jonah seeks is a myth and no solution to the problem of living. Perhaps that is the idea behind the cryptic remark of Nachman of Bratzlav, when he too speaks about the narrow path we tread during the brief time given us on earth: "This entire world is but a narrow bridge - but the essential thing is never to be afraid."

KING ALFRED'S COLLEGE
LIBRARY